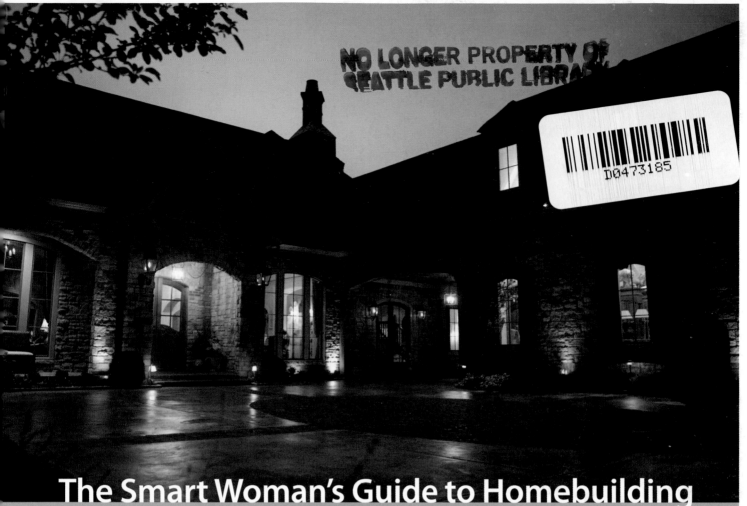

The Smart Woman's Guide to Homebuilding

An Essential Reference For Homeowners and Builders

DORI HOWARD

BETTERWAY BOOKS
CINCINNATI, OHIO

Distributed in Canada by Fraser Direct
100 Armstrong Avenue
Georgetown, Ontario L7G 5S4
Canada

Distributed in the U.K. and Europe by David & Charles
Brunel House
Newton Abbot
Devon TQ12 4PU
England
Tel: (+44) 1626 323200
Fax: (+44) 1626 323319
E-mail: postmaster@davidandcharles.co.uk

Distributed in Australia by Capricorn Link
P.O. Box 704
Windsor, NSW 2756
Australia

Visit our Web site at www.fwpublications.com for more resources about home-related topics.

Other fine F+W Books are available from your local bookstore or direct from the publisher.

12   11   10   09   08   5   4   3   2   1

Library of Congress Cataloging-in-Publication Data

Howard, Dori.
  The smart woman's guide to homebuilding : an essential reference for homeowners and builders / by Dori Howard.-- 1st ed.
        p. cm.
  Includes index.
    ISBN-13: 978-1-55870-817-4 (pbk. : alk. paper)
  1. House construction. 2. Contractors--Selection and appointment. 3. Consumer education. 4. Women consumers. I. Title.
    TH4815.4.H69 2008
    690'.837--dc22
                                        2007046014

Acquisitions Editor: David Thiel
Senior Editor: Jim Stack
Designer: Brian Roeth
Production Coordinator: Mark Griffin

WEB SITES

210 Home Warranty Protection, www.210.com

American Society of Interior Designers, ASID, www.asid.org

American Society of Landscape Architects, ASLA at www.asla.org

Better Business Bureau, www.bbb.org

Forest Stewardship Council, www.FSC.org.

Leadership in Energy and Environmental Design, LEED, www.usgbc.org/LEED

Old Republic Home Protection, www.orhp.com.

National Association of Home Builders, NAHB www.nahb.org

National Association of the Remodeling Industry's NARI web site: www.nari.org

National Council for Interior Design Qualification, NCIDQ, www.ncidq.org

www.constructionweblinks.com

www.uslegalforms.com

PHOTO CREDITS

Front cover house: French Normandy-style home features a custom-made front door with iron grill, cedar timbering common to Normandy design and a turret, accented with native Tennessee stone. CASTLE CONTRACTORS, REED BROWN PHOTOGRAPHER

Table of contents, page 4. Woodmeister, BPC Architecture and Interior Designer Victoria Harris created this award-winning home within the strict guidelines of the Historic District Commission on Nantucket. Characteristic of many Woodmeister homes, there's a private widow's walk. WOODMEISTER MASTER BUILDERS, GARY SLOAN PHOTOGRAPHER

Introduction, page 6. This lot was challenging due to its steep slope. Conceptually, this home had to be designed on a linear axis to take advantage of the panoramic view. NANCY HAYDEN ARCHITECT, RICHARD LEO JOHNSON PHOTOGRAPHER

Chapter 2, page 28. Award-winning home built by Woodmeister Master builders overlooks Nantucket. PHOTOGRAPHER: GARY SLOAN GENERAL CONTRACTOR: WOODMEISTER MASTER BUILDERS ARCHITECT: BPC ARCHITECTURE INTERIOR DESIGNER: VICTORIA HARRIS

Chapter 7, page 94. Custom home with poplar wood ceiling, natural ash floor, native Tennessee farm-stone fireplace surround, local craftsman made the hammered-copper mantle. PHOTO CREDIT: SANFORD MEYERS, GENERAL CONTRACTOR: FORTE BUILDING GROUP, ARCHITECT: SCOTT WILSON

Chapter 8, page 104. This kitchen incorporates both a clean-up area for storage and prep area for that is conveniently located by the pantry, fridge and sink. PHOTO CREDIT: GARY SLOAN, ARCHITECTURAL MILLWORK: WOODMEISTER MASTER BUILDERS, GENERAL CONTRACTOR: KISTLER & KNAPP

DEDICATION *To all homeowners who desire to build your own homes — may this book inspire you to reach for your dreams.*

ABOUT THE AUTHOR

Dori Howard, author and speaker, grew up in Minneapolis, Minnesota, in a family of homebuilders and artisans. After a successful career as a commercial actress in Los Angeles, she moved with her musician husband and their young family to Nashville, Tennessee. She appeared on the Oprah Winfrey Show for a segment of *Kitchens With a View*. Having gone through a harrowing "learning experience" of building her own home, Ms. Howard developed a passion for bridging the huge communication gap between homeowners and the professionals in the homebuilding and remodeling industry. Through her web-based company, Dori Howard Enterprises, she has created the Proactive Homebuilding Method™, assisting both homeowners and professionals in making the best choices when building or renovating a home.

ACKNOWLEDGEMENTS

All my love to my husband Tom and my kids, Katie and Joseph. I am grateful to you for all that you have done to support me on this incredible journey.

The experience of researching and writing this book has been blessed by the generous and gracious help of some very special people. My gratitude to each one is immeasurable. Dr. Brad Gray, my mentor and friend, has brought constant encouragement and wisdom to this process. Sam Watson, my business advisor, has had the right words at the right time. I also want to thank the Band of Brothers at Holy Smokes, my St. B's family, my sister Becky and my friend Paula for your support throughout this journey.

Thank you, Sigmond Brouwer, for believing in me early on and sharing your insights as an author. Thanks also to my editor, Jim Stack and the staff at F+W.

HOMEBUILDING PROFESSIONALS

I'd like to thank the following homebuilding professionals for their generosity in granting me some their time to share their knowledge and insights about the business of homebuilding:

- Jim Catlin, Senior Account Executive for Woodmeister Master Builders
- Kimberley Collins-Ripmaster, Mortgage Loan Officer & Certified Builder Representative
- Todd Panther, Attorney, Tune, Entrekin & White, P.C.
- Carol Pedigo, Honary AIA, Executive Director for the American Institute of Architects Middle Tennessee
- James Edwards, Architect
- Duo Dickenson, Architect
- Nancy Hayden, Architect
- Benjamin Nutter, Architect
- Kevin Hale, Owner of Hale Insurance Agency, LLC
- Will Forte, Forte Building Group, LLC
- Alan Looney, President, Castle Contractors
- Evy McPherson, Interior Designer
- Don Silvers, Author, Chef, Kitchen Designer and Cooking Instructor
- Richard Dykman, Architect/Contractor Executive Vice President, Boran Craig Barber Engel Construction Co., Inc.
- Salem Forsythe, Remodeling Contractor
- Sharon Lester, Retired Contactor

For more information on the homes featured in my book and the people who worked on them please visit my website.

contents

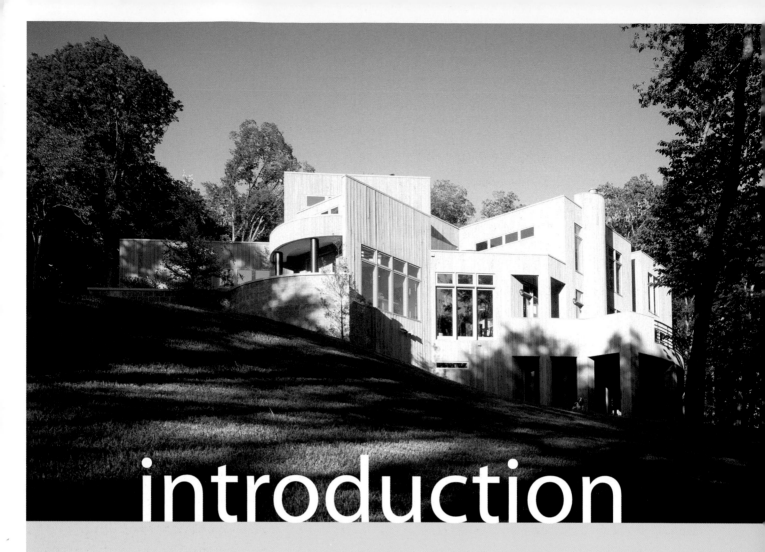

introduction

Simply stated, women make up the majority of homeowners who spend the most time with their builders, architects, interior designers and the other members of their homebuilding team, yet most women have never set foot on a building site, let alone their *own* building site. Along with managing the affairs of your household and family, you *can* manage the building team for your new home. That's where this book comes in. *The Smart Woman's Guide to Homebuilding* removes the shroud of mystery about building a house and ultimately, helps you to become the CEO and overseer of the building of your own home.

WHY WOMEN? THE INFORMATION IN THIS BOOK IS PERTINENT TO EVERY HOMEOWNER TAKING ON the challenge of building or remodeling their home. However, the fact is, women make up the majority of homeowners who are most likely to be on the building site at any given time, representing their family's needs to the homebuilding professionals hired to design, build or remodel their homes. This means that on a daily basis, women who have never set foot onto a construction site will be called upon to provide the information necessary to keep the job progressing in a timely manner. Women are most likely going to be the ones meeting with vendors to pick out products and materials that will be used in creating their home's ambiance. They invest the most time and energy balancing the needs of their family's day-to-day activities alongside the responsibilities of managing a building project.

I, along with every other homeowner who has built or remodeled their home, have experienced the frustrating consequences of not having an adequate management system available to assist in managing a homebuilding or remodeling project. I think it's time that homeowners, especially the woman homeowner, be provided with a set of essential homebuilding tools that are specifically designed to meet your needs within the context of any homebuilding project, assisting you in the daunting task of managing what is likely going to be the most costly investment of your lifetime. By creating the Proactive Homebuilding Method™ I have made it possible for you to keep you and your family's priorities intact while successfully integrating your newly-found responsibilities within your homebuilding project.

In this book, I've combined my knowledge of homebuilding and remodeling along with other homeowners who have gone through the process and added insight from industry professionals. You'll learn, from interviews that I've conducted with other homeowners and homebuilding professionals, how you can make the most of your homebuilding or remodeling experience. This will help you to avoid some of the most common mistakes homeowners make when they take on the challenge of building or remodeling their homes. The best aspect of these homebuilding essentials is that they all communicate the homebuilding process in a language you'll understand, homeowner-to-homeowner.

While gathering information from the industry professionals, I focused on the homebuilding essentials that speak directly to how building a new home or remodeling an existing home will personally affect you, your family and your financial investment. By addressing the homebuilding processes in this manner, I put you in the position of being able to attain key information about the homebuilding process that historically eluded the homeowner new to the experience until months into their project.

CHAPTER one

PROACTIVE HOMEBUILDING METHOD™

your tools for success

Your Conundrum

Homebuilding is set up in such a manner that the end justifies the means, and what you don't know can indeed hurt you and your project. As a homeowner new to the homebuilding or remodeling process, you are entering your project from the "back door". There's a huge gap of information between the completed-project photos you gather for reference purposes for your new home and the actual new home. From day one you will have to start making costly decisions on things you know little or nothing about. Yet it is these decisions that will ultimately determine your project's destiny.

My Conundrum

Having experienced firsthand the pain and frustration of living through a horrific homebuilding experience, I know what you need to know to avoid your own homebuilding nightmare. I also know that if you are new to the homebuilding/remodeling process, you have no way of relating to or identifying with your need for this information. So, how can I help you recognize the value of venturing beyond the typical picture-gathering process and into the more substantial elements that you are ultimately responsible for? I needed an incentive that you can readily identify with. I think I found it — your money!

Avoiding Litigation, Arbitration or Mediation

At the beginning of our homebuilding project, I purchased a number of books that were written by professionals for homeowners who were building or remodeling their home. They were full of information on how a house is built and what we could expect during the process. I'd begin reading them in anticipation of discovering something that would excite me about this new venture. What was my job going to be? How would my family be involved? Try as I might, I had a hard time relating to this experience through the eyes of the professional. Because I had not actually built my own home before, my desire for personalizing the process wasn't developed through the technical aspect of the homebuilding. I'd read a few chapters of one of these books, and soon lose interest. I felt like an outsider looking in. I enjoyed tearing into the home design magazines and collecting pictures that represented what we wanted to have our house look like much more than studying a glossary of homebuilding terms to better relate to an architect or contractor. Compiling these pictures was a tangible contribution that I could make to this overwhelming project. It was fun and I could readily identify with these visuals versus the hypothetical experience that an industry professional was laying out for me. It provided me with a sense of order, this was an area that I could manage and control.

Recognizing the fact that other homeowners are going to have the same experience that I did when they attempt to educate themselves about the process of homebuilding, I was aware of the obstacles I faced when it came to writing a book that was going to hold your interest from beginning to end. I knew it had to be real page-turner. Fun, yet suspenseful, informative yet easy to digest, while still providing you with the riveting information that, until now, homeowners hadn't read about in all the other homebuilding books currently sitting on the store shelves. I needed a reality-show-type challenge (in a book format) that every homeowner across the country would want to take part in. It had to be based on a concept that we all relate to, no matter what size homebuilding project you are considering. What might inspire homeowners to delve into this book and absorb its information in hopes of bettering their homebuilding experience? How about an avoiding-litigation challenge?

Record numbers of homebuilding projects are ending up in *litigation, arbitration* or *mediation.* When you build or remodel your home, it is an all-encompassing experience. This means that what *you* experience, your family experiences along with you. You want to take the appropriate actions now to help prevent you and your family from having to expend valuable time, emotional energy and financial resources that any of the three situations would require.

How I Got Started

It wasn't long after our homebuilding fiasco that I started to receive calls from friends and acquaintances that wanted to build or remodel their own homes. In hopes of avoiding the same fate, they thought it wise to consult with us first. I was asked to help them review their options before they committed to anything. I began looking over kitchen designs, blueprints, pictures and listening to their comments on what they were hoping to accomplish on their projects. I walked through newly built homes and gave my opinions as to what this homeowner may want to consider before making the purchase.

I was receiving many calls from people who knew of someone who was currently in a bad homebuilding experience or just recovering from one. They would relay the tragic news and how devastating it was to the family. I am not an architect or contractor, and I would not presume to advise as one. Nor am I in a position to offer legal advice. I do know, however, from firsthand experience, what the future holds for the unfortunate homeowner caught in the middle of a homebuilding nightmare and the stress it can have on her and her family. In those situations, as they began picking up the pieces, my role became one of listening, consoling and offering the insight I have gained.

One evening my husband asked. "Did you get a call from Sarah yet?" I said, "No, why?" "She has some friends who just built a home in Atlanta. Apparently, it's not quite finished and they can't get the builder to come back and do the work. Sarah said they're just worn out and want the experience to be done with. They've moved in and, as an incentive, they paid their contractor in full, hoping he'd make good on his word to finish out soon, but they haven't heard from him in months."

I talked with a woman who works in a media position that affords her the opportunity of meeting people who are in the process of building or remodeling their homes who also had what she would call a horrific experience. She said that when someone comes to her with their eyes full of hope and anticipation she wants to yell at them, "Don't do it!" She said, "I begin to tell them my story and I can see the expression on their face change. Their eyes glaze over and I know they're thinking to themselves, 'I'm not you, my experience will be different.'"

I picked up a popular woman's magazine a while back because one of the subtitles on the front cover was how to "Manage The Perfect Remodel." I was intrigued and bought the magazine in anticipation of learning something. However, the more I read, the more disappointed I became. By the time I was finished with the article, I was downright angry. I was hoping for some real guidance and insight that would enable a woman to enter into her project from a place of knowledge and understanding that would allow her to effectively manage her project. Instead, what I walked away with was that the only option to surviving your remodel successfully was to submit to the fact that your contractor was going to be late showing up, as well as late to finish your project and that you were going to go way over budget. It also insinuated that if, while working on your project, either your architect or contractor were to make a mistake resulting in an upcharge to your project, that you should expect to have to take out your checkbook to pay for the corrections. The writer actually made light of this type of setback and said it goes with the territory.

Homeowners ill-prepared for and unknowledgeable about the homebuilding process are quick to acquiesce and assume financial responsibility, or overlook and excuse, less than professional standards under the guise of, "That's just the way it is with home construction.". Not true. As a matter of fact, I have talked with many architects and contractors who hold themselves and their peers to a high standard of professionalism and cringe at the thought of being portrayed as one of the workers who gives this industry a bad name.

Even with all the material available to the homeowner today via books, magazines, web sites and other media resources, homeowners are entering ill-prepared into the single most costly investment they are likely to make in their lifetime. I have talked with people across the country; successful professionals who are embarrassed or ashamed when giving accounts of the decisions they made on their failed project. Often I hear what I have now come to call the homeowner's homebuilding lament: "If I knew then what I know now, I would have done things differently."

The commonality of all homeowners new to the process of homebuilding is this lack of experience with which we enter our projects. And yet it's from this vulnerable position and entry-level perspective that we attempt to make executive level decisions — like assembling a team of professionals to design and build our homes. I know of no other venture where one is willing to risk taking financial responsibility, to the extent of possible ruin, solely on the basis of trusting in another, who professes to be, professional, to do the right thing on our behalf.

In the process of developing my company, I have had the good fortune of meeting top-notch industry professionals. The good news for homeowners is that they're out there! There are people who work very hard to deliver a successful homebuilding experience to their clients. The not-so-good news for many homeowners is that it's obvious we have a difficult time identifying who they are. I've created a homebuilding method that will begin tipping the scales in your favor by helping you identify the problem areas that most commonly trip up the homeowner new to the homebuilding process. I call it the Dori Howard Proactive Homebuilding Method™ — key word being *proactive*.

Proactive Homebuilding Method™

I have been developing the Proactive Homebuilding Method™ (PHM™) over the last four years in response to the real-time problems encountered by the Homeowner as they embark on any construction project, be it a new build or a renovation. The attendant issues are always the same; those having to do with navigating one's way through a professional (and foreign) environment, information management, sched-

uling, and some of the more hidden matters, such as maintaining emotional control in the midst of overwhelming and relentless requirements for crucial day-to-day decisions to be made quickly and intelligently. The Homeowner needs help. REAL help. They do not need one more in a plethora of "building books" which hand out advice and technical information to the reader who is vulnerable and inexperienced, trying to work within a complex industry. This is why I have developed a Method, a revolutionary and practical way of walking through this daunting process.

The Proactive Homebuilding Method™ is a well thought out, deliberate set of actions that are supported by organizing specific products relating to the needs of the homeowner. It also engages a very concise method of communication between the homeowner and the people they hire to design and build their home. Providing real-time Web-based assistance and updates that document the ongoing ever-changing communicative process between the homeowner and the people who will be working on their project.

Every professional that you hire to design and build your home is dependant on a set of tools that are specific to their needs in order to get their job done. These tools help organize and manage the different elements that come into play throughout the life of the project. The same holds true for a homeowner. A homeowner needs tools specific to their needs that will help them to organize and manage their responsibilities to their project.

It is not enough for a homeowner to simply maintain a calendar and organize their samples, receipts, draw requests, scheduled meetings, etc. If it were that easy, we wouldn't be experiencing the record number of projects ending up in court and disgruntled homeowners loosing millions of dollars annually due to mismanaged projects. Correspondence, invoices, draw sheets, product receipts, meeting dates, product samples, CDs, photos, manuals, contracts, construction payments, etc. are an example of the types of information you will begin accruing on a daily basis. Homeowners that I have talked with start out with the best intentions. They begin by putting the details of their project in a drawer, file or box in the attempt of keeping track of everything. However, after a couple of months of keeping up with the project's normal demands, organizing this information becomes an overwhelming challenge, even for the most diligent homeowner.

The difficulty of keeping this mounting data under control becomes evident the first time you spend an entire weekend rifling through the numerous drawers, over-stuffed files or toppling boxes in hopes of finding an email, receipt, or picture detailing the 1800's period fireplace mantle you wanted to include in the design of your living room.

My Proactive Homebuilding Method™ walks you through the ever-elusive homebuilding process pointing out what's most important for you to know along the way. I continue to provide you support on my Web site, www.proactive-homebuilding.com. Having the opportunity to build or remodel your own home should be one of the highlights of your family's lifelong experiences together. Providing you with the essential tools to assist you in the process is what the PHM™ is all about.

A Bit of Eye-Opening Homebuilding Trivia

I've provided the following information to help jumpstart your thinking process and introduce you to the benefits of my Proactive Homebuilding Method™. Unlike the limited perspective of the typical homeowner new to the homebuilding and remodeling experience, you will learn the importance of going beyond the basic picture sharing elements of the interview process and on into the significance of identifying with and acting upon the CEO responsibilities you inherit with your project.

The following chart is a typical example of who brings what to the first interview meeting.

At first glance, it's easy to understand why you, the homeowner, can get intimidated and feel like your leadership abilities are out of

HOMEOWNER
Pictures

HOMEBUILDING PROFESSIONAL
Professionally designed Portfolio
Professional contract
Legal representation
Insurance policy backed by conglomerate
License / registration from the state, city or county
Credentials
LLC or Incorporated business structure
Accounting procedure
Association memberships
Referrals

skew with the professionals you are interviewing. That's only because you don't understand (yet) how all this business related information the professionals provide for you is essential to establishing your own professional identity within your homebuilding / remodeling venture. From the get-go, the very first interview, the majority of homeowners misinterpret what their role is going to be throughout their project. The homeowner often assumes that because the professional knows more about homebuilding than they do, that they should take the back seat in this process and wait to be told what to do. While it's true that you will need to count on these professionals to help guide you through the process, they're depending on you to step up and take the lead. Someone has to make the decisions that drive the project forward. By assuming you are not qualified to make these decisions, you set yourself up to start abdicating your responsibilities to the people you hire to design and build your home from the onset of your project. If you are not willing or able to be in the driver's seat of your project, it is likely to go in a direction you didn't anticipate.

The Dori Howard Proactive Homebuilding Method™(PHM) will teach you how to gather the pertinent information necessary to assure you greater success in assembling the right team of people that you will be dependant on to design and build your home. My PHM™ will teach you how to begin your project communicating your intent, which is to hold all who work for you to a high standard of professionalism. The people you hire will appreciate this. It shows that you have an understanding of, and can appreciate how hard they work in order to provide you with the level of quality you desire.

From your lender's perspective or yours, if you are fortunate enough to be able to pay for the cost of your project, the following represents who will be financially responsible for all that happens on your project.

HOMEOWNER
100%

HOMEBUILDING PROFESSIONAL
Architect
Contractor
Contractor's subs
Codes department
Contractor's insurance provider
Manufactures that warranty the products used on your project?
0%

You are financially responsible for whatever the outcome is on your project. You took out the loan, you hired the professionals, you OK'd the design, you made the decisions that had to be made, and you paid for the work that was done. Good or bad, wonderful or horrific, when all is said and done, you will be paying a mortgage on whatever you end up with.

Foursquare Homebuilding Analogy

Making sense of you and your team's responsibilities is mere child's play.

It was early in the morning and I was out weeding around our front steps when I heard my neighbor call from across the street. I looked up to see her gesturing for me to come over; it was obvious she wanted to tell me something.

When we got within earshot of each other she yelled out, "I hear you're writing a book about homebuilding." I said, "Yes, I am." "Kyle and I are thinking about building a house," she continued, "would you be willing to come over and talk with me about it?" "Sure, I'd be happy to," I said.

At our first meeting, to help me better understand the type of home Brenda and Kyle were going to build, Brenda brought out a notebook of pictures she had been accumulating over the last year or so. Just like my notebook, the pictures were encased in plastic sleeves that were tabbed accordingly, room-by-room, representing what she and her family wanted to have built into their new home.

Brenda laid the book on the table and started talking me though each page, pointing to the pictures and explaining how each one related to some aspect of what they were hoping to build. Then she proceeded to tell me about the lot they had purchased. It was one of the first lots to open up in this newly developed piece of land. This was going to be the home of their dreams. The home their children would grow up in, and their grandchildren would come to visit.

Amidst the excited anticipation of building their new home, Brenda expressed some concerns she and Kyle had about the process. They have two daughters, twelve and fourteen years old. She and Kyle had opted to homeschool their girls over the next few years and Brenda was really enjoying the time and opportunities that homeschooling was affording them. One of her concerns though, was how she would continue to prioritize her family's current needs while taking on the new responsibilities of building their home. I told Brenda that this is an important question for any family to ask themselves when they decide to take on the challenge of building or remodeling their own home.

Some homeowners, having gone through a homebuilding project, will liken the time commitment and demands it makes on your daily routine to that of taking on a full-time job. Realizing this, a calendar will help minimize the potential for you to miss out on what's most important to you at any given moment.

Castle Contractors custom-built mantle, wood coffered ceiling with metallic finish, walls painted blue with chocolate glaze faux finish, furniture by At Home Nashville.
PHOTO CREDIT: REED BROWN, GENERAL CONTRACTOR: CASTLE CONTRACTORS, ARCHITECT: KEVIN COFFEE

I had one such unfortunate experience with regard to my son's schedule while in the process of building our home. I was up on our lot meeting with our contractor about the incorrect application of the brick on our house. During the meeting, I happened to remember that this was the same day of the Thanksgiving celebration at my son's school. He was in the fourth grade and was asked to read the paper he had written about what Thanksgiving meant to him, in front of the parents and kids in the auditorium. The celebration began at 11:00 and it was now 11:35. I quickly finished up my meeting and rushed over to my son's school. As I entered the auditorium the kids were filing out. My heart sank. I happened to catch my son's eye and we smiled and waved at each other as he was exiting the auditorium. Gauging from the look on his face, all went well and he was not aware that I had missed it. (I'm going to have to make sure he doesn't read this book. Fortunately my husband had captured the event on video.)

One of the key elements to the successful integration of this new homebuilding venture and your everyday life is going to be your ability to keep up with your usual obligations — especially where kids are involved. You want your project to be inclusive versus intrusive of your family's lifestyle.

It was clear that Brenda, like most homeowners, had a good grasp of the visual aspect of her project, as evidenced by the book she had compiled. This type of information is readily

available to homeowners in the form of magazines, books and cable television.

What Brenda wasn't clear on was the business side of a homebuilding project, which is the practical aspect of homebuilding as it relates to her role and responsibilities. This information is *not* readily available to homeowners. To help Brenda understand the business aspect of homebuilding and to see her project as a homebuilding venture that she is going to manage, I used my foursquare homebuilding analogy.

Do you remember the game of foursquare that we played when we were young? You had one large square that was divided into four smaller squares. Four people would play; one per square. Each person had to stay within the boundaries of their square throughout the game. The game began when the server (homeowner) bounced the ball from their square into another's (architect, contractor, etc.). In order to stay in the game you had to keep passing the ball to the other players. If you dropped the ball or hit it out of bounds you were out of the game. I use this foursquare analogy because it parallels the homebuilding team and helps to clarify a number of things for a homeowner.

It demonstrates the importance of defining boundaries. Each square contains a title or job description that represents an area of expertise. It also helps to delineate what the person in that square will or will not be responsible for. Anything outside of their square is not their job to take on. In order to keep the ball moving (project progressing) the team members have to recognize their interdependence on one another's expertise to accomplish their goal, i.e., to design and build a home to the homeowner's specifications within their budget and on schedule. If someone drops the ball, by either stepping outside their square and into someone else's (getting in someone else's business — this includes the homeowner) or doesn't fulfill their own responsibilities, the entire project suffers.

Here's a breakdown of the titles and job descriptions for you and your team members within the foursquare homebuilding chart.

PHM™ FOURSQUARE HOMEBUILDING ANALOGY CHART

CEO Homeowner	**CFO** Loan Officer directed by CEO
COO Contractor	**CDO** Architect

Chief Executive Officer – CEO

(Homeowner)

This is the senior manager who is responsible for overseeing the activities of an entire company.

The homeowner is the CEO and the head of the project. This does not mean that they have to know everything about building or remodeling a home. It means that you, being the CEO, have to do the homework that is necessary for you to hire the right people who know how to do that for you. The significance of making the right choices cannot be underestimated, as it is these team members who you are dependent upon to advise you throughout your project.

The point I made to Brenda was that, once you have your PHM™ homebuilding team in place, you can begin enjoying the process. Your homebuilding team will assist you in making all of your decisions on the front end of your project, in a relaxed environment where you are in control of how your money is going to be spent.

Chief Financial Officer – CFO

(Loan Officer – directed by CEO)

This is the senior manager who is responsible for overseeing the financial activities of an entire company. This includes signing checks, monitoring cash flow and financial planning.

I have included the homeowner in the CFO square as well as the CEO square because it is your responsibility to oversee the managing of your homebuilding budget throughout the life of your project. This is an area of responsibility that the typical homeowner falls short on. They often make the assumption that they can hand this task over to their contractor and be done with it.

Chief Operating Officer – COO

(Contractor)

The senior manager who is responsible for managing the company's day-to-day operations and reporting them to the chief executive officer (CEO).

Hiring the right COO (contractor) will help you maintain control of your homebuilding process. An honest contractor, who is experienced with the homebuilding process, will do all they can to assure that you get the home you desire. They will assist you and your architect or home designer in making realistic cost effective choices when creating a design that will fit within your budget. There will be no surprises or costly changes due to a dishonest bid. If you do decide to make a change, you will be able to assess the affects it will have on your budget and your project's schedule before committing to it.

Chief Design Officer – CDO

(Architect)

The senior manager who is responsible for producing the construction documents that provide the information needed for a contractor to build a project specific to the client's requirements. This can include construction administration services and revision of drawings request (architectural corrections) of the project in accordance to the client's needs.

The CDO is responsible for taking all the elements that you want to incorporate into your house and creating a set of documents or plans that represent these specifications to the contractor. The majority of homes today are built without using the services of an architect. In my opinion this is one of the reasons we have so many homebuilding projects fail. Contrary to popular belief, using an architect's services on your project can actually save you money in the long run. An architect welcomes the insight that a contractor can provide regarding the pricing of products used in a home design. The architect takes that information to create a design within the homeowner's budget parameters.

Although not accounted for in a square, an interior designer is just as essential to a project. The interior designer can work within the parameters of the CEO, COO and CDO squares on behalf of the homeowner. The interior designer's contributions assist the architect and contractor in esthetically designing spaces specific to the homeowner's needs and desires. If a space has to accommodate a special piece of furniture, the interior designer will help make sure that happens. They can also organize meetings and pick out product and materials on behalf of the homeowner. The interior designer speaks the language of both the homeowner and the homebuilding professional, making them a valuable asset on any project.

After going over this information with Brenda, I assured her that she was not going to be responsible for anything that she couldn't already make a decision on today. Brenda looked at me from across the table, teary-eyed and said, "I can do this. I don't have to put it off anymore." I am happy to say that Brenda and Kyle hired an architect shortly after our meeting. They are on their way to a family-focused homebuilding experience.

PHM™ Homebuilding Mantras

The following three phrases are for you to use at any juncture of your homebuilding or remodeling project. They are simple, to-the-point action phrases that will help you approach every decision you will make on your project.

- Don't Assume — Confirm
- Don't Abdicate — Delegate
- Defend What You Spend — Is it really worth it?

All three of these phrases are geared to keeping you in a proactive frame of mind. This means that in any given situation, no matter how stressed, pressured, indecisive, rushed, excited, flustered or overwhelmed you may become, reciting the phrase that best suits your situation at the time will help you to better focus in on the reality of your priorities before making a hasty or ill-informed decision you may regret later.

Don't Assume — Confirm

This phrase can be applied to almost any circumstance or phase of your building project. Because the nature of all homebuilding projects is dependent upon human beings interacting with each other, the potential for miscommunication at some point is inevitable. Keeping the lines of communication open and productive between you and the people you hire to design and build your home is not only going to produce a better quality product, it's going to keep you properly informed, in control of your responsibilities and relaxed. This is essential for you and your family's wellbeing.

Adopting the *don't assume — confirm* way of thinking will prompt you to proactively engage yourself within your project, ensuring that your needs and desires are being effectively communicated and carried out. The homebuilding professionals, i.e., your architect, home designer, contractor and interior designer all expect you to have questions. More importantly, they know the value of working with a homeowner who is knowledgeable about the homebuilding process, so they welcome the opportunity to answer them. *Don't assume — confirm* helps create a win-win environment.

Don't Abdicate — Delegate

Not understanding the significance of this phrase opens you up to becoming one of the "homebuilding horror of fame" statistics we've all heard about. Both words, abdicate and delegate, are verbs. Action words. The homeowner has to actively make a decision to abdicate or delegate responsibility. *Abdicate* relates to your responsibilities and *delegate* relates to the professional's responsibilities. Homeowners

Castle Contractors added authentic antique pieces like the stair newel post and refurbished 1920's light fixture for Old World charm in a newly built home. PHOTO CREDIT: REED BROWN, GENERAL CONTRACTOR: CASTLE CONTRACTORS, ARCHITECT: KEVIN COFFEE

who abdicate their responsibilities hand over or entrust to their professionals the decisions that they themselves are responsible for. Doing this can jeopardize the final outcome of your project. You may either fall prey to an unscrupulous homebuilding professional or you could become the source of the problem on your project.

Delegating the portion of your project that the homebuilding professionals are responsible for is appreciated. This puts the homeowner in a position to protect their home's assets and experience a positive homebuilding or remodeling experience.

Defend What You Spend — Is It Really Worth It?

Go into your project with the understanding that the market is always going to be introducing "new and improved" ways of using products in the homebuilding industry. This doesn't mean that the faucets that you loved and had installed last week are not going to rinse your dishes off as well as the new version this week.

Think back to all the big events in your life — getting married, having your first baby, buying your first home. Do you remember how many people became experts as to how you should best handle the event? The same thing is going to happen once you begin designing and building your home. Everyone (most likely the same person who told you what natural childbirth really means) is going to have a better way of doing what you are going to do. Unless they're on your payroll, don't make the mistake of changing things to appease a visitor in your home. Stay focused. You are making decisions about the design of your home based on you and your family's needs only.

The most important decisions you are going to make are about the professionals you hire to help you design and build your home. If you have a high expertise need in your home, such as an over-the-top kitchen, like I did, hire the right kitchen designer to design that space. A kitchen designer who cooks and knows how to use the appliances that are on the market (see the chapter about specialty designers) is an expert in what they can do.

Four Phases of Homebuilding — Not Unlike Childbirth

Every building project can be broken down into three to four phases of development. Your architect, home designer or contractor may label those phases differently to better suit their business terminology, but in general, your project will be defined within these phases. To personalize it, here's a birthing analogy.

Pre-conception/Pre-design

This is when you are first thinking about the possibility of building or remodeling your home. You haven't made any real commitment at this point. You are just beginning to explore all your options and gather information.

Conception/Design

You've made the decision. Yes, I want to begin working on this new addition to our family. You don't know what all is going to go into it at this point so you need to start putting together a picture book and hire a specialist (architect, home designer) who is skilled at developing a plan (blueprints) to help the staff (contractor and subs) to bring this project full term (building your house).

Transition/Construction

Transition is the longest and most formidable (labor intensive) phase of the project. All the preparation work you did (reading and acting upon the information in this book is like taking part in the best Lamaze class available) during the first two phases come into play here. The *transition/construction phase* starts out at a pretty slow pace. Then things start picking up and you quickly begin to see your home taking shape. If you've hired the right team to assist you in the delivery of your home, and you've prepared well during the *conception/design phase*, you will experience less setbacks (labor pains) and more fun in the process (the epidural!).

Delivery Process

Once your project is completed and passes all its inspections, you will receive a certificate of occupancy. This is your home's equivalent to a birth certificate. You will have a six- and twelve-month checkup from the contractor and continue to keep up with your home's needs by checking into our web site for long-term maintenance.

A Hard Lesson to Learn — What You Don't Know *Can* Hurt You

I knew a couple, Nick and Lynn, who had a homebuilding fiasco. During the litigation process, they began receiving and reviewing a vast influx of information, that was pertinent to their project, but that they had not seen before. This information also contained important details regarding the contractor they had hired. This information was public record but they didn't know to ask for it when their project began. When Lynn and I were talking about her experiences she said, "Knowing what I know now, hiring a contractor without first following up on this type of information makes about as much sense as walking into a hospital for open-heart surgery and choosing your surgeon based on his likability quotient." Unbeknownst to a homeowner who has not built before, it is this lack of forethought that the dishonest contractor is dependent upon to succeed in taking advantage of their clients.

One afternoon, Lynn had a man from the codes department come to her home to review some information. When he looked at a page requesting that their builder fill in the amount of money that he had determined it would cost to build their house, Lynn said that he paused, looked at it again and said, "This guy (I'm substituting the language here) knew exactly what he was doing the day he came in to pull this permit!" Lynn said that it was clear from his exclamation that he was able to read between the lines and ascertain why their contractor, when asked to fill in the amount it cost to build their home, lied. He had written in an amount that was two hundred thousand dollars less than what he knew it to be.

One of the contractors who came to give an estimate of what he thought it was now going to cost to correct the work done by their first builder told Lynn that he knew their first builder. He proceeded to tell her that he had done a check on that builder's license status before he came to meet with Lynn. This contractor asked Lynn if she and Nick were aware that at the time their house was built, their builder was not licensed to build a home that cost as much as theirs did. This meant that Lynn and Nick's builder would have taken on their project knowing that he was neither qualified, due to his lack of experience, nor did he have the financial strength that his license required him to have, when he signed on to build their home. Lynn and Nick, like typical homeowners heading into their construction project, trusted what their builder told them to be true. Also, they were limited in their knowledge as to what information that they should follow up on *before* hiring a contractor.

They didn't know the significance of a builder's financial strength until their builder's attorney informed their attorney that their builder had no financial capitol, and what little assets he did have, he had put under his wife's name. It became clear to Lynn and Nick that they were going to be responsible for the majority of the financial loss that they incurred due to hiring this contractor to build their home.

Because the degree of success you will have on your project is based upon the quality of professionals that you hire for your building team, I have developed a method for interviewing the professionals that you are going to hire for your project (see chapter 2).

The Common Homebuilding Experience vs The PHM™ Experience

The Common Experience
A homeowner has decided to either build or remodel their home. They drive around town and find a development that they want to build in, or purchase a piece of land to build their home on. If they are living in a home and the neighborhood is one that they like and can sustain the cost of their renovation, they decide to stay and add on to their existing home.

Most of these homeowners will bypass the services of an architect when they begin their homebuilding venture. If, when driving around the development they happen to see a house under construction that they like, they go up to the workers on the lot and either meet the builder or ask for a card from one of the subs to follow up with the builder later in the day. The person who wants to renovate proceeds in the same manner. They will talk with neighbors who have recently renovated and ask who they used to do the work. This is what I call pre-concept/pre-design.

At this point, the homeowner will follow up with the contractor responsible for the projects they were interested in and enter the conception/design phase. Upon meeting this contractor, if they like them, they will want to set up a meeting to go over what they would like to accomplish with their homebuilding project. This meeting may be at the homeowner's home, at the contractor's office or back on the site where the homeowner originally got the contractor's name. Some developments have a set list of builders that they work with, and, if you happened to go into that development, you would most likely meet in the main office of the development firm. In any case, they would meet with a representative who would walk them through their homebuilding process. This type of setup may include an architect or two on staff who also work for this development, keeping the homes that are being built in this neighborhood to a specific size, comparable style and resale value.

Often, in an upper-end development, contractors will have their own set of pre-designed plans that they have built before and are comfortable with. They will offer these to a client for review. These plans are similar to the other homes currently being built in the same neighborhood in size and design content. The contractor knows that this design is going to fit or be very close to the building budget that the homeowner is looking to spend because the development has set its prerequisites on the size of homes that can be built there. Once the homeowner is given their final set of plans, they would then receive what the builder considers to be the *cost estimate* or amount of money needed to build this house. Within this budget, the contractor would have provided *allowances*. This is the amount of money that the contractor has allocated to specific areas of the budget amount. For example, the contractor may have allowed $20,000 for appliances, $15,000 for plumbing fixtures, $17,000 for tile, etc. The homeowner agrees and the project begins.

Preparation of the lot begins. The footings and foundation are set. The homeowner begins the process of picking out their items. The builder may have given them a schedule of what to expect, or the project gets rolling along and the builder contacts the homeowner and lets them know when they are beginning a certain phase and what they will need from the homeowner during this phase. This is the beginning of what I would call the *transition phase*. You are transitioning from the *design/conception phase* on into the *construction/transition phase*. In the beginning of the *transition phase* things are moving along relatively slowly so you don't feel the push to have to get your decisions made right away. Your contractor has probably asked you to choose your windows, doors, shingles, exterior material, etc. Then you move on into framing. This begins the skeletal structure of your home, i.e., walls, stairs, roofing, etc. — getting everything ready to receive your exterior choices.

As the exterior is coming together, your contractor is getting their subs for the mechanical aspect of your project scheduled and in place, i.e., rough-in plumbing, water heater, electrical, HVAC (heating and air duct work), furnace installation. You are now choosing: interior doors, knobs, hinges, doorstops, switchplates, plumbing fixtures, light fixtures, ceiling fans, thermostats, intercoms, cabinets, wall tile, floor tile, carpet, wood flooring, crown molding, appliances, countertops, bathtubs, commodes, mirrors, entertainment centers, etc., for every room of your house. However, you realize amidst this whirlwind of decision-making that the allowances that your builder provided for you in your budget don't line up with the actual cost of the items that you are picking out for your home. At first you are okay because the floor tile you were looking at in the showroom is marked at $10 a tile, which fits within your allowance. Then, as you begin to talk with the sales rep, they explain that that price is just for the tile itself. It does not include the installation cost, which is an additional $9 per square foot. When you tell them what your allowance is for that area of your house, you both determine that this allowance is not enough to provide for the tile you were looking at. They take you to an area of the showroom that has tile in your price range (in the range of your allowance). These tiles (in your price range) don't fit with what you had planned on buying — it is a different color pallet, texture and size from what you were planning — this new tile is not going to work with the other areas of your home. You realize that if you were indeed going to use this second choice tile, you would have to change the wall color in that room to be a better match. Then you would have to change the wall color in the adjoining room as well. In fact, the rug and furniture you had planned on using in this area may not work as you had hoped either.

To stay within budget, you now have to rethink what you are going to do with this tile purchase, so you thank the sales rep and go home to regroup. The next day you go out to look at light fixtures and the same thing happens. Plumbing fixtures, too. This has thrown a major wrench in the works. You have to make a decision, or a sacrifice. Do you stay within budget and sacrifice what you really wanted — which is better quality — or do you purchase what you want and sacrifice your budget?

These overages are going to have to come out of your pocket. If you're lucky, you have the cash to compensate (some contractors know this). If you are not so fortunate, the money may have to come out of your savings, the money allocated for furniture or, worse yet, your kid's college fund or your IRA. Those of you who have yet to be in this position may think this wouldn't happen but, the fact is, it happens to homeowners more often than you think. For those of you who have just begun your project, are maxed out on your construction loan and have not yet confirmed your allowances, you need to take the next day or two to finish this book before making any more decisions!

The insulation and drywall begins to go up. Having to reselect some of the items that you are picking out due to the cost of everything has caused delays in deliveries. So, your contractor has had to shuffle his subs to adjust to the new schedule demands. This means that you also have to adjust because you need to get the items that these subs need versus the items you were originally focusing on. The stress of keeping this project managed, along with your family's everyday needs, is taking its toll. When your phone rings, the last person you want to talk to is your contractor. You can't wait for all this to be done!

When your contractor presents you with their monthly draw sheet, included is a number of change orders for upgrades to your project. You ask for an explanation and your builder tells you that you made changes that exceeded your original budget. The tile you picked out exceeded the budget allowance by $11,000. Your lighting is over by $14,000, your plumbing fixtures are over by $9,500 and you still have four months to go before your project is completed.

Your project is winding down and you think you have a pretty good handle on your costs. You know you've gone way over budget but at least you're seeing a light at the end of the tunnel. Then your contractor tells you that you still have two outstanding invoices and those will be higher than usual because it's at the end of the project and everything that hasn't been accounted for yet will be added on here.

Over 90% of current homebuilding projects go over budget — way over budget. Sometimes to the degree that the homeowners can't finish the entire project as originally planned or they end up losing it all together. These overages are due to the homeowner not knowing enough about the homebuilding and remodeling process to make the right decisions on the front-end of their project, beginning with who they hire and why. Even with the copious amounts of books, magazines, television shows and Internet information about the subject of homebuilding that is available to the homeowner today, our country is experiencing a record high number of failed building and remodeling projects. And, homeowner's are the ones left holding the bag. Being one such homeowner, I felt challenged to come up with a homebuilding process that would enlighten homeowners.

The PHM™ Experience
The PHM™ experience is much different than the common experience. It starts with assembling a team to help you make your dream home a reality. The first person on the team is the loan officer who pre-qualifies the homeowner for their building budget. The second is the attorney. The third is either the architect or the contractor, or both. Then the homeowner hires the interior designer, specialty designer and anyone else that their project requires. These people may or may not know each other, but they would all agree on the importance of being a team player and value each other's contribution to this project on behalf of bettering the homeowner's homebuilding experience. Chapter 2 will teach you how to interview and select your team members.

The homeowner has made known to everyone what their financial cap is going to be for this project and calls a meeting with everyone attending. At that meeting, everyone reviews the reference material that the homeowner has put together and they begin to define their roles and responsibilities. They discuss how each person will contribute to the design of the house in order to arrive at an end project that will be within the budget amount that the homeowner has allocated.

With the homeowner's budget in mind, the architect, contractor and designer can begin to give the homeowner a realistic perspective as

Charleston single style home built by Castle looks like it's been nestled on this hillside for years.
PHOTO CREDIT: REED BROWN, GENERAL CONTRACTOR: CASTLE CONTRACTORS.

to what they can expect out of this project; how many square feet, what types of materials will be used, etc. Given their combined experience, they are able to assist the homeowner in making value judgments that the homeowner would not know to make on her own. This is how hiring an architect and interior designer can actually save money as opposed to costing more.

The architect begins the design process. The contractor and interior designer consult with the architect as the design progresses to confirm that the materials being specified are going to meet and not exceed the budget parameters of the project. The homeowner is going to pay for the services of the architect one of two ways. Either they pay with their own money that was allocated for this purpose before the project began or, they have worked out a loan product with the loan officer and contractor to include this amount as a line item of their construction loan, still paying the architect the design fee upfront, but getting reimbursed for this amount at the end of the project.

If an architect is not going to be used for this project, the homeowner using my PHM™ understands that a pre-designed set of plans comes with many hidden or unforeseen costs and takes on the responsibility of those costs before construction begins by enlisting the services of their interior designer and contractor.

Because this homeowner has taken a proactive role in organizing their project, and knew how to interview and hire the right people for their team, they are able to make their choices for all their items upfront, as opposed to trying to accomplish this task amidst the whirlwind of the construction process. This homeowner is able to take their time, not be rushed by last minute phone calls from a contractor who needs something purchased for tomorrow and is in control of what they want to purchase; they know what their choices are and can make them with the help of their team members' expertise. If they run into budget limitations, they can meet with team members and get creative alternatives instead of making sacrifices.

If, during the design process, the architect calls the homeowner and says they either need to cut back on some of the square footage on this plan or pull back on their appliance budget, the homeowner is in a position to say, "Okay, let's bring in the square footage" or "I'll keep both because I know I can afford the $12,000 overage that the appliances are going to cost." This homeowner knows that they are currently three quarters through with their choices for their new home and so far, they've only gone over on their appliances.

It's been six months and the third set of drawings is finished. The homeowner signs off on it and construction is scheduled to begin in two weeks. Almost all of the items that the homeowner is responsible for have been chosen already. There are a couple of paint samples still outstanding that they want to decide on once the spaces are constructed.

The family is excited about the process. This homeowner has used my PHM™ to help them organize all their paint samples, color swatches, pictures of their knobs, lights and plumbing fixtures. As things progress, they are able to keep track of everything they picked out and watch as their home starts coming together. Their family comes up to visit in the evenings and on weekends throughout the next few months to watch the progress. Aside from the periodic calls to confirm this or that, the experience is going smoothly. The home-owner is able to continue with their normal day's activities while the house is being built.

The homeowner meets with their interior designer and architect at the homebuilding site and they start reviewing where all the furniture is going to go. Thanks to this designer's input on the front-end, the architect was able to incorporate specific design details to customize this homeowner's plans to suit the needs of their lifestyle.

One day the homeowner comes to the site and realizes that the light over the island is not as bright as they thought it would be. They decide to add some recessed lights. Their contractor meets with them and they go over what

this change is going to cost. The homeowner discusses the lighting change with whoever designed the kitchen. They decide that the change is worth the added expense. The following day the contractor hands the homeowner the change order to review. They sign off on it and write the contractor a check for the work to be done.

The house is almost finished. The homeowner needs to pick out the paint for their new office and the adjoining library. The interior designer meets the homeowner at the site with the perfect paint samples and their work is done. The homeowner is impressed that their home is complete, and, aside from the few changes that they made, and the minor price adjustments on some of the materials, they are able to get their home built within their budget.

True or False?

You purchased a lot and construction is underway, creating what the insurance company calls an _attractive nuisance_. (This is not a cute subcontractor that whistles in your direction when you come onto the building site). An _attractive nuisance_ is the dirt pile that is sitting on the side of your property. A neighboring child is riding his bike on the dirt pile, falls off and breaks an arm. The insurance your contractor carries will cover this accident. TRUE or FALSE?

False. Your contractor's insurance provides coverage to construction related matters. For this accident you would most likely have needed to take out a _premises liability policy_ from your homeowner insurance agent. According to Kevin Hale of Hale Insurance Agency, "Most homeowners make the mistake of assuming that it isn't necessary to get premises liability coverage until they actually move in. If you own the land that your home is being built on, you need to have it insured to protect you from property related accidents."

You have a general contractor who has hired numerous subs to work on your project. The general contractor, along with each sub working on your project, carries at least a

$1,000,000 general liability insurance policy. You file a claim to repair an incorrect installation by a worker. The cost to repair the work is estimated at $50,000. You're confident that in proving the insured worker's installation was defective and caused the problem to begin with, their insurance provider will cover the repair costs. TRUE or FALSE?

False. Making this assumption can have dire consequences to a homeowner. Not all insurance policies offer coverage that will respond to a construction-defect related claim. It's important that you ask your contractor how damage to your home resulting from faulty workmanship would be covered if it were to occur on your project while working with him and the subs that he hires. Hiring the right contractor from the get go will make all the difference if this type of scenario were to happen on your project. The preview, interview and review section of this book will help you make a more informed decision. If, after talking with your contractor, you still have questions, follow up with the agent who is providing the insurance policy. Their contact information will be on the insurance certificate that I have you receive upon your first interview.

The insurance certificate your contractor provided to you states that the policy effective date is Nov. 1, 2008 and the expiration date is Nov. 1, 2009. You have a subcontractor fall off your roof on Sept. 7, 2009. They are seeking funds to live on for the next 6 months while recovering. Upon hearing their employer (your contractor) has no insurance coverage, they come to you for this money. You call your contractor's insurance provider and they tell you that the policy was canceled 4 months ago due to non-payment of premiums. You state, yes, but the date the subcontractor fell off our roof was before the Nov. 1, 2009 expiration date, provided on the insurance certificate from our contractor.

This worker will be covered under your contractor's insurance policy. TRUE or FALSE?

False. Your contractor's insurance provider is not legally responsible to notify you of canceled coverage due to non-payment of premiums. And you can be sued if an accident occurs and your contractor's insurance has been canceled unbeknownst to you while they continued working on your project.

There is a fire on your building site halfway through your project and $350,000 worth of damage is done. Your contractor has a builder's risk policy in their name. They assure you that this policy will cover all the damages. The insurance company issues your contractor the check and your contractor takes off with the check in hand. You call the insurer and provide proof that it was your property the contractor was working on when the accident occurred. The insurance provider will either stop payment on the check, or pursue the contractor for reimbursement, and issue a new check to you for the damages. TRUE or FALSE?

False. The check will be issued to the insured party. If your name is not on the policy along with your builder, the check will be issued to your builder only. When we were building our house, I was talking with a neighbor who was just finishing up their home. She told me a similar story. The work that was damaged was in her kitchen. The contractor received a check to replace all the cabinets, counters and appliances and then he skipped town. When you hire your contractor, you will want to request that your name is listed as the additional named insured party along with them on all policies. It's important that you specifically include *additional named insured* party as opposed to *additional insured* party to be able to receive the equal and exact coverage that your contractor has. Then, for your own records, ask for a certificate indicating that this has been done. Hiring the right contractor along with taking this type of proactive responsibility will help you protect your homebuilding assets.

You are going to begin shopping for a construction loan for your project. You are focusing in on one of two lender's options. One advertises that they specialize in selling construction loans. You decide to go with the lender who specializes in construction loans because they will have the agents who know what your project's needs are going to be when it comes to helping you watch over your building budget. TRUE or FALSE?

False. Homeowners often make the mistake of not interviewing their construction loan agent just as they would anyone else on their homebuilding team. According to Kimberley Collins–Ripmaster of Franklin American, "When purchasing a homebuilding loan, you want to find someone who specializes in construction finance. Lending institutions may specialize in homebuilding loan products but not all loan officers do. Your regular mortgage loan officer is not going to know enough about the construction process to ensure that the customer is protected throughout the project."

If I build from a pre-designed set of plans that I order out of a design book, I will save more money than if I hired an architect to design my home from scratch.

While this is not necessarily true or false, the number one reason that projects go over budget is because of changes and upgrades that are made by the homeowner during the construction process. Homeowners assume they are going to save money if they build from a pre-designed set of plans rather than hiring an architect. However, those plans do not provide the specifications (specs) — the detailing of materials and such that help to define a solid budget. Homeowners inexperienced with the homebuilding process underestimate the amount of time and energy it takes to make all the decisions and choices necessary to construct their home.

Working with an architect or experienced home designer will provide you the opportunity to spend the time making better-informed decisions before you begin building.

Congratulations! Simply by reading this much of my book, you have already learned more about the practical business aspects of homebuilding than the majority of homeowners who are well into their projects know!

interview

Jim Catlin
*Senior Account Executive for
Woodmeister Master Builders*

Jim Catlin is responsible for up-front interaction with the customer at Woodmeister Master Builders. Jim, being a sales representative, interacts with everyone on a homebuilding team. He gave some great insight from both the homeowner's and the professional's perspectives.

We started as custom, hand-crafted cabinet company, working on interiors, doing cabinet and millwork throughout an entire home. As such, you're touching every wall in that home and interacting with every other subcontractor in the home — electrical, plumbing, HVAC, wiring, painting — everything. And because of our good level of detail and preparation up front, our customers have basically pushed us into doing construction. It seemed the natural thing to do. We've evolved from 26 years of being a cabinet company to the past 12 years of being *Master Builders*. We wanted to create this unity of team right from the beginning, which is the *Master Builders* approach to a project. We work with an architect, a designer, the builder, the interior specialist and a landscape designer. This is an important thing — right from the beginning.

Some people come to us with an architect and ask us to be their builder and interior specialist. Others come to us and say they want us to build them a home. We will help them find an architect that will suit their design needs and that understands the power of collaboration. Also, if they don't have a designer, we'll help them find one.

DO YOU FIND THAT HOMEOWNERS HAVE AN UNREALISTIC PERSPECTIVE OF THE AMOUNT OF TIME IT TAKES TO PROPERLY PREPARE ON THE FRONT- END OF THEIR HOMEBUILDING PROJECT BEFORE CONSTRUCTION BEGINS?
People have a preconceived notion of how it's going to go and they want it right away. Our process is to educate them as to what will happen. Once you tell a customer their role and their responsibility in this process,

they understand. They didn't realize how much time it takes and that it won't happen as quickly as they thought. That's why it's important to have the right team that they respect and trust. Then they say, "You're right. It doesn't make sense to rush into the project." When we get into a project, expectations are consistent.

I DEVELOPED THE FOURSQUARE ANALOGY TO HELP HOMEOWNERS MAKES SENSE OF THEIR ROLES AND RESPONSIBILITIES AS WELL AS THOSE OF THE OTHER TEAM PLAYERS. FOR EXAMPLE, MY NEIGHBOR, I WANTED HER TO SEE THAT AS A HOMEOWNER SHE IS RESPONSIBLE FOR *HER* JOB. SHE NEEDS TO LET THE OTHER TEAM MEMBERS TAKE CARE OF THEIR OWN RESPONSIBILITIES.

I find that homeowners can get overwhelmed with construction. They say, "I don't get it." They don't understand that there are many things involved. There's no way for them to read a few books or look on the Internet and understand what these professionals have learned in their twenty years' experience. And why should they? Their job is not to know how to nail on shingles or know the difference between shingles. That's our job. For the benefit of the homeowner, it's key that everyone in the industry is aware of this.

There's only one ego that's important in the process and that's the customer's. Everybody wants to strive to appease it when creating a home for that customer. If you get a customer, a contractor and an architect from the beginning that respect each other and understand each other's roles, that's good.

I TELL HOMEOWNERS TO HIRE PEOPLE WHO CAN WORK ON A TEAM AND USE YOUR TEAM MEMBER'S EXPERTISE ON THE FRONT END OF YOUR PROJECT. DON'T COMPARTMENTALIZE YOUR TEAM'S CONTRIBUTIONS FOR SPECIFIC PHASES. EVERYONE NEEDS TO BE INVOLVED AND ON THE SAME PAGE EARLY ON TO BE THE MOST EFFECTIVE IN HELPING YOU DESIGN A PROJECT THAT MEETS YOUR BUDGET.

I think you've hit on something that is key in this industry, and I've said before, something that has to change. A lot of people are recognizing it, and I see more and more architects are starting to realize and are advocating to get a builder involved from the beginning. They're refraining from answering the customer's question as to how much is this going to cost. They're coming back and saying, "That's not my line of expertise," which is great, because it's helping to set realistic expectations. We're all craftsman, architects, designers and builders. We all want to provide our crafts, but we've got to do it in a collaborative manner. An architect is great at designing the home and creating space and function. The builder brings validity to all that, including budget. Architects don't do pricing on a day-to-day basis. Their pricing is from the last job that they did with the last contractor that they did it with. Every project is different. I tell homeowners to get the builder involved early on and, when using an architect and builder, make sure that there's a synergy between the two. Get the two together in the same room and have a conversation about how this process is going to take place and make sure that you don't get the awkward facial expressions or squirming in the seat from either party saying "I don't know if that's going to work for me." Because if it's not going to work for them, then they are not the right person that you want to hire for your project.

The tagline of our company is "To Experience the Difference of Collaboration and Craftsmanship." The old linear approach to construction is when you hire an architect, get together and spend three or four months coming up with a plan. Then you say, "Oh, this is beautiful. I love it." You can't wait to build it. Then you think, "Oh, yeah, we should get a builder involved." When you get the builder involved and they say, "this isn't a $4 million home; this is a $6 million home." Now you have to go back and try to get your design in line with what you want to spend. You begin feeling, "Gee, you know, I'm not quite as excited as I was." Then you're moving along with the building process and you say, "Gee, I need furniture in this house," or "I need a kitchen design," and you call the designer. The designer comes in and says, "I've got to put couches here, a bed there and it doesn't fit under the sloped ceiling in the second floor. And, I don't have enough room for side tables on either side. There's no electrical outlet for a lamp. The drapes don't fit because it's too tight for the inside wall." Now you start to sacrifice things that you wanted because you didn't have those players on the same page from the beginning.

I HAD A FRIEND WHO WAS JUST FINISHING HER PROJECT. WHILE WE WERE TALKING HER PHONE RANG. WHEN SHE LOOKED TO SEE WHO IT WAS SHE ROLLED HER EYES AND SAID "IT'S MY BUILDER. I HATE WHEN HE CALLS."

That's because you're sacrificing what's important to you and your family's lives and you start to resent the project. You're frustrated with the builder or the architect or the designer — whoever is calling. "I hate it when he calls me. Can't he just do this without me?" And the builder is saying, "Don't they understand I need this information?" The project ends and everybody's ready to move on. The homeowner may or may not have gotten what they wanted, they don't know who to trust or who to blame and they're going, "Man, I hated that."

SO BY EDUCATING THE HOMEOWNER TO WHAT THEIR ROLE IS, HELPING THEM SET REALISTIC EXPECTATIONS, ASSISTING THEM IN MAKING THEIR DECISIONS EARLY ON TO MEET THEIR BUDGET, THE TEAM SETS THE HOMEOWNER UP TO BE A PRODUCTIVE CEO IN MANAGING THEIR PROJECT. THIS IS SO IMPORTANT IN MAKING THE OVERALL EXPERIENCE INCLUSIVE VERSUS INTRUSIVE WHEN IT COMES TO BALANCING THE PROJECT WITH THEIR HOME LIFE.

That's exactly the point. If nothing else gets changed in the industry, I would love to see people get more excited about their projects. Like you say, it's something people look at and say, "Oh, gosh, I've got to do this. I don't want to do it." It should be something that's exciting. It's like, "Wow, I have the wherewithal to do something for my family. I have the money, I have the need and the desire to do this. I can't wait to do it. I want to make it mean everything."

There's so much media access for people to see all these wonderful things that they can incorporate into their homes. They should be able to and it should be an enjoyable process. I agree, if the homeowner understands early on and says, "Okay, I'm going to do this!" And they're going to devote one day a week or two hours a week to a meeting with the architect, designer, builder, whatever the group is that they are going to work with, then they can properly schedule it within their life. Rather

than all of a sudden a builder calls up and says, "I need a faucet picked out tomorrow or you're holding everything up and costing yourself all this money," That's pressure, and the homeowner is going to end up sacrificing something.

IT'S IMPORTANT FOR HOMEOWNERS TO UNDERSTAND THAT, ONCE THEY HAVE DONE THE PROACTIVE WORK ON THE FRONT END, IT'S IMPORTANT TO HIRE THE RIGHT PEOPLE FOR THEIR PROJECT. THEY NEED TO TRUST THOSE PEOPLE TO DO THE JOB THEY WERE HIRED TO DO.

Yes. Homeowners often come into this process not trusting. They may have had friends or relatives say, "Boy oh boy, you're getting into construction? What a pain in the neck! Don't trust the contractor. Don't trust the architect. Don't trust this or that person." They go into it with that attitude of not knowing who to trust. Customers say, "This is what I want, and if I can't have it..." The professional is looking at it saying to themselves, "This will look drastic. They could get what they want for a whole lot less." When a builder or architect says, "This is what you said you wanted, but if you did this, you'd hit it pretty close", a lot of times the customer's red flag goes up. "They're trying to take advantage of me, they're trying to give me something less than I want," so they push back saying, "No, that's what I want." This is the struggle. My recommendation to customers is to pick a team that you can trust and then trust them. Make sure they're listening to you, but make sure you're speaking up. You need to have this back and forth communication. Just like any good relationship in your life. You're going to be married to this group for the next one- or two-year process. You've got to feel comfortable. You don't jump into a marriage unless you're comfortable that it's going to work for the next thirty or forty years. Don't jump into a project unless you're comfortable that it will work.

CHAPTER *two*

PROACTIVE HOMEBUILDING METHOD™

the interview process

Proactive (prO-'ak-tiv), adj, 2. Controlling a situation by causing something to happen rather than waiting to respond to it after it happens

What separates the Proactive Homebuilding mindset from the typical homebuilding mindset is the manner in which a homeowner and a homebuilding professional approach a project. The word proactive means to control a situation by causing something to happen, rather than waiting to respond to it after it happens.

Characteristically, homeowners have entered into their homebuilding projects with great enthusiasm, high expectations, hopeful and emotionally charged! A few months into it and they are totally overrun by the process.

Once the homeowner begins their project, their decisions start lining up in sequence like dominos. Nothing takes the fun out of a homebuilding project faster than having to run in front of the dominos, always feeling rushed and pressured to make last minute decisions. It's usually about halfway into their project when the homeowner catches on as to how the homebuilding process works. Now, with the benefit of having this knowledge, it serves only to exacerbate an already overwhelming situation because they are now in the position to make better decisions but the work has already been done. The key to my Proactive Homebuilding Method™ is having the tools that you need on the front end of your project to assist you in making the decisions and managing the environment that causes your project to go in the direction that you want it to go.

I have developed a method of interviewing that gives you the greatest potential for identifying the right professionals for your project. The information that I've provided for you in the Preview and Review sections of my PHM™ Interview process will establish a basis of knowledge that far surpasses what a homeowner typically brings to their interviews. You will begin your process from the empowered position that knowledge generates, as opposed to the vulnerable position that a lack of knowledge generates.

The following chapters will prepare you for your interview process. They break down the business component of each professional into an easy-to-understand, easy-to-relate-to fashion. For your architect and contractor, you will have a preliminary review and first interview list that establishes the items and information you will require from this professional at your first interview. The items on this list are then broken out into an interesting-to-read format that helps you understand the importance of what you are asking for and why you need it. Included in all of the homebuilding team member chapters is a follow-up review process, complete with a handy checklist to help you confirm that the people you are talking with at these interviews are on the up-and-up.

Helping you prepare for your interview process in this manner is what sets my Proactive Homebuilding Method™ apart from other homebuilding references. This due diligence will provide you with the answers to the questions that the typical homeowner doesn't know to ask before their project begins. Better yet, you will know what to do with the information once you get it. How cool is that!

The First Interview

Call the professional to set up an interview, introduce yourself and briefly describe your project to them. Ask if this is the type of project that they would be interested in. Make sure that their schedule fits with yours and that they're not too busy to take on your project. If this sounds like an individual that you want to meet with, set up a time to meet. Let them know that you have some items that you will need for them to have available for you at this meeting.

Some professionals may not be used to homeowners asking for this information up front. If you are met with any reservations from someone when asking for this information, a simple, "This is a business venture for me. I'm sure you can understand that, given the amount of money I am investing in this project, it is in my best interest to hire the right people who are best suited for the job. This information will help me determine who that is."

If you are still met with reservations or any negative response, my suggestion would be to pass on hiring this individual. They have already given you an indication of what you will be dealing with throughout your project, were you to hire them.

The goal of this first meeting is to learn all you can about this potential team player and focusing on them and what they have to offer will help you maintain productive control of your decision making process. Whereas dispersing information, i.e., focusing on tons of pictures (especially this early on in your home-building process) becomes all about you and allows for the emotional excitement to take over. This can distract you from asking important questions and registering the answers.

Maintaining a clear objective is important to making the right choices of the people you will hire for your project. At the outset of your project you will want to determine whether or not the qualities of the professional you are interviewing are those you want for this project.

When you first meet this professional, let the introductions take place. Then, ask if you can receive the information you requested during your phone conversation. Don't take up a lot of time going over details on everything you've received while at this meeting. If there is any information from your checklist that has not been provided, ask why.

You will know, from your preliminary preview of the information listed for this professional, the importance of acquiring it and the negative impact it would have on your project if it was missing. For example, when you meet with a contractor who does not provide you

with his insurance certificate, you know you cannot consider hiring this person until you receive that information. Ask when you can expect to receive it. They may have a legitimate explanation. It could be that they simply forgot to get you a copy. In any case, you need to let this person know that you will need to receive this information before you can schedule a follow-up interview with them.

Here are some general questions you can ask during your first interview to help you establish a rapport with this professional:

- How long have you been working in residential construction?
- What percentage of your work is made up of residential projects?
- Can you give me a general history of how you got started in this industry?
- How will your expertise benefit my project?
- What are your strengths?
- What are your weaknesses and how might you compensate for them?

(This is an interesting question to ask anyone. It's not meant to be a trick question or a question that has some deep philosophical meaning to life, it's just interesting to hear how people respond to it and it gives you a bit of insight into their character, self awareness and willingness to be honest about it.)

- How will you help me head into my project with realistic expectations?
- What are your feelings about working on a project with other professionals in a team-like environment?
- Have you worked in a team environment on other projects? If so, tell me how it went.
- It's important for me to have a clear understanding of how much money this project is going to cost me. How will you assist me in arriving at a realistic building budget at the onset of my project?

During your first interviews, you are not trying to sell your project to the professional!

Brownstone, under construction, the interior is custom per client's request while exterior is built true to 1800's architecture in Historic downtown Franklin. PHOTO CREDIT: SANFORD MEYERS, GENERAL CONTRACTOR: FORTE BUILDING GROUP, ARCHITECT: SCOTT WILSON.

• It's important to me that I understand my role and responsibilities on this project. How will you assist me in gaining clarification as to what they are?

• How will you assist me in maintaining my role as CEO throughout the life of my project?

Combine these questions along with some of your own and the questions that I include at the end of each chapter that are specific to the professional that the chapter is about. I also include a follow up and review check list to help guide you through all the materials and referral questions you have gathered from your first interview.

The purpose for asking these questions is to give you a perspective on how this person communicates and how you feel about the answers you are receiving. Are they clear? Are you confident that this person's personality is one that you would be comfortable with? Are you relaxed in their presence? Are they listening to you? Are they able to take the lead or are you doing most of the talking? Once you begin your project, you may be asking a lot of questions — possibly about the same topic a number of times. You want to work with someone who appreciates the fact that you are new to this process and that you need clarity as to what you can expect.

At no time do you want to feel like you are being spoken down to, or that if you were to ask too many questions that this person would take offense at you not recognizing their potential to do the job. You are not selling your project to this professional! Architects often refer to being awarded a project from a client. I like that. When you decide whom you want to hire as part of your homebuilding team, you will award them with the opportunity or privilege to work on your project. Creating an environment of mutual respect between you and the people you hire is the way you want to begin your project.

Ask to see their portfolio and point out things that interest you. Be open to hearing about a project that you may not be drawn to initially if this professional thinks that something about this project may be of benefit for you to consider. If you are drawn to a specific project in the portfolio, ask if these clients are included in the references you asked for. Resist the temptation to tie up this time describing things that you did not bring with you. Remember, if after the second meeting and follow-up review process you decide that you want to hire this person, you will have plenty of time to go over your entire Dream Book in a relaxed, enjoyable state. For right now, the items you've compiled in the interview section of your Dream Book, along with your interview questions, will provide plenty of stimuli to get what you need from this meeting.

At the end of your first interview meeting, make sure to thank this professional for their time. Let them know that you are interviewing other potential candidates as well and that you will be taking this next week or two (depending on how many people you have scheduled to meet with) to review all the information you have received. At that point, you will contact them as to scheduling a follow-up interview. This provides you with enough time to properly review the information you have gathered from all your candidates while letting the people you have interviewed know when they should expect to hear back from you.

The information you have gathered from this first meeting will provide you with the material you need to do your follow-up review of this potential team member. It's this type of information that is not a part of a typical homeowner's hiring process, but it should be. You will have a preliminary follow-up review checklist to guide you through this follow-up process. You can take your time and check off the follow-up information as you get it done. If you have any questions resulting from this follow-up, jot them down to go over at your second interview.

Get Help Reviewing Materials

Your loan officer and your attorney can begin to assist you with reviewing the information that you've received during this beginning phase of your interview process.

Your loan officer can help you assess an accounting procedure and review any examples of project estimates that you may have received. They can also help you follow up on the financial strength of your contractor and explain the process to you if you have any questions. They may know of this builder or architect from other clients and can provide you with some insight into their past work via those clients.

An attorney can help you go over the contract examples that you've gathered and begin making suggestions for you to consider when drafting up your own contract or attaching an addendum to the one that your contractor or architect provides for you.

You can also bring in the copy of the insurance certificate to your insurance provider for their review to get an idea as to what you may need to compensate for. This is where you will begin to realize the benefit of including these professionals as part of your homebuilding and remodeling team. You can relax knowing that you have a number of people who are assisting you and are looking out for your best interest.

Another important aspect of this initial following-up process is contacting the clients that your candidate provided as references for you. I have compiled some questions that you will find after each chapter to get you started and there are additional questions on my web site that you can review. I suggest that you choose twelve to fifteen questions to ask. Read through the rest of them to help give you an idea of the types of information that you are looking for.

The professionals I've interviewed offer their insight and suggestions as to what types of information you will want to acquire from someone you are considering for your project. Many of them say don't ask any specific questions at all. In their opinion, asking questions may be too leading and the professional may respond by giving you answers that they think you want to hear versus the way things really played out. You may want to try both avenues and see what works best for you. Combine the professional's information along with mine and add some of your own to customize this process to suit your personal needs.

Taking the time to follow up like this is an area that homeowners typically don't attend to. This PHM™ follow through of your review process gives you valuable information that helps you determine whether or not this professional has a personality that you would like to work with and if they handle their jobs in a manner that you would be comfortable with. While the case can be made that if a professional provides you with an extensive list of referrals, they must be successful at their job. Do not let this deter you from calling at least three of these contacts. Take the time to visit a couple homes that this professional has worked

The very nature of homebuilding is set up in such a manner that the end does justify the means, and what you don't know can hurt you (and your project).

on. Proactively follow up and hear what these clients have to say. Your opinion of what constitutes a great work environment may differ from theirs. It doesn't necessarily mean that this professional is any less qualified, it simply means that this professional may not be best suited for you and your project.

Once you've completed your reviewing process from the preliminary information that you received at the first interview, and confirmed that this professional is someone you want to consider for your project, you can head back into your second interview with the confidence that any CEO would have when beginning a project of this magnitude. If you have determined that this person is not someone you would like to follow up with, you can notify them and let them know that you have decided on someone else who better suits your project and thank them for the first meeting.

The Second Interview

At this second interview, bring along the notes and questions that arose during your follow-up review of the materials from your first meeting. This would include any documentation that the professional gave you when you first met, such as their contract, a copy of their insurance certificate, their accounting procedures, etc. These are items that you have reviewed with your attorney or with your loan officer or your insurance agent or your family. (Visit the Proactive Homebuilding Method™ web site for additional tools to help with this process.)

After this second meeting, you should have a good idea of whether or not you would like to work with this individual. You should also have received enough information to determine if this person qualifies as a PHM™ professional.

The final thing that you need to confirm about this individual — before you hire them or

before you sign your contract — is that they are a team player and that they will work well with the other people you are going to hire to work on your project.

As Jim Caitlin noted in his interview in Chapter 1, "There is only room for one ego on a project and that's the homeowner's."

Meeting of the Minds

Once you have decided on a professional that you want to work with, let them know that you are very excited about the possibility of working with them. However, before you sign your contract let them know that you would like to invite them to meet with you and the other professionals that you want to hire for your project. Your team may consist of only an architect, contractor and yourself. It may include three other individuals such as a designer, specialty designer and landscape architect. Regardless, you want to establish that there is compatibility. You want to get an idea as to how each potential team member interacts with the others. This is the first "meeting of the minds."

If you have access to a conference room, use that space. If not, ask the architect, contractor or designer if they have a space that would be compatible for this purpose. If you are doing a remodel, you could meet in your home if you are comfortable with that.

You will be heading up this meeting, this gathering of possible candidates. This should in no way make you uncomfortable. It's not a presentation. It's a group of people getting together to meet each other with the anticipation of working together on your project. It should be a fun meeting.

You can now lay out some of the pictures that you have gathered for your project. If there are any specialty areas such as the need for a music studio, photography studio, art studio, home office, chef's kitchen, infinity pool with extensive architectural landscaping that ties back into the house or an elite sound system setup — anything that may present a challenge to the normal design and construction of a home — now is the time to bring it up.

Maybe it's the location or the site conditions where the house is going to be built. Are you doing renovation on a historical home? Are you building with sustainable Green products or using a sustainable design that will require mechanical engineering knowledge for installation of the products? The reason for presenting this information now is to provide a conversation platform. What you want to get out of this meeting is a sense of how these people are going to work together. Does information flow between parties cohesively and productively and is everyone contributing to the conversation?

Here are some additional points that I suggest you ask to start this meeting:

• First off, have everyone introduce themselves and what their contribution is going to be to the project.

• What is the timeline for beginning and completing this project? Is everyone in agreement with that?

• Does everyone understand the importance of having a design that is going to fit your budget before you begin building?

• Does everyone understand that you want to make your choices on the front-end of your project to confirm that the money allotted in your budget provides for what you want?

• How will they assist one another to ultimately help you in achieving this goal?

• If you are having an architect design your home, at what point will the contractor and the designer, etc., be included?

• Do any of them see any specific challenges to this project?

• Is working on a team like this new to anyone present?

• Does everyone understand the value of working together on this project?

Be prepared for the possibility of discovering that one of these personalities may clash at this meeting, but if you've taken care in choosing the right people this probably won't happen. However, be open to accepting it if it does happen. It's important that you go with your instincts on this. If you sense that one of the individuals at this meeting is not as cooperative, forthcoming or compatible with the others as you would like them to be, make note of it.

Follow Up to the Team Meeting

Follow up by calling the other people who attended the meeting and asking them how they thought things went. By you following up with them and allowing them to provide you with their professional opinion about the team, you will help put the other team members at ease. This will help them when they are confirming their decision to work with you. It will indicate to them that you are perceptive and able to assume leadership of the project. It also indicates the level of professionalism that you want to put forth with everyone you hire.

Keep all comments in confidence and take personal responsibility for the choices you make with regard to your project.

Some of you may be uncomfortable with the thought of having to tell this person that you have reconsidered and you are not going to use their services for your project. Let them know that you have determined them not to be the right fit for this team and in being fair to them and your project, you will be hiring someone else. This is a business venture and you have a lot of money invested in the outcome of this project. Part of your responsibility of being CEO includes having to make some difficult choices for the sake of your investment. I cannot tell you how many homeowners make poor judgment calls just to "save face." The assumption is that they can "ride out" a worker's bad behavior and, once the house is built, they won't have to deal with them any more.

Overlooking someone's professional shortcomings because it would be uncomfortable to let them go, or hiring them to work on your project in hopes that they will change once things get started, would be just as successful as entering into a marriage based on the same principles. Whether it's ten months or ten years, having to relate to an individual who does not respect or relate to what's most important to you, day-in-and-day-out, is an experience that you want to avoid. And the easiest way to do that is to not get married in the first place. There are too many good professionals who would welcome the opportunity to work on this project with you and your team. Do not settle for less than you and your project deserve.

Once this meeting is over, thank everyone for coming and let them know that you will be contacting them in the next day or two. When you talk with these individuals one-on-one, confirm that they felt comfortable with the other team members and let them know how excited you are to award them this project.

REVIEWING CONTRACTS

You are now ready to go into the contractual stage. The degree of details in the contract or contracts that you will be signing are going to be determined by the amount of team members you hire and the services that they are going to provide to your project. You need to review these contracts with your attorney before signing them. For some people, sitting down and reading through a contract is as much fun as reading an owner's manual for a new appliance. If your eyes start to glaze over and you want to give way to the, "I'm sure this is fine" syndrome, don't! If you give in to it now, you may be kicking yourself six months into your project when the consequences of not having taken the two to three hours upfront to go over this type of information comes back to "bite you in your budget!" This is the time to get everything clearly spelled out and understood.

I cannot stress enough the importance of you following through with an attorney and making sure that you are properly protected before you begin your project.

PHM™ Interview Method Overview

PRELIMINARY REVIEW AND INTERVIEW LIST
☐ Items that you will ask this person to provide to you at your first interview meeting.

INITIATE FIRST INTERVIEW
☐ Phone call.
☐ Introduction.
☐ Brief description of project.
☐ Confirm that this is a type of project that they are interested in.
☐ Confirm that their timeline coincides with yours.
☐ Schedule a meeting date and request that the items on your preliminary interview list be made available for you at this meeting.

FIRST INTERVIEW
☐ Gather the information that you requested from your list and put it in the interview section of your Dream Book.
☐ Go over your interview questions with this individual.
☐ Review portfolio.
☐ Take notes.

FOLLOW-UP REVIEW CHECKLIST
☐ Go over the items on this list and check them off as you get the follow-up completed.

SCHEDULE SECOND INTERVIEW
☐ Go over reviewed material, documents and additional notes that you have compiled from doing your follow-up review.
☐ Set up a meeting with other potential team members.

MEETING OF THE MINDS
☐ Go over project expectations, roles and responsibilities, project schedule and determine this is the team of people you want to work with.
☐ Call individuals and set up a time to sign the contracts and award the project to the professionals.

CHAPTER three

YOUR PHM™ HOMEBUILDING TEAM

your loan officer

Protecting Your Money — Don't Blow It

We entered our loan process like most homeowners do. We focused on getting the funding we needed to start building. A friend told us about a well-known bank with a loan department that we should check out. We set up the appointment and met with the vice president and a loan officer from the creative lending department. The creative element of this lending department was that it specialized in financing self-employed people who worked in a creative capacity. We have always been self-employed and we like to think of ourselves as being creative, so this seemed like a logical fit. After an hour or so of going over our options, we left with our homebuilding loan in place.

A couple of months into our project, the VP called us in for a meeting with our builder. We had barely begun the actual construction on our house and we were already $30,000 over budget. Needless to say we were flabbergasted. We looked at our builder and said, "This cannot happen! We haven't made any changes to a thing on our home and already we are $30,000 over budget?" Our builder began explaining to us that the lumber prices shot up from the time he bid on our home and actually got started framing. There were a number of other reasons he provided for this unusual price hike as well. He assured us that everything was on schedule and we need not be concerned. After that initial meeting we heard nothing else from our banker or the loan officer who assisted with our loan so we assumed things were indeed back on track.

Both my husband and I dislike accounting. We have always hired someone to do our taxes and handle our Individual Retirement Accounts (IRAs) and insurance accounts. At the time we were building we were fortunate enough to have a savings account built up, a solid IRA and consistent employment to pay for our construction loan. When the builder presented us with a draw, we signed it and faxed it on to our bank. He didn't review it with us and we didn't spend a lot of time going over it — we trusted him.

At one point I asked him about receipts, stating that our accountant suggested we keep them for resale purposes. He said that that was a highly unusual request — none of his previous clients had needed receipts from him. They all trusted him implicitly. The awkwardness of the conversation lingered for a few moments and I said, "Oh, well, that's what she suggested and we would appreciate it." As our budget overages continued to grow we would request a meeting to get some clarity. Our contractor would go over the items explaining why the numbers we were looking at didn't really represent what was actually going on. We would walk away more confused than we were at the beginning of the meeting. We assumed he knew what he was talking about. The topic of the receipts was not brought up again until weeks before we dismissed him from the project.

Months passed and we started heading into a rainy season. It was during these rainy times that we began to see the degree of damage to our home. I came onto the site early in the morning after a storm. We had a ten by twelve foot pool of standing water in the middle of our living room floor. Granted, it was only plywood at that time, but by now, our home was to be weatherproofed. We had our roof, shingles, chimneys, brick, electrical, plumbing, insulation and drywall all installed. The trim carpenter was putting up crown molding and the painters were painting the rooms. Water was leaking from the chimneys down the walls, alongside the mantles across the floors, and on down to the rooms below. Naturally I called my contractor and told him how concerned I was. Both my husband and I, the architect who designed the house, along with the contractor and the sub he put in charge as the superintendent met on the site to discuss the problem and what was going to be done to resolve it. Things continued to go downhill.

For an outsider looking in, the obvious thing to do would have been to fire this contractor and hire someone else to finish up the work. We checked into that. We had numerous contractors come to the house and give us their take on the situation. Not one was willing to warran-

Water damage in kitchen eating area.

Demolition/reconstruction began nine months after moving in.

My husband's office leaks from outside chimney. All three chimneys torn down.

Front porch, columns, stone balustrades and wrought-iron balcony demo.

ty their work because they didn't start the job in the first place. One contractor put it this way, "As troubled as I am with what I see, I'm more concerned with what I can't see." Another said, "The best thing to do would be to tear it down completely and start over." Can you imagine? We were advised by our attorney to do what we had to do to get moved in and work things out afterwards. So, that's what we did.

Fast forward. Things did not get resolved. And the more we pursued our contractor for receipts and accounting information, the more belligerent he became. Finally, one day he marched up onto the site and dropped a box of paperwork down on the kitchen counter. "Here," he said, "here's your receipts!" And he stormed off. My husband and I started going through the box of paperwork to try and make sense of where our money had gone. By the end of the week we had sorted through everything. What we found was alarming. Our attorney set us up with a construction accountant. After reviewing the information, she confirmed what we had suspected. According to our contractor's paperwork, we had close to $200,000 of our money

that was unaccounted for. Money that we had paid this contractor, assuming it went into our house. To make matters worse, he was asking for another $160,000 in overages that he couldn't produce receipts for.

Money is what gives life to your project. Your money pays for the materials that are needed to construct your home. Your money puts bread on the table of your banker, your architect, interior designer, contractor, the subs, the venders, the city, county and even your state. Mismanaged money will have dire consequences for you and your project. The first proactive step in the important process of protecting your money is to identify with, and then act upon your responsibilities. Along with being the CEO of your project, you are also the CFO. It's in your best interest to make sure you have a clear understanding as to how your money is going to be spent.

If you are used to having your finances managed by an accountant or other financial advisor, continue that practice with your homebuilding project. If you have the type of work and social schedule that won't allow you the appropriate time to manage your budget, get some assistance. Accounting on a construction project is not like a typical check-and-balance-procedure. There are varying degrees of percentages and estimates that are always fluctuating. And it's easy for a homeowner to get overwhelmed, confused or misled and simply not want to put in the time that's necessary to manage it. Sometimes the homeowner will pass on following up with their contractor because they are embarrassed to admit they don't understand how their money is being spent. Enlisting the services of others who are knowledgeable in construction financing is what the PHM™ teaches you to do. It's a great business practice to hire someone who can advise you accordingly.

interview

Kimberley Collins-Ripmaster
Franklin American Mortgage

One of the nation's leading construction loan experts, Kimberley Collins-Ripmaster, has received numerous awards for No. 1 sales nationwide. Her clients have benefited from her expertise in the business of homebuilding and have made the most of their investment while maintaining control over their building budget.

I first met Kimberley when we were picking up the pieces of our homebuilding fiasco. We needed to get a second loan on our newly built home to help pay for the costly corrections.

HOW WOULD YOU SUGGEST THAT A HOMEOWNER GO ABOUT FINDING A LENDING OFFICER TO HELP MANAGE THEIR LOAN?

When a homeowner calls a lender, they should ask for a construction specialist in their area. You also want to work with someone who has a good relationship with the builders and who understands the homebuilding process so they can keep you informed and help prepare you upfront for the process ahead.

If you get on the phone and somebody says that they are indeed a construction loan specialist, then I would ask them for three references from homeowners that they have worked with on construction loans. The homeowner then needs to follow up on those references to see how the process went. Basically, you are interviewing this loan officer in the same manner you do an architect or contractor. This is important information for a homeowner to have because a bad lender in this process can be just as bad as a bad builder, in your case you had both.

AS A LENDER WHO IS EXPERIENCED IN THE HOMEBUILDING PROCESS, WHAT ARE SOME OF THE MOST COMMON MISTAKES YOU SEE HOMEOWNERS MAKE WITH REGARD TO FUNDING THEIR HOMEBUILDING PROJECT?

Homeowners make too many assumptions. They assume that because they are with a lending institution that specializes in homebuilding loans that the loan officer who is helping them acquire their financing is going to understand the construction process. And, that this loan officer will be on the lookout for their well-being and watch over their building funds throughout the construction of their home. I've taken over a lot of construction loans on behalf of homeowners who didn't get the help they needed from their first loan officer and I've had to rework them, as in your case.

WHAT SHOULD A HOMEOWNER BE LOOKING FOR IN A LENDING INSTITUTION WHEN PURCHASING A HOME BUILDING LOAN?

The homeowner needs to find someone who specializes in, and has a history in, construction finance. Lending institutions may specialize in homebuilding (loan product) however, not all loan officers are specialists in construction finance. Your regular mortgage loan officer is not going to know enough about the construction process to ensure that the customer is protected throughout the project. The homeowner wants to work with someone who has a good relationship with the builders, knows the process, keeps the customer informed and tries to prepare them upfront for the process ahead.

THAT'S INTERESTING. JUST BECAUSE A LENDING INSTITUTION OFFERS A CONSTRUCTION LOAN TO A HOMEOWNER, THAT DOESN'T MEAN THAT THE LOAN OFFICER SELLING THAT LOAN WILL KNOW HOW TO HELP THE HOMEOWNER MANAGE IT.

It's important for the homeowner to understand that before they purchase their loan. The loan officer you get may be providing a product that that institution specializes in, but they're not a specialist themselves, and that's who you're going to be dealing with on a daily basis. A lot of loan officers, unfortunately, will view this as another commission on a loan, and they're done with it once the loan closes. Construction loans frighten some loan officers because they don't know the answers to the questions that homeowners ask when they need help. They're just lucky that they got the loan closed.

DO DIFFERENT LENDERS OFFER DIFFERING DEGREES OF INVOLVEMENT TO THE HOMEOWNER THROUGHOUT THE CONSTRUCTION PROJECT?

Yes, and that's why you want to make sure you talk to someone who has a strong history in construction finance. Otherwise, you could be in the wrong hands, as you were. If homeowners work with a loan officer like myself who specializes in construction finance, that loan officer can review their allowances up front and make sure that the contractor was being reasonable and honest in their bid. They could ask the homeowner if they had followed up on these allowances by making their choices on the front-end of their project to assure that these allowances were adequate. That way, they can begin their project confident that they can stay within their budget.

WHAT MIGHT A CONSTRUCTION FINANCE LENDER OFFER THAT MOST HOMEOWNERS DON'T KNOW TO TAKE ADVANTAGE OF?

A good construction finance lender will offer support to the homeowner throughout the process. If you have any questions during construction, they should be able to help you or will know someone who can. I would call them for anything. If you've got a question on what the builder's doing, if you don't agree with how they're handling the situation or the cost on something that you received on your monthly statement, you can ask this loan officer about it. Bring it to their attention. I always want to know the customer has signed off on everything before I receive a draw request from the builder. I want to make sure that happens before the funds are disbursed. That way, if something were to happen, we'd have more to work with.

Note: I have come to the conclusion that home-owners lack the emotional connection with their building funds that they have with their personal accounts, which leaves their money vulnerable. You can secure a building loan relatively quickly. Within a week you can have hundreds of thousands of dollars available for your project. You get a checkbook and away you go. Whereas your personal accounts, such as savings, checking, and IRA, have taken you years to build and you're protective of that money.

I would venture to say that if you had a friend or even a family member ask you to give them $20,000 from your savings or IRA, that you would want some assurance as to where that money was going and when you would get paid back. If there were high risk involved, you would

say no. Yet with a homebuilding loan, a homeowner who knows nothing about the homebuilding process often writes out checks triple that amount and hands it to their contractor without any regard to accountability. Following through on your draw requests does not represent distrust of your contractor; it's being proactively responsible with your money. You can bet that if you were to shortchange your contractor on their fee they would follow up with you. It's good business practice.

HAS IT BEEN YOUR EXPERIENCE THAT HOMEOWNERS ARE LESS EMOTIONALLY CONNECTED TO THEIR BUILDING FUNDS THAN THEY WOULD BE IF THE CONTRACTOR'S DRAWS WERE COMING FROM THEIR PERSONAL ACCOUNTS?

Absolutely. That is one of the most serious problems with regard to budgeting issues. Homeowners do disconnect with their funding. They don't see it as being their money right now. More often than not, I would be doing my job, but the customer was completely disconnected from the process. To help customers better connect on the front-end of a construction loan, I would give my customers a budget on an Excel spreadsheet with the months at the top and the amounts on a line item basis. I would have them either check it off or put the amount in each month that was coming from the category we were reviewing. Then they could see that they don't have anything else left in electrical, plumbing, etc.

Note: I am a big fan of the Turnkey method of homebuilding custom homes. The team of people that gather together along with the homeowner on the front-end of a project to get all the aspects of that project's needs laid out within budget exemplifies what the Proactive Homebuilding Method™ is all about. If, however, your contractor is working on cost-plus basis, (cost of the labor and materials plus a fee) you are going to have to put in more effort to assure that the sum provided in your contractor's bid balances out with what you want to have built into your home.

If you are getting bids on your project, have your architect prepare construction documents that define details. The follow up on the bids.

Walk through homes in your area that are on the market for the same amount of your bid. Find out if you like what is in these houses. Do they have the quality of product that you expect to include in your house? If you walk through a home that is listed for the same price as one of your bids and you are saying to yourself, I could like this house if I added or changed this and that and used better quality, you are sending yourself signals. Pay attention to them. This bid is most likely too low. You are already upgrading in your head. That can translate into costly change orders on your project. If you walk into a home that represents a bid and you feel like this house is over the top for you, then that may signal that this bid is too high.

If however, you walk into a home and decide that you can live with pretty much everything you see in this home — the quality of craftsmanship and materials used — then you know that this bid is representative of what you want in your home. Don't make the mistake of assuming that you can build a house for less than you can buy it. In a lot of cases it's going to be more costly for you to build.

Bidding on a project can be a frustrating process for the contractor or building team whose bid represents a realistic price for the homeowner. It is going to be that much more important that you step up to the plate and take charge in the managing of your budget.

Finding the Perfect Loan Officer — Be Choosy

Kimberley Collins-Ripmaster suggests that you find the lender and loan officer you want to work with is by calling a lending institution and ask to speak with a loan officer who specializes in homebuilding loans. Describe the project you want to have built and ask them about their experience in dealing with construction loans. Ask them to provide you with three references of recent construction loans that they have handled. Follow up with those references, ask the homeowners about the experience they had with this loan officer and if they would recommend them. Questions to ask the homeowners:

☐ Did this loan officer review the budget, before construction began, to check their allowances with the clients?

☐ Did the clients have any concerns or questions regarding the handling of their building funds, monthly draws or overages by their contractor at any time during construction?

If so, how did this loan officer help them?

☐ Did the client go over budget on their project? If so, was the loan officer aware of this and did they bring that to their attention?

☐ How often did the loan officer meet with the client to go over their budget throughout the duration of their project? (Kimberley reviewed the building budget once a month with her clients.)

☐ Did the loan officer visit the building site to match the draw requests to the work that had been done, to make sure that the funds being disbursed were going toward the items specified on the builder's draw requests?

☐ Is there anything else they would have liked their loan officer to do or to do differently on their behalf?

Kimberley says that her hands-on approach with her clients is not the common procedure with loan officers, so doing your homework before settling with someone will help ensure that you and your investment are in the right hands. She adds, "The only thing worse than getting with an incompetent builder is getting with an incompetent loan officer as well."

CHAPTER four

YOUR PHM™ HOMEBUILDING TEAM

your attorney

interview

Todd E. Panther
Tune, Entrekin & White, P.C.

Very few homeowners consult with an attorney on the front end of their project. This was one of the mistakes we made. When you begin your project, no matter what your budget is, no matter what degree of work you are having done, it is imperative that you have a contract that has been reviewed by an attorney who is knowledgeable and experienced in construction law. There is no justifiable reason that you can provide as to why you would not hire an attorney before singing a contract that any homebuilding professional has provided for you. I speak from experience.

Todd is Co-Managing Partner at his firm and one of the areas that Todd specializes in is Construction Law.

Todd recommends interviewing an attorney as you would anyone else you're hiring for your building team and to interview multiple candidates.

WHAT SHOULD HOMEOWNERS LOOK FOR SPECIFICALLY WHEN HIRING AN ATTORNEY?

Someone who knows about residential construction. Ask them questions about whom they represent. Ask them if a significant portion of their practice is construction related and if they're conversant with construction contracts, with the lien law of the state that they're in and that they know how to litigate or arbitrate construction related disputes.

These are the areas that, at some point, they may want the lawyer's advice on and neither the homeowner or the homebuilder wants the lawyer learning for the first time on their project. They may be a great lawyer and great litigator, but, if the lawyer doesn't know, in general terms, the lien law, the contractor's licensing law, the arbitration act, what the state law provides concerning warranties or statute of limitations, then don't hire them.

WHAT IS THE DIFFERENCE BETWEEN INSURANCE COVERAGE AND A BOND?

In order to get to the insurance, I've got to go through the contractor first. I've got to prove that the contractor is liable, then the insurance will pay. With a bond I don't have to do that.

The bond stands in front of the contractor. If a contractor has given a performance bond or a payment bond, and the contractor doesn't perform, doesn't pay, I have the absolute right under that bond to go directly to the surety company and say, "Your principal has breached the contract so I'm making a claim under the bond." Unlike insurance, the bond is a direct avenue for whoever is the beneficiary under the bond. The liability of the bonding company is limited to the bond amount, so the bonding company will have to pay no more than that.

I have represented some builders who had some code errors. The homeowners knew enough to contact the codes officials and they resorted to the bond.

WHY DON'T CONTRACTORS CARRY HIGHER BOND AMOUNTS LIKE THEY DO WITH INSURANCE COVERAGE?

Bonding companies don't want to be at risk. A bonding company is not going to issue a surety bond that will hold them responsible to perform a contract without sufficient security from the builder. If a claim is made on the bond, the bonding company has somewhere to turn so that they're not left holding the bag.

WOULD THE BONDING COMPANY TURN TO THE CONTRACTOR'S ASSETS?

Correct. Let me give you an example. I filed a lawsuit on the sale of a piece of property. I represent the buyer of the piece of property. The seller decided that they could make more money if they didn't sell the property to the people who I represented and they were going to sell it to somebody else offering more money. When I filed the lawsuit, I asked for a temporary restraining order. Under the law you have to post a bond in order to get the temporary restraining order. It was an $800,000 piece of property and the court set bond at $50,000. I then called my client and said: "I've got good news and bad news. The good news is we're going to get the TRO (temporary restraining order). The bad news is you've got to find $50,000. Get a $50,000 bond." So they contact their insurance company.

"We need a surety bond."

"No problem. How much does it need to be?" "50,000 dollars."

"Great. All we need is an irrevocable letter of credit for $50,000 and you need to pay a bond premium of 1%."

"Okay. How do I get the letter of credit?"

"You need to contact your bank."

So they contacted the bank.

"I need an irrevocable letter of credit for $50,000."

"No problem. We'll be glad to do it. What you need to do is set $50,000 aside in an account that you cannot touch and pay us the fee for the irrevocable letter of credit."

They're like, "What!?"

That's the reason most contractors don't get payment in performance bonds, because of the extra costs involved.

HAVING BUILT YOUR OWN HOME, WOULD YOU RECOMMEND THAT A HOMEOWNER ASK FOR RECEIPTS TO ACCOMPANY THE DRAW REQUESTS THEY RECEIVE FROM THEIR CONTRACTOR?
"We insisted upon it, and we drafted a contract to provide it. For certain types of contracts it's more important than others. If you're in what's commonly called a cost-plus contract where you pay for the cost of the labor and materials plus some fee, having that backup documentation, not because you distrust the builder but because as a prudent business person, you would want to make sure that a mistake hasn't been made and you're charged for materials that belong on some other job. That happens. That's not someone being dishonest. It's someone being human. If someone is unwilling to provide that backup documentation to you, that should raise a red flag."

WHAT WOULD YOU CONSIDER TO BE ONE OF THE MOST OVER-LOOKED SERVICES AN ATTORNEY CAN OFFER A HOMEOWNER WHO IS BUILDING OR RENOVATING THEIR HOME?
Very few homeowners have an attorney look at the contract before they enter into it.

WHICH IS A MISTAKE?
I think it's a huge mistake. A lot of homeown-

ers have the misconception that it may seem adversarial if they involve an attorney on the front end of their project.

SHOULD A HOMEOWNER BE CONCERNED THAT PRESENTING A CONTRACT PREPARED BY THEIR ATTORNEY WOULD BE OFF-PUTTING TO A CONTRACTOR?
It's not adversarial but rather good business practice to protect your homebuilding investment, and a professional would understand.

It's most likely that the builder has had an attorney draft their contract, and, make no mistake about it, when I draft a contract for a builder, I draft it from their perspective. If the homeowner were to present a contract wanting to have a clear understanding about our agreement, which is really the true reason to have a contract, it doesn't have to be adversarial.

CAN A HOMEOWNER HIRE ANY ATTORNEY TO REVIEW THEIR CONTRACT?
They need to hire someone who knows something about residential construction. A significant portion of the attorney's practice should be focused on construction related matters so that they're conversant with construction contracts and the lien law of the their state. They should know how to litigate or arbitrate construction related disputes. Those are the areas that they might need their lawyer's advice about. Neither the homeowner nor the homebuilder, the client, wants the lawyer learning for the first time with this particular client.

WHEN YOU ARE ASKED TO REVIEW A CONTRACT ON BEHALF OF THE HOMEOWNER, WHAT TYPES OF THINGS ARE MOST COMMONLY CHANGED TO BETTER SUIT THE HOMEOWNER'S NEEDS?
I would strike the arbitration provision, strike out the provision that final payment is acceptance of the work and strike out the consequential damage provisions.

CONSEQUENTIAL DAMAGE PROVISIONS?
For example, in the current version of the AIA standard agreement form, the general conditions say that the contractor and the owner waive any consequential damages. What that means for homeowners is that if the builder fails to complete construction on time and you lose the lock on your loan or you can't move in on time and that results in rental space on your

furniture or rental space on the apartment, those damages are waived. Typically, that provision helps contractors more than homeowners — that's why it's generally something that is struck. I would also suggest taking out any deadline-driven provisions that require responses within a certain period of time or where the contractor is given the unilateral right to terminate the contract.

Note: This is a good example of how an attorney who is well-versed in residential construction law can help a homeowner better understand what is in their contract before they sign it.

HOW DETAILED SHOULD A CONTRACT BE?

Extremely. What I'm finding is that the trend is to have longer, more detailed contracts. I see that not just with custom homebuilders who are building a few houses a year, but I'm seeing that with speculation (spec) builders as well. The reason for this is to make sure there's a clear understanding with regard to expectations. With more information the homeowner understands things. There may be a meadow behind them now but there may not be a meadow behind them a year from now.

Longer contracts, though more burdensome to read, are more explanatory, and, if they're done right, they start the parties off knowing what is expected of each other, and that education stands the parties a greater chance of the contract being put in a drawer and never coming out again.

SO IT'S AN IMPORTANT PREVENTIVE MEASURE.

Right.

HOW WOULD A HOMEOWNER FIND AN ATTORNEY WHO SPECIALIZES IN CONSTRUCTION THAT CAN HELP THEM WITH THEIR BUILDING PROJECT'S NEEDS?

Most people that contact me are from word of mouth. A homeowner can call their local homebuilder's association, ask who represents them and call that attorney. Some state bar associations allow you to designate your practice areas as well, so consult with your state bar association and ask them.

Attorney Follow-up Review

☐ To confirm the reputation and level of construction expertise of this attorney I suggest you visit the American Bar Association at www.abanet.org.

Click on lawyer locator and fill in the attorney's information where specified. If you provide a name, county, state and country, it will be enough to pull up the attorney's information. You will see a description that breaks down the areas of law that this attorney practices in.

You will want to see construction-related listings for this attorney. For example, Todd Panther has Real Estate, Commercial Litigation, Land Use, Business Litigation and Construction Litigation listed as areas in which he specializes.

You can also call your local Homebuilder's Association and ask if they are familiar with the attorney you're seeking to hire.

Attorney's Client Reference Questions

☐ Name

☐ How did you first come in contact with this attorney?

☐ What services did this attorney provide for you?

☐ Were you happy with their service?

☐ Were they able to provide you with these services expeditiously?

☐ Was this attorney well versed in residential construction procedure and law?

☐ Were they well versed in construction contracts?

☐ Did you feel like they were able to help you gain a clear understanding of the information that they assisted you with?

☐ What did you find most beneficial about enlisting the services of this attorney?

☐ Would you recommend using this attorney for my homebuilding project?

CHAPTER five

YOUR PHM™ HOMEBUILDING TEAM

your architect

I am an advocate for architects. If more homeowners used them, we would have fewer problems with our projects. I learned to appreciate the value of hiring the right architect when we had to hire a second architect to correct some of the work that was done by our first architect/builder team. The difference between them was their experience and construction administration abilities.

Preliminary Review and First Interview List for Architects
- Architect's Registration
- Architect's Credentials
- Insurance
- Contract
- Information on their fees and levels of involvement
- Example of budget or accounting summary used for clients
- An example of architectural supplemental instructions
- An example of an architect documented revision
- Business procedures of Company overview
- Experience with implementing Green Building materials in Home Designs
- Experience with designing Sustainable housing
- Portfolio
- References (3 – 5 clients) current, one-year-old project to 3-year-old projects

Working with a *registered architect* versus a *home designer* or a *contractor's draftsman* can be significant, given the needs of your project. The difference between the *registered architect* and *home designer* is their training and credentials. *Registered* (you may be used to hearing *licensed* as opposed to *registered*) *architects* are held to a higher degree of standards than *home designers* who have no governing body to which the are accountable.

To become a registered architect you must attend an accredited college offering an architectural degree. Completing this course as a full-time student can take five to six years. Within two years after receiving one's architec-

tural degree, the graduate is required to continue his education by apprenticing under the direct supervision of a registered architect. This process can easily add six or more years to the interning architect's training experience.

When I began researching the architect's credentials for this book, I had a limited amount of knowledge as to the rigorous training involved in acquiring the title *Architect*.

Just as it would be illegal for a medical student, who has not successfully completed all requirements to become licensed in the field of medicine, to advertise themselves to the public as a doctor open for business, it's illegal for the architect student, who hasn't met the required training necessary to become licensed, to advertise themselves to the general public as an architect open for business. The student architects need to complete their registered training in the time allotted by the National Council of Architectural Registration Boards (NCARB) to become a registered architect.

The Registered Architect

Only after the interning architect has completed the hours of training required by the Intern Development Program (IDP) in the various aspects of architecture is the architect eligible to take the rigorous architect's registration exam (ARE). Those requirements include:

1. Programming
2. Site Development
3. Engineering Systems Coordination Building Cost Analysis
4. Code research
5. Design Development
6. Construction Documents
7. Specifications and Materials Research
8. Documents Checking and Coordination
9. Bidding and Contract Negotiation
10. Construction Phase office
11. Construction Phase Observation
12. Project Management
13. Office Management
14. Professional and Community Service

After passing the exam, they go in front of the state registration board for an oral exam, along with giving verification of the completion of their IDP training.

Although the ARE exam is recognized as the standard registration test given across most of the US, some states may vary as to the minimum number of authorized requirements they specify necessary to achieve and maintain registration within their state. It is the responsibility of the architect seeking registration in that state to comply with these requirements.

As the architectural climate is always progressing, registration requirements may change to meet higher standards of design. What was deemed acceptable when an architect first sought registration may no longer meet the board's requirements. In this case, the architect will be expected to study, learn and adapt this new information with what they already know. Meeting this requirement is necessary for them to maintain their registered credentials.

It is not unusual for an architect to be licensed in numerous states across the country. This enables him to continue to work with clients owning multiple dwellings. If a state is prone to specific modifications in architecture due to the nature of the terrain i.e., California and earthquakes, an out-of-state architect wishing to become registered in California may be required to take additional testing and/or give oral documentation of their work and/or solve a problem pertaining to earthquake design, etc.

In understanding the training required to achieve a registered status, a homeowner should be able to better understand the level of professionalism an architect is able to bring to their project. One of the most common reasons a homeowner declines the assistance of an architect on their project is the perceived excessive cost it adds to the project. In my opinion, making this decision without first meeting with and considering the contribution this professional can make to your project is one of the first mistakes homeowners make when they enter into the homebuilding process.

In our current homebuilding climate, the majority of homes are being built without the assistance of an architect — an estimated one out of every one hundred homeowners makes use of an architect. This means that the homeowner is dependent upon their contractor to implement the follow through on the design interpretation of a home as well as building the home. To quote *This Old House* general contractor Tom Silva, "Contractors are not designers, and in my opinion should not be designing houses. But architects are not builders — they can't possibly be on top of all the latest construction techniques and materials. When builders and architects share input from the beginning, houses are invariably better." This team perspective is essential to establishing a PHM™ environment.

When you are considering the possibility of building your own home or doing an extensive remodel on the house you're currently living in, it is in your best interest to interview architects for your project.

First, determine if your architect is registered. If they are advertising that they are an architect, it is most likely that they are. However, in not wanting to assume that that is the case, visit the National Council of Architecture Registration Boards web site. www.ncarb.org/stateboards/index and click on the link. Type in your architect's name, or call and talk with a local representative.

Any credentials that a professional carries are to the benefit of the homeowner. It tells you that the professional you are interviewing is serious about their profession. The most common accreditation that an architect will carry is an AIA. AIA stands for *American Institute of Architects*.

Insurance

You will want to confirm that your architect, home designer and interior designer carry insurance. The type of insurance your architect is going to carry will most likely be *errors and omissions (E&O)*, also referred to as *professional liability insurance* coverage. Unlike your contractor's liability coverage, E&O insurance covers the architect, employees and those who are

(continued on page 50)

interview

Carol Pedigo, Honorary AIA

Executive Director for the American Institute of Architects, Middle Tennessee Chapter,

Carol Pedigo has been the Executive Director for the American Institute of Architects, middle Tennessee Chapter, since 1994 and has served the organization nationally in many leadership areas. Currently she is the vice president of the *Council of Architectural Component Executives*, a volunteer position to which she was elected by her fellow peers spanning 287 components across the US and abroad. As vice president she is currently developing resources for the AIA and its components both nationally and internationally.

WHAT IS THE AIA ORGANIZATION?

The American Institute of Architects (AIA) is a professional organization for architects in the United States. Organized in 1857, the Institute conducts various activities and programs to support the profession and enhance its public image. There is a full-time CEO that resides in Washington, D.C. The staff in Washington is about 225. Each component may have between 1 to 12 staff members, depending on their geographical area. In California, for example, their council has about 50 people on staff. Here in Tennessee we have about 15 staff people statewide.

DOES THE AIA OFFER EDUCATIONAL FORUMS THAT WOULD BE OPEN TO THE PUBLIC?

Yes. In April our Nashville AIA component hosted a public forum luncheon. We brought in a residential designer from Maine who was here for a book signing, as well as participating in a question-and-answer period. Some chapters across the country open up their offices to the public to take classes. For example, what to expect when you start working on the design process with an architect. The public can go to the web site. AIA.org, which will provide them with a link to their city and state for more information about these classes.

WHAT ADVANTAGES WOULD THE AIA OFFER TO AN ARCHITECT?

The opportunity to network, to share information and to see trends that are coming from across the country or even out of the country. By providing this forum of information, the AIA helps prevent stagnation, and provides an opportunity for those architects that may feel isolated in their practice to connect with others in their field on a local, regional, state and national level.

WHY WOULD IT BE OF BENEFIT FOR A HOMEOWNER TO HIRE AN ARCHITECT WHO IS CURRENTLY AN AIA MEMBER?

The AIA has a code of ethics, which our members are expected to abide by. We also adhere to strict regulations for continuing education — making sure that our members stay up to speed with trends that affect the building environment. Having that regulatory arm of mandatory continuing education is a way that homeowners or commercial developers can be assured that the AIA architect knows what they're talking about.

If the architect you are considering hiring to design your home is not a member of the AIA, I would ask them why. Sometimes you'll find wonderful architects that have never joined the AIA. I recommend that you follow up on any architect you're considering hiring. These AIA standards apply to all states.

CAN AN ARCHITECT EVER LOSE THEIR MEMBERSHIP TO THE AIA?

Absolutely.

HOW MIGHT THAT HAPPEN?

By not keeping up with their continuing education credits. The AIA expects that architects have a minimum of 18 hours of continuing education, with the majority of those hours being in health, safety and welfare. Also, if they don't adhere to the code of ethics they can lose respectability from their clients. If they do something illegal, immoral or unjust and they are brought before an independent council, they can be relieved of their AIA status.

(continued from page 48)

subcontracted by them. If any of these people or the architect themselves perform work on your project that is not within the scope of what they were contracted to do or is not to the industry standards or fails to perform as intended, the architect's E&O policy will provide coverage. It also covers the architect's legal costs. Ask if your architect carries such a policy. They will have an insurance certificate demonstrating that they are insured.

Contract for Title

Ask the architect you are going to be interviewing for a copy of their standard contract for your review. This will familiarize you with their contractual process. Once you decide to hire the architect, you can make contractual revisions as needed for your project.

The documents your architect uses are generally AIA documents. These documents are available to you from the AIA component in your area or directly from the AIA web site (AIA.org). Most likely, your architect is using an AIA contract formatted for architects. If not, they may have had an attorney develop a contract for them.

You'll want your attorney, who is well versed in residential construction and familiar with architectural contracts, to review any contract on your behalf before signing it. It will also be to your benefit to understand how your architect's contract may or may not have any inclusions that pertain to the contractor you hire. You can walk through this information with the architect, take notes if necessary and review them later with your attorney.

Level of Involvement

Architects have numerous ways of charging for a project. Depending on the scope of work you are going to require from them, I recommend using an architect on a full-service capacity. This will give you the advantage of having a pair of eyes throughout your project that are trained to see things you don't see. Even though you may be a bit hesitant when first hearing the architect's fee for this full service, wait until you have thoroughly reviewed a detailed description of what this would include on your behalf before declining. Amortize this fee over the length of time it will take for your project to be completed. You can then determine a monthly rate for these services. I can tell you from experience that a competent architect will be well worth every dollar spent. They will save you time, money and emotional energy while adding value to your homebuilding investment. You want to conserve and reinvest these in your family as much as possible when the transition/construction phase begins.

Recently, I was interviewing an architect and he began relaying a story. He was asked to design a home for a contractor. This contractor was building his own home in an area that specified he use the services of an architect for the house plans. This contractor considered himself to be an accomplished contractor who rarely used the services of an architect for his clients. He would use a set of pre-designed plans or a hired draftsman when necessary. However, after receiving this architect's plans and working from his design, this contractor was converted! He called the architect and said, "I had no idea how different it would be working from a set of plans drawn up by architect! The job went smoother and the quality and detail you integrated into the design added value to my home."

I had an architect tell me recently that she was originally awarded a project for the full scope of architectural work. This meant that she was hired for all four phases of architectural services — schematic design, design development, construction documents and construction administration on the front end of the project. After the schematic designs were completed, the architect received a call from her client. The homeowner said, "My contractor told me to tell you that we do not need any more drawings from you, so I guess I won't need any more of your services." And she let this architect go. Later on in the project, when problems started to arise, this homeowner contacted the architect and asked her to provide more detailed services — for free. The architect declined.

This would not be a PHM™ move for a number of reasons. First off, you would have called a meeting with your team at the beginning of your project. At this meeting, everyone would have established what their roles and responsibilities were going to be with regard to your project. The contractor would have a clear understanding of the level of involvement that the architect would play over the life of your project. They would also know that it is your decision as to whether or not another team member's services were to be terminated. If a contractor or any other team member would counsel you to terminate the services of your architect or another team member before they have completed your project's requirements, it would be done for the sole reason that in keeping this architect or other team player involved, it would jeopardize the outcome of your project.

The fact that this homeowner was willing to forgo the services that she and her architect had originally agreed to, solely on the advice of her contractor, without any indication that this architect was not performing well, is a clear indication of her lack of understanding as to the value that the architect would bring to her project. More importantly, it also indicates the disconnect that this homeowner had regarding her role in managing and protecting her home-building venture. Unless you have hired an architect for schematic design drawings only, a contractor who advises a homeowner to dismiss an architect's services once construction is set to begin would be suspect to me.

From the above example, we can most likely conclude that the contractor did not want to have to give account to the architect. It's much easier to have control over a project when you are the only one calling the shots. It's also much easier for the contractor to begin cutting corners to save themselves money unbeknownst to the homeowner. This homeowner has put herself in the position of being one-on-one with her contractor and his crew. If the project had begun with this type of arrangement on the front end, the homeowner would have gone in on a different level of communication with her contractor. As it stands now, she is going to be playing catch-up throughout the entire project. This puts her in a vulnerable position when it comes to understanding the intentions of her plan. All the decisions from here on out are going to be made by either her, based on her limited knowledge, or by her contractor. The architect, the person who knows her home best, is now out of the picture. If the construction process does not follow the design or specifications that her architect had originated, she is most likely not going to catch it. If she does, she may need to re-hire that architect to come in and rectify what they could have managed if they were involved throughout.

If you hired an architect with the intent of them following through to completion, it is in your best interest to honor that agreement. If your contractor asks or suggests that you let the architect go, you need to ask your contractor why. If they tell you that they have sufficient information in the drawings to finish the job, the PHM™ teaches the homeowner that their architect's services extend far beyond the drawing phase. The most common reason given to the homeowner by the contractor to discontinue an architect's services would be to save the homeowner time and money. This is why it is good for you to be clear on the front-end of your project regarding the value of this architect's services to your overall project.

Bear in mind, no one should be calling the shots with regard to your project but you.

Budget and Accounting

Ask the architect you are interviewing how they usually charge for the different level of services that they provide. The majority of architects that I've met don't like to work on a design and consult on an as-needed basis because the consult often comes as the result of a problem. Having not been involved from the onset of the

(continued on page 55)

interview

James Edwards
Architect

I first met James when we were seeking advice on the corrections we had to make to our newly built home. James is partner and one of the three owners of Edwards + Hotchkiss Architects and he was instrumental in developing my appreciation for what an architect can bring to a homebuilding project. James was also the first professional that granted me an interview for this book, for which I am very grateful.

CAN AN ARCHITECT LOSE THEIR LICENSE AND STILL BE ADVERTISING HIMSELF AS A REGISTERED ARCHITECT UNBEKNOWNST TO THE HOMEOWNER?

Practitioners, regardless of education or former registrations), are not allowed to use the term *architect* or any derivative of the word, unless they hold a current license in their state of practice. Furthermore, licensed architects are not allowed to use the word architect, or practice or advertise as an architect, in states in which they do not hold registration.

I WAS SURPRISED AT HOW LONG ONE HAS TO STUDY TO BECOME A REGISTERED ARCHITECT. IT'S SIMILAR TO A MEDICAL DOCTOR'S DEGREE. THE GENERAL PUBLIC DOESN'T COMPLETELY UNDERSTAND THAT.

I have, in the past, read statistics on timing and duration of training time after securing a college degree prior to license or first sitting for the exam, and I'm not up to date on the current, but my strong belief is that the average length of time between graduation from college with an accredited degree and securing an architectural license for those architects practicing today is more than eight years after college. There are numerous reasons for that.

In order to satisfy the training requirements to qualify for architectural licensing examination, the candidate would need to be in a professional environment that would expose them to precise amounts of experience in the various qualification categories. While the minimum requirement is three years after graduation, when working under the direction of a licensed architect, the time required to collect the minimum time in each professional experience cate-

gory is usually six years or more. There are currently sixteen different experience items in four categories that must be satisfied. There's also a diligence aspect. The exam is passed by a small percentage of people the first time, so there's a reluctance to do it. I believe there's pride in taking the exam, so those who take it tend to prepare well, in spite of the low initial pass rate. Those individuals that eventually become architects do so about eight years after college.

HOMEOWNERS OFTEN PREPARE A NOTEBOOK FULL OF PICTURES TO USE AS A VISUAL REFERENCE THAT WILL HELP THEM DEFINE WHAT THEY WANT TO INCLUDE IN THE BUILDING OF THEIR HOME. WHEN IS THE APPROPRIATE TIME TO PRESENT THIS TO THE ARCHITECT? WOULD IT BE AT THE INITIAL MEETING?

No, not at the initial interview. That meeting is to learn about the architect and try to establish a feeling as to whether or not you're comfortable with them and can establish good communication. That starts the process. Once you have determined that this is the architect you want to design your home, you can then introduce the information you've gathered in your *dream book*. The homeowner can say, "Here's some of my initial thoughts." Often the architect will ask if you have any initial thoughts so you can learn more about each other and they can understand your expectations.

WHAT ARE THE MOST COMMON MISCONCEPTIONS THE PUBLIC HAS ABOUT HIRING AN ARCHITECT?

• That the mere presence of having an architect on the job is going to make the building budget go up too high.

• That the architect is going to cost them a lot of money.

• That if they go to an architect, they're going to spend money they wouldn't normally spend.

• That the value of the services offered by the architect are not values they'll ever realize either from their own realization or future value of the house relative to resale.

• That hiring the architect's going to eliminate any potential problem.

• That a good architect can make up for a

bad builder. So, if you get a good architect and have a good design, then they're going to get in there and make the builder perform and your house is going to be virtually perfect.

• That architects are megalomaniac designers who want to create monuments to themselves. That's absolutely a falsehood.

• That architects are in it for the money and that their fees are high. They're not. For example, you wouldn't go to an attorney that would only charge you $25/hour, would you? An architect has more and higher training requirements, more educational requirements and a more difficult examination process than an attorney. For most homeowners, their house is the most expensive thing they'll ever buy, so don't hire someone that's charging you $25/hour.

WOULD YOU SUGGEST THAT A CLIENT HIRE AN ARCHITECT AND A BUILDER THAT WORK TOGETHER?

You mean that work in the same company?

CORRECT.

Cherry cabinetry by Woodmeister add to the warm tones of this kitchen, curved design helps to soften open space and provides ample storage for homeowners. PHOTOGRAPHER: GARY SLOAN, ARCHITECTURAL MILLWORK: WOODMEISTER MASTER BUILDERS, GENERAL CONTRACTOR: CONRAD & SULIVAN

No. There are architects that try to be builders and offer design/build services. Part of my objection is that it's contrary to the basic interests of the parties when the architect and the builder are one business entity because it has a tendency to conflict the architect in their decisions about things. They're not as free to represent the homeowner in an impartial manner.

WHAT ARE SOME COMMON REASONS A CONTRACTOR WOULD BE RESISTANT TO THE IDEA OF HIS CLIENT ENGAGING THE SERVICES OF AN ARCHITECT?

There's a belief in the industry by some contractors that architects complicate the issue. Some contractors and builders believe that architects complicate and make their job harder, more difficult and more expensive. For those builders with more of a suspicious or paranoid

bent, I believe that there is a fear that they're going to be held accountable to a higher degree. Not that they're held to a higher standard, but that they will be held to a standard that maybe they don't want to adhere to in all cases.

IF THERE IS A DISAGREEMENT BETWEEN THE ARCHITECT AND CONTRACTOR ABOUT SOMETHING ON THE JOB SITE, WHO ULTIMATELY MAKES THE DECISION AS TO HOW TO CARRY ON?

Traditional owner/contractor agreements specify what the responsibilities of the architect are going to be relative to the project, and the contractor agrees to that because he has signed that owner's agreement. The architect represents the owner during the construction phase and acts on his behalf in dealing with the contractor. A common mistake that architects make is when they get into conflict situations with the contractor, they interpret that conflict to the owner's favor. That's not their job, and that's contrary to their professional responsibility. The contractor has an agreement to do this scope of work as defined by the architect. If something is not explained or fully defined, then the contractor doesn't have the ability to include that within his thinking and pricing. So if something is not defined and a modification is made or an interpretation is made that is not fairly or clearly shown in the construction drawings, then the contractor should be paid extra for it.

IF THE QUESTION ARISES REGARDING THE PERFORMANCE OF A CONTRACTOR OR ARCHITECT DURING THE PROJECT, TO WHOM WOULD A CLIENT TURN FOR INSIGHT OR GUIDANCE AS TO HOW TO CONTINUE?

If, during the construction of a project, the builder is not performing properly and, if the architect is doing construction period services, it should be the architect that brings it to the owner's attention first. If the owner and the architect have a good relationship and the builder is not performing, there would normally be discussions between the two on how to address the problem as to whether or not to terminate the builder's services. Certainly, you consult with the builder to see what can be done. Often it's a subcontractor problem that the builder may not be aware of.

If, during the construction of a project, the owner thinks he has problems with the architect's performance, that would normally be known because the builder's making a lot of complaints about the drawings. Or, there seems to be a lot of omissions or it seems like they're having to make a lot of corrections to make up for problems in the drawings. Then, if the owner has a strong relationship with the builder, he might want to go to the builder first and say, "Listen, I think you're trying to do a good job here and it seems to me that you've got some problems with the documents and I suspect that there may be some performance issues or quality issues with the documents. What should we do?"

Beyond that, if one of those two cases doesn't exist and the owner doesn't feel comfortable or in a position to consult one about the other, then most owners go to an attorney. That's not necessarily my recommendation. My recommendation would be that if a homeowner is having trouble with his architect, then he consults with another architect that he's had a recommendation on. Just sit down with them and say, "Sir, I'm here to pay for a couple of hours of consultation with you. I don't want the content of this conversation to go beyond this room, but here is what I perceive my problems to be. Would you tell me if I'm right or if I'm wrong? Please share your advice with me." I've had that happen a number of times. If the homeowner is having problems with the builder and the architect is not helping and the homeowner has confronted the architect and said, "We need to get rid of this guy," and the architect said, "No, let's string him on," then I believe an attorney should be consulted.

AND IT'S IMPORTANT TO GO TO AN ATTORNEY THAT'S KNOWLEDGEABLE IN CONSTRUCTION?

Yes, it is.

IS IT REALISTIC FOR A CLIENT TO COUNT ON AN ARCHITECT TO HELP WITH COST ESTIMATING?

No. An architect may be experienced with general construction costs, i.e., $200/foot vs. $400/foot given the style and materials a homeowner may choose, but to make more realistic, detailed cost estimates the homeowner should rely on the contractor.

TWO THINGS: I'VE INTERVIEWED THREE ARCHITECTS AND I'VE DECIDED TO HIRE ONE. IS IT IMPORTANT FOR ME TO FOLLOW UP WITH THE TWO I AM NOT HIRING?

Yes.

HOW MIGHT I DO THAT BEST AND WHY IS THAT IMPORTANT?

It would be good information to the unsuccessful individuals to know if there's any reason why. It's just courtesy. Of course, when you call, if you hated the guy, you're not going to say, "I hated you. I'd never hire you to do a dog house." You just say, "We're really impressed with this other firm and I wanted to pay you the courtesy of letting you know that we elected to proceed with so-and-so. Thanks for meeting with me."

(continued from page 51)

project, it's more difficult and costly to undo what they could have properly managed in the first place.

Your architect may charge you a percentage of your project, an hourly fee — or both. Whatever the fee is, you want to have a clear understanding of what services are going to be included before your project begins. It is also important for you to understand when you are going to be expected to pay for your architect's services. Generally, architects are paid upfront before construction begins. This means that homeowners are going to be responsible for this design amount without having the benefit of a loan. Depending on the fee, this can be the determining factor as to why many homeowners bypass the services of an architect.

There is good news for those of you who would like to use the services of an architect but don't want to let go of that cash in addition to the construction costs. Alan Looney, one of the contractors that I feature in the contractor preview section of this book, describes how he includes the architectural fee in his overall project bid. In accounting for the design fee in this manner, that sum of money is now considered to be part of your overall project fee. Kimberley Collins–Ripmaster, a loan officer and construction financial advisor, says that if this agreement is worked out with your loan officer on the front-end of your project, the design fee for the architect is not unlike earnest money paid on the front end of the project. This amount is refunded to the homeowner at the end of the project. You can then use it for other expenses.

Once you have gone over the different ways that your architect would charge for their services on your project, you now want to understand the schedule in which you will be billed. At what point would you expect to pay for these services? Ask to see a draw sheet. You want to see how they lay out the work of their services when they request funds. This will help you better familiarize yourself with their accounting procedures and your project's progression.

Architectural Supplemental Instructions

Change orders are most commonly used by contractors during the construction process. Nancy Hayden, an architect, says that she issues what she calls an architect's supplemental instructions. These are changes to the job. A change may result in a credit, it may be an add-on that creates additional charges to the project or it may not involve any money at all. Nancy says that she gives this to the contractor and the contractor then issues the homeowner a change order. It's important for the homeowner to get this change order, whether it's a credit or an increase to the cost of their project. On Nancy's supplemental instructions document, she states that the contractor is to notify the client if there's a change in price prior to proceeding with the work being done.

This is important because you want to have full understanding of the ramifications of this change. It may be minimal or it may be substantial. By requiring a signature from you, your contractor and your architect will make sure that everyone involved is up to speed with what is happening on your project before the change takes place. Keeping the lines of communication open like this will assure smooth transitions if change is necessary.

Architect Documented Revision

Ask your architect what would substantiate a price increase on your project and how they will document this change on your behalf. For example, you may have the design documents completed or near completion and you decide to make a change. Would you need to pay extra for this change? If so, how would your architect be compensated for having to take the time to make this change? It's most likely going to be on an hourly basis. It could be a 20-minute change, a 2-hour change or a 20-hour change. You need to understand this going in.

Depending on how far into the design process your project is, making changes can cause additional design time that was not provided for in your original design fee. Re-designing a set of plans can have a domino effect on your drawings. These changes may also result in a more costly construction budget as well. Ask your architect if they use a Computer Aided Design (CAD) computer program that helps to facilitate these changes. If so, they may offer to email you a PDF file or make you a CD of the changes so you can study them before deciding. These are "view only" files. They can't be changed.

Business Procedures or Company Overview

Find out how your architect will conduct their design services throughout your project. Are they the ones who you will be doing business with or do they have other people in their firm that will be working on your project as well? If they will be using other people to assist them on your project, you want to know who these people are. And you want references from other clients that they have worked with.

Experience with Implementing Green Building Materials in Home Designs

If you are interested in building or remodeling with green homebuilding materials, ask this architect to have examples ready for you that represent work they've done on other projects. Some of these projects may not be LEED certified, however, they met the homeowner's requirements or needs for their lifestyle. If this is the case in any project that your architect shows you, ask them to go through the work with you that was done. What you want to confirm at your first meeting is that this architect has experience with and understands how to incorporate green building products into a home design. Ask for references from this architect to follow up with the clients that this architect did the work for.

Experience with Designing Sustainable Housing

If you are interested in building a sustainable home, you will need to hire an architect who is well versed in implementing the design requirements beginning with the initial design phases —- no on the job training with your project. You also want an architect who can offer construction administration services to throughout the life of your project, assuring that you will reap the full benefits of a sustainable design.

Portfolio

When you are looking at an architect's portfolio you want to see work represented that is similar to what you want for your project. This can be an arguable point, because all architects are trained to design structures. So it is likely that any architect can design any style of home. If you hire an architect who specializes in modern design and you want French Country, you may be forfeiting some of the esthetic qualities and nuances that brought you to this style in the first place. Architects may develop their own style of interpretation and that may be what you are attracted to. Give yourself enough time and interview a number of architects so you can compare what each one would bring to your project. Compare men and women architects as well. Just as men and women may approach life differently, men and women architects may approach design differently. The artist in the architect interprets design elements differently. Being exposed to the talent of numerous architects is going to inspire you and help assure you of not settling for less than you deserve.

An architect may ask you to bring pictures that you have gathered or other items that would help give them a visual or emotional representation of what you want to build. The information I have outlined for you to bring for this first interview will be enough for you to review at this meeting. An architect unfamiliar with the PHM™ may ask for all the information that they know the typical homeowner identifies with — lots of pictures laid out in a notebook to review. You could easily spend hours with numerous architects going over this visual material and still walk away not really knowing if they are the architect for you and your project. You would also have limited your opportunity to find the ultimate match.

Duo Dickenson , a good example

I first met Duo Dickenson, an AIA architect based in Connecticut, a couple of years ago while he was the guest speaker at an AIA luncheon. Duo is the author of numerous books, including *The House You Build* and *House on a Budget*. Duo is also one of the founders of Congress of Residential Architects (CORA) and contributes regularly to the television series, *This Old House*. What struck me most about Duo were his approachable personality and his ability to incorporate brilliant architectural design with a common sense appeal to it.

When I began writing this book I was able to talk with many different professionals and homeowners that were experienced with homebuilding and remodeling. One thing that came up numerous times was the difficulty of working with an over-inflated ego. Ego within any member of a team can be obtrusive and will most likely cause tension and frustration throughout the project. This type of personality will hinder the creative process that should evolve when working with a team of people. It's also at odds with the most important goal of the project — which is to focus on the homeowner's needs. Duo focuses on educating the homeowner to the homebuilding process and evidences the value of hiring an architect to enrich their overall experience. This should be the focus of every professional you hire.

If you are drawn to hiring a celebrity architect, contractor or interior designer because of the work you've seen represented in publications or in another media format, treat your interview with them as you would with anyone else. Go in open-minded and properly focused. Be proactive with your follow-up review of your meeting. Monitor your motives for making your decision. If you are confident that this is the person you should hire for you project, great! If you are hesitant, pay attention to those feelings as well. Remind yourself that there are many other talented professionals that you haven't seen. Regardless of the level of notoriety of an individual, always bear in mind that you are footing the bill and you and your family will be living in the space and sharing it with your friends and loved ones. Your home is an extension of who you are, not the people you hire to design and build it. They may put their imprint on it, but it's your heart-felt decisions that give it life.

If you meet with an architect, contractor or designer who makes you feel less about yourself and your project in their presence than you do outside of their presence, walk away. Finding the right fit for you will be well worth your time and effort.

I talked with Duo again in a phone interview and asked him what were the most important things that he would suggest a homeowner bring to their architect when they are ready to begin the design process. Duo's answer was to bring anything and everything that will help the architect get a better idea of what your likes and dislikes are. "You can learn just as much about someone from their dislikes as you can from the things they like." While most homeowners bring in photos of houses and rooms, Duo suggests that they bring in subject matter that can elicit an emotional feeling as well. For example, one of the most helpful items that a homeowner brought into a meeting with him was early on in his career. A woman brought in a photo of a section of a stone wall. "That was it, nothing else was in this picture but this stone wall. She said, 'I don't know why, but I really love this picture.'" Duo said that that one picture spoke volumes to him. It represented texture — materials that he could incorporate into the house. It showed colors and an overall feeling that he could create to match the emotional response that this woman had when she looked at this picture. "It was very strong."

Another point that Duo made was that he, of course, is flattered when a client comes to him and says, "I like your work and I trust you to design my house, so do whatever you want." While flattered, he likes the creative process and energy that comes with the give and take when a client participates in the design process of their home.

interview

Nancy Hayden
architect

Nancy Hayden was one of the first women architects that I met when I began this project. I appreciated Nancy's insight and candidness in her approach to designing a client's home. Homebuilding is a male dominated industry, however, statistics show that a higher percentage of architectural students are now female. That's exciting news! Nancy is a great example as to why you should expand your team search to include women in the industry as well as men.

YOU HAVE WORKED ON BOTH COMMERCIAL AND RESIDENTIAL PROJECTS, HOW DOES THAT TYPE OF BACKGROUND BENEFIT A HOMEOWNER HIRING AN ARCHITECT?

It's not unusual for an architect to have worked on both commercial and residential projects. For me, the advantage I can bring to a homeowner is the knowledge of materials. I have the ability to work with materials other than wood. This gives me the advantage of being able to handle projects that someone else may be uncomfortable with — like historical homes that call for the integration of materials not commonly used in new home construction.

WHAT SHOULD A HOMEOWNER LOOK FOR IN AN ARCHITECT WHO THEY ARE CONSIDERING FOR THEIR PROJECT?

First off, their personality; you need someone that is respectful.

They're going to be in your house for a long time, especially if it's a renovation addition, and if you don't get along with them and they irritate you, it's not going to be a good experience. I tell my clients that about contractors, too. Second, style of architecture. There are some architects that only design in one style, and if you don't like that, it's not a good idea to work with them. I like designing in different styles and variety. It's challenging to me.

IF I WERE A HOMEOWNER CONSIDERING HIRING AN ARCHITECT TO DESIGN MY HOME, WHAT WOULD BE SOME OF THE BENEFITS OF HIRING YOU?

I've had kids, I grew up in a family of five, I cook, I know how a house works and I know how a house works throughout the family cycle. Beginning with no children, to infants, to tod-dlers and on into teenagers. I haven't gotten to the college part yet. So I have an understanding about space and design for a family who wants to renovate their house in anticipation of having a child. I can walk them through the thought process of reconsidering level changes and long expanses because it's just not going to work for awhile; they don't want to have to be running after their child every second.

I think about all these things that make your life simpler. How your house works makes your life flow. Organization and enough space but not too much space.

Where do you put the tub toys? How do you feel in this space? What do you want this space to feel like? How does your family work? How do you enter your house? How do you leave your house? How do you live? Do you entertain formally, informally?

There are a lot questions that I think I bring to the table that a lot of other architects may not think about, especially kitchen design. When I design one, I consider things like where do the storage container go? Do you have a lot of serving trays, do you have a lot of dishes, do you have a lot of linens — that kind of thing.

WHAT DO YOU THINK A HOMEOWNER SHOULD TRY TO ACCOMPLISH ON THEIR FIRST MEETING WITH AN ARCHITECT?

My first meeting with clients is to decide whether they want to hire me or not. And the second meeting is for images of what they like and want in their home. I ask to meet in their house because it tells me about their taste and it tells me a lot about how they live.

SO, YOU LIKE TO MEET IN THEIR CURRENT LIVING SPACE?

Yes, even if it's an apartment, or their first home and they want to renovate. If it's a couple, I ask them for any ideas they might have, if they can sit down and think about each room individually and then together. How they work together, how they want it to feel, do they want a lot of windows or not — are there privacy issues? Sometimes they have different ideas as to what they want, and, if you can get them to talk, you can discover what issues may cause conflict, and then that can be avoided later on in the design process. If they don't talk it can be very problematic. I've had a situation where a husband called me and said, "I don't want this in the design," but he didn't say it in the meeting, and that puts me in an awkward position — I'm not the counselor.

WHAT ARE SOME IMPORTANT QUESTIONS A CLIENT SHOULD ASK THE ARCHITECT DURING THE INTERVIEW PROCESS?

Ask enough questions to find out if they're open to designing a house for you, not for them. Find out what type of experience they have. Do they only design in one style or are they open to designing in other styles? Ask for references and follow up with the references that you are given. Find out if they're open to your ideas, because it is your house and you know how you live. Are they open to understanding how you live? If they're not, then they're not the architect for you.

MY PROACTIVE HOMEBUILDING METHOD IS BASED ON THE IMPORTANCE OF TEAMWORK. HOW IMPORTANT IS IT TO INCLUDE YOUR CONTRACTOR AND OTHER TEAM PLAYERS ON THE FRONT END OF THE DESIGN PROCESS?

It's very important to have the contractor and everyone else involved at the beginning and build that team right from the start, which is sometimes hard, especially if it's a big project and you want to involve a landscape architect, etc. It's hard to get the homeowner to understand how beneficial it is to have everyone on the same page from the beginning, even at the initial meeting, to bounce around some ideas.

WHY WOULD THAT BE BENEFICIAL FOR THE OWNER?

They need to understand how important it is that we all work to make all these elements come together. When you build your home, you don't finish it and then say, "Okay, now I'm

The intersecting window dormers create an illusion and cast shadows that add to the romantic mood of this bedroom space. PHOTO CREDIT: RICHARD LEO JOHNSON, ARCHITECT: NANCY HAYDEN

going to paint it." A lot of architects are not interior oriented but I am, so, at the beginning of the project I'm thinking about paint, finishes and tile etc.

HOW CAN YOUR ABILITY TO SEE THE BIG PICTURE HELP THE HOMEOWNER ARRIVE AT A REALISTIC BUILDING BUDGET?

I send them out early on to start looking at lighting and plumbing fixtures and make them aware that you can spend thousands of dollars in one little bathroom, so you have to prioritize. Some people want the new convection range. Well, okay, if you get the new convection range, you may not be able to afford the silver or gold-plated faucet that you wanted in the bathroom.

There are some compromises. You don't have to spend thousands of dollars on every little thing to make your house fabulous. There are things that are in a mid-range price level that are beautiful. You can use granite — just don't pick exotic. It typically runs the same as Corian, which people don't know, especially if you use just a straight edge. I start trying to educate them on materials. Go look and see what you like. Some people are just so overwhelmed; they're like, "I can't do it. Just pick it." So I tell them, "I'll be glad to go with you in the beginning, you and your interior designer can go or you can go look first and then decide what you want to do." That's most helpful because the amount of tile and plumbing fixtures out there today are amazing, and that's only one choice that the homeowner is trying to make.

IS GOING OVER BUDGET A COMMON THING FOR HOMEOWNERS TO DO BECAUSE OF UPGRADES AND CHANGES? IS THIS BECAUSE THEY DIDN'T UNDERSTAND AND DIDN'T DO THEIR HOMEWORK TO PROPERLY PREPARE THEMSELVES ON THE FRONT END?

They need to take the time up front to look at the choices that are available to them. The contractor has given them a specific building budget to build their home and they need to understand what that budget entails and if it allows this much money for the kitchen countertop, then that's what they have to stick with if they're already in the building process. However, if they do their work ahead of time, and they go out with their architect, designer or they go out on their own, they'll understand what Formica, Corian, Silestone, granite or exotic granite is going to look like and determine whether or not they can work within that budget. They can decide then, okay, do I want to upgrade now or do I want to keep the cost where it is and use that money somewhere else? Am I okay with this allowance? By doing this process early on they have a realistic picture going in as to what the overall expense is going to be, versus a third of the way through the construction process, they've upgraded, and they're $30 - 40 - 100,000 or more over budget.

Before I send out the final drawings, I like to have all these questions answered: What are the exact appliances the homeowner is using?, Are we using granite? Are we using tile? What kind of tile? Then there's a realistic allowance number in their budget that covers the tile choice the homeowner can live with. Don't put yourself in a panic situation because you didn't prepare properly. Don't wait until the middle of the job and have a contractor show up at 7 in the morning needing a light fixture by the afternoon. Then you only put yourself at risk of buying something you don't like, or spending too much money — only to want to change it out later on.

I once heard a contractor say, "The palette of colors is like a wardrobe." The palette he is referring to is everything that goes into your home. He's talking to women — helping them get a visual of putting their ideas and choices for their home together. You take care and time to choose your wardrobe so it coordinates and looks good together. That's the way you need to look at the decisions you make with this house too. You need to take your time to make the right choices. Because one choice is going to affect another choice, everything affects everything.

I think this is very important for women to understand about being panicked to get something done or a choice made on the spot. The contractors are pushing and pushing because they have a deadline to meet: "Can you just give me the foundation drawings so we can get started?" I may have to say, "No, I cannot." I had one job where I had a problem because the homeowners let the contractor get started without my drawings. They had no contract, no drawings, nothing, and it was a nightmare. Sometimes the homeowners don't listen to the people they hire to help build their home. They need to respect their architect, respect their building team and their knowledge and their experience. They need to listen to them.

The homeowner needs to determine what they want. It's their house. Let your designer help you, or in my case, let me help and guide you to pick something that *you* like, not what everybody else likes. It's a problem when the homeowner starts asking other people's opinions.

how to select an architect

Items You Should Ask the Architect to Have Available at First Interview

- ☐ Registration information
- ☐ Credentials information
- ☐ Copy of insurance certificate
- ☐ Copy of Contract example
- ☐ Example of budget or accounting summary used for clients
- ☐ Information on their fees and levels of involvement
- ☐ Sample of architectural supplemental instructions (see page 47)
- ☐ Architect documented revision (example of what would substantiate an additional charge to project)
- ☐ Business procedures of company overview information
- ☐ Experience with implementing Green Building materials in home designs (If applicable)
- ☐ Experience with designing sustainable housing (If applicable)
- ☐ Portfolio
- ☐ References (3 – 5 clients), (from a current and a 1-year-old project to 3-year-old projects)

Architect Interview Questions

- ☐ How long have you been an architect?
- ☐ What is your position in this firm?
- ☐ Will you be the main person I would be dealing with in the design development of my home or renovation?
- ☐ Would you be using anyone else to work on the design of my home or renovation? If so, what will they be doing?
- ☐ Will I be interacting with this person throughout the design development of my project?
- ☐ Can I meet them, and can you provide me with some references of clients who they have done work for?
- ☐ How busy are you at this time?
- ☐ Do you use the newest technology available to architects today in the design process? If so, how will this technology be of benefit to my project and me?
- ☐ How will you approach the design process with me?
- ☐ How will you help me to understand the different development stages of the design process?
- ☐ How will you help me in understanding my role and responsibilities as CEO of this home-building venture?
- ☐ Do you consider yourself to be a team player when it comes to working with a contractor on a project?
- ☐ Can you tell me about some of your past projects where you have worked as a collaborative team member for a project?
- ☐ Have you used the services of a contractor to secure cost estimates in the early phases of design development?
- ☐ If so, can you provide the names of some of your clients that have benefited from these services in your references for me?
- ☐ How do you feel about having a contractor come in on the early stages of design development to give input on cost requirements?
- ☐ I'm new to the concept of reading blueprints. If I have to ask you to review something for me several times, how will you handle that?
- ☐ What are specifications? How would they benefit my project?
- ☐ A lot of homeowners build homes from pre-designed plans that either their contractor has provided for them or that they have purchased from a design book. What will your services provide for me that a pre-designed set of plans would not?
- ☐ In your opinion, what might be some of the hidden costs of working with a pre-designed set of plans?
- ☐ Tell me about the different level of services that you provide.
- ☐ How do you charge for these services?
- ☐ What do you estimate the fee for this project to be?
- ☐ What is the schedule of payments for your services and will I receive from you in writing the services you will provide upon receipt of payment for these services?
- ☐ When do you expect to be paid for these services?

☐ Have you ever worked on a project where the architectural fees were included as a budget item in the overall construction loan by the contractor so that the homeowner is reimbursed for their cost of design fees at the end of the project? (See chapter 3 for and explanation.)

☐ Is your work guaranteed?

☐ Tell me how my making changes throughout the design process are handled. Will I be charged for any of these changes?

☐ After hearing about and seeing some of my ideas for my project, how do you think your services will most benefit me?

☐ What are some of the challenges that you see in my project?

☐ Are you insured? Can I get a copy of your insurance certificate?

☐ Are you a member of the AIA or any other accredited organization?

☐ How will you gain information about the needs of my project?

☐ What do you want from me to help in the development of my design?

☐ Have you ever had a conflict with a contractor in any given project? If so, what was it about and how was it resolved?

☐ What will be your availability to answer questions on the project as they arise for me or for the contractor?

☐ What will be our method of communication throughout the project?

☐ How do you follow up with a client once the home is completed?

Architect Preliminary Review Checklist

PHM™ MINDED

☐ Decide if the architect is a team player.

☐ Decide if this architect will have a PHM™ approach when working with me and my contractor to establish a homebuilding design within my budget.

☐ Follow up on architect's registration

CREDENTIALS

☐ If AIA member, call your local component, confirm membership and check to see if there have been any complaints against this architect. If they hold other credentials, go online to see what they are.

INSURANCE CERTIFICATE

☐ Call insurance agent and ask if this policy is up to date. Has this architect kept up with their insurance premiums? Has this architect ever had their insurance policy canceled?

CONTRACT REVIEW

☐ Only review contract if this is the architect you're thinking of hiring.

☐ Review the contract with a construction attorney and clearly understand what it says with regard to the services the architect is going to provide.

☐ Obtain a clear understanding as to how this contract relates to this architect working with my contractor or others on my building team.

☐ Obtain a clear understanding as to how this contract does or does not protect my interests with regard to this project. Include any additional changes to this contract that your attorney has provided and include these changes for review by the architect.

☐ Don't sign anything until your attorney reviews the final document with you. I am confident that this architect guarantees their work.

Services Provided by this Architect

☐ I Understand the level of services that this architect is going to provide on my project.

☐ I Understand the importance of maintaining this agreement throughout the project.

Fee

☐ Review the fees that this architect is going to charge for their services and understand how I am going to be charged.

☐ Talked with this architect about including the design fee in my contractor's building budget (see Alan Looney's interview page 82. I understand that I am responsible for paying this architect's design fee as soon as I receive the services of the architect and that I will be reimbursed at the end of my project. (Please log onto my web site, www.proactivehomebuilding. com and review the information provided by Kimberley Collins-Ripmaster about financing the design process of your project. Also read the chapter 3, Protecting Your Money — Don't Blow It.)

ARCHITECT DOCUMENTED REVISION

☐ Understand how this architect is going to handle changes that I make during the design process of my project and what would constitute an additional fee for those changes.

ACCOUNTING PROCEDURE

☐ I understand how the design phase of my project is going to be billed by this architect.

BUSINESS PROCEDURES AND COMPANY OVERVIEW

☐ I Understand the design philosophy of this architect and the firm that they work with.

☐ I have a clear understanding as to who I will be interacting with throughout the design process of my project. If this person is not the architect that I interviewed, I have met with this person and I have followed up with references from other homeowners who have used this person's services on their project.

EXPERIENCE IN DESIGNING GREEN AND SUSTAINABLE HOMES

☐ I understand what it means if this architect is *Leed Certified* and whether or not that will have any bearing on this architect's ability to design with *Green* materials or implement sustainable design.

☐ I am confident in this architect's ability to design a home with *Green* product. I am confident in this architect's ability to design a sustainable building.

PORTFOLIO

☐ I feel great about the work represented in this architect's portfolio and I believe that their work represents work that is consistent with the work that I will require on my project.

REFERENCES

☐ I have received 3 – 5 references from other clients of this architect. I have followed up with these references on the phone. I have visited the homes of some of these references and I like the quality of detail and design that this architect provided.

Architect Client Reference Questions

☐ Name of client. What level of services did the architect provide for this client?

☐ Did this architect design a home that stayed within the client's budget range?

☐ Did this architect use the assistance of a contractor and/or interior designer during the design process? Does the client think that this architect has a team mentality or would they rather work independently?

☐ What might the client have had this architect do differently on this project?

☐ Did this client feel like they had a clear understanding of what their home design was going to look like before it was built?

☐ Do they feel that this architect was able to capture their design desires successfully?

☐ Did this architect help this client choose a contractor for their project?

☐ Were they happy with this contractor?

☐ Did this architect provide construction administrative services and review draw requests submitted by the contractor? If so, was the client happy with the way things were handled?

☐ Did this architect provide this homeowner with an insurance certificate?

☐ Did this architect respond to the contractor's needs on the project in a timely manner?

☐ Would the client be willing to let you come to visit their home? Would the client recommend this architect?

☐ You will find more questions for your review on my web site.

CHAPTER six

YOUR PHM™ HOMEBUILDING TEAM

your contractor

Your contractor is the person you are going to be spending the most one-on-one time with, so you want to make sure you are very comfortable with them. That doesn't mean that you adopt them into your family. Contractors by nature are going to be congenial people. That's what draws them to this business and helps them to succeed. It's also the part of their personality that makes you want to invite them to your next BBQ to meet all your friends. Don't make the mistake of interpreting your contractor's willingness to be helpful and upbeat with you as a sign that your relationship is uniquely special. Yes, they want your project to succeed. Yes, they want to be the one to help you make it succeed. It's their job, and helping you achieve your goal puts bread on their table.

Handholding — having to introduce and walk the homeowner through every aspect of the homebuilding process — is important to the contractor because it keeps the project moving forward and assists in keeping it on schedule. Handholding begins at the first meeting. It's a professional and strategic move on the contractor's part.

A professional contractor will prove to be a competent leader who successfully manages all the details of your project's needs while helping you, the stressed-out homeowner, navigate the ebbs and flows of the homebuilding/remodeling process more easily. They will take your hard-earned cash and transition it into your family's new dream-home, while helping you protect your investment.

The dishonest, incompetent contractor is just as congenial as the legitimate professional, if not more so. Unfortunately, if you make the mistake of hiring them, it's usually months into the project before you, the unsuspecting homeowner, are able to identify the problem areas. Depending on how much damage has been done, your hard-earned cash may or may not be enough to salvage what's left of your project.

By reading and acting upon the information I've provided in the following pages, I am confident that you will be prepared to hire the best-suited handholding contractor for your project!

Preliminary Review and First Interview List for Contractor

- Current License
- Credentials
- LLC
- Bond information
- Insurance certificate
- Contract
- Example of their Budget / Accounting summary to be used on your project
- Are they paid Cost + or set fee
- Value analysis or value–engineered bid
- Copy of Change Order to be used
- Business procedures or company overview
- Portfolio
- Building Green or Sustainable Housing experience

Ask if there is anything specific that they want you to bring.

Current License

Your contractor's license or registration information should be on their business card. *Do not* do business with a contractor who will not provide you with their license information. A contractor has to be licensed to pull building permits or to receive bond and insurance coverage. *Do not* do business with a contractor who asks you to pull a building permit for your project in your own name.

The *National Association of State Contracting Licensing Agencies* (NASCLA) has recently relayed information about a scam in New Orleans involving dishonest contractors who asked homeowners, trying to rebuild their homes after Hurricane Katrina, to obtain building permits in their own name so as "not to delay the rebuilding process." In this scam the homeowner signs an affidavit that allows them to pull the permit without being a licensed contractor. The homeowner then pays the dishonest contractor money for work done or work to be done. That contractor then takes the money and runs. The unfortunate homeowner has no recourse because they fraudulently signed a notarized affidavit to illegally obtain a governmental permit to perform the work. This prevented the licensing board from telling that homeowner that this contractor is not legally licensed to work on their project.

This type of practice is not limited to New Orleans. It is widespread across the country. Individuals looking to take advantage of the unsuspecting homeowner offer to provide construction services at a savings or in record time. These predators are well-versed in their manner and approach. Be aware and follow through with the necessary precautions when it comes to verifying any potential contractor that you are considering hiring, especially if this contractor has not provided you with referrals and projects that you can visit. I continue to address this issue in the remodeling section of this book. A large percentage of homeowners who have experienced problems with contractors are on remodeling projects. Homeowners who are remodeling their homes tend to be less likely to follow-up on the legitimacy of a contractor. If you are considering doing a remodel on your home, read chapter 12 to help you prepare for your project.

The requirements for receiving a contractor's license vary from state to state. Some states require that the applicant give proof of actual work experience as well as pass a written exam. Other states or counties require little more than filling out an application. Do not assume that just because you are interviewing a "licensed contractor" that you are interviewing someone qualified to do the work on your project.

There are states across the U.S. — Colorado, for example — where construction work is not licensed or regulated through the state. If you happen to live in a state that does not require the contractor to be licensed, follow up on a local level. Your city or county is most likely going to have the information you need.

There are web sites you can go to when seeking information regarding your contractor's license. One such site that I have found to be very helpful is: www.constructionweblinks.com. Click on state agencies and then click on your state. Your state will provide you with an information page that will link you to the information you need.

You can also find your state licensing information online at contractors-license.org. You will get the option to click on Contractor's License Reference Site. Click on that site and it will provide you with a page of the U.S. Click on your state and click on the web site that directs you to the licensing information for your state. You can either read the information once, typing in your contractor's license number, or you can call the number listed for your licensing board and talk with one of their representatives.

What your contractor's license/registration tells you (once you have confirmed that it is indeed current) is that they are complying with the state, county or city requirements and working as a contractor in a legal capacity. By contacting your state, city or county licensing board and asking about a contractor's current license status, you can inquire as to how long your contractor has been working in your area, and the amount of the license bond that your contractor carries, as they vary from state to state. (See information on bonds below.) Have there been any liens, license suspensions, fines or court proceedings that have been filed against this contractor? You will also be able to confirm that this contractor is licensed to build within the scope of your project's budget.

Credentials

A contractor's credentials range from project awards to Building Associations. The most common association for a contractor to be a member of is the *National Association of Home Builders* (NAHB). This organization offers great information for the homeowner as well. I suggest that you visit their site, Nahb.org. The NAHB offers a *Certified Graduate Builder* (CGB) designation. A contractor who receives this designation tells you that he has taken the initiative to go beyond the normal contractor's requirements. If your contractor has a list of credentials, awards and accreditations, follow up on what they stand for to assess the value they offer to your project. Don't make the assumption that just because you see a picture and an award in the paper that that contractor is reputable or that the award is of much merit. It may be an award that is given on photographs alone. Call the paper that provided the article and find out what qualifications were required to receive the award.

I know of a homeowner who was recovering from a horrific homebuilding experience. She sat down to read the paper and upon opening it up, saw a spread about how wonderful her contractor was. Other awards are legitimate achievements recognized by the industry. If your contractor displays an award, title or credential in their portfolio or business brochure, ask them to tell you about it. What did they do to achieve it?

Limited Liability Company (LLC)

Your contractor may have LLC after their name on their business card or any other form of advertisement that they use. If a contractor has LLC after their name, it is used to designate that they (as many independent business owners) have chosen to form a LLC as a separate and legal entity. Your contractor can now obtain a tax identification number, open a bank account and do business all under their LLC's name. Along with other tax and business related benefits for forming an LLC, it sets your contractor's business assets apart from their private assets, protecting your contractor from personally being held liable if they were to be sued.

Upon doing an interview with an insurance provider not featured in this book, I was told that some contractors form LLC's only for the life of a project. Once the project is finished, they dissolve that LLC and open a new one. If something goes wrong on the project that the original LLC was developed for, that homeowner has no recourse or funds to collect for damages. You may want to ask your contractor how long they have had their current LLC in place.

Bond Information

There are numerous types of bonds that are available to your contractor. (See the interview on page 73.)

LICENSING/CONTRACTOR'S BOND

The licensing/contractor's or *permit bond* is most common. When you see licensed, bonded and insured on a contractor's business card, it is most likely one of these types of bonds that they are referring to. Before a contractor can receive an active license, most states (not all) require them to maintain a *surety bond* for the benefit of consumers and employees. Some states only require a license bond for home improvement or remodeling contractors. Tennessee, for example, requires remodeling contractors to carry a $10,000 licensing bond.

On a local level — meaning city or county — your contractor may be required to carry a permit bond. This enables them to pull the necessary permits to do the work on your project. These types of bonds protect the city, county or state from being sued and the bond will cover the cost to repair a road, curb, or other city-owned property that may get damaged from the contractor or one their workers while on a project. This bond is also a source of funds that an employee who is rightfully due payment can go to if the contractor doesn't pay them for work they have done. Lastly, this bond is in place as compensation for a homeowner as well as protecting consumers and employees. They are meant to provide a measure of protection for you, the consumer, in case your contractor defaults or causes damage to your project due to defective construction or other license law violations.

The amount of this bond varies from state to state. For example, in the state of Washington, it is $12,000. In the state of California it was just raised from $10,000 to $12,500. Williamson County, in the state of Tennessee is $30,000. Some states require additional bond protection for you from your contractor. Arizona requires that residential contractors also provide a consumer protection bond of $200,000. You can inquire as to the amount of your contractor's licensing bond before your interview by calling your state, county or city licensing board.

PERFORMANCE OR PAYMENT BOND

If you deem it necessary to request that your contractor carry a bond to supplement their licensing/contractor's or permit bond amount, you would request that they obtain a *performance* or *payment bond*.

The performance bond assures that your contractor and their subs perform work according to their contractual obligations. If work is not done satisfactorily or is done defectively by either your contractor or their subs and results in damage to your property, the performance bond will cover the damages or the cost for repairs (providing it is a sum that is sufficient to cover those costs).

A payment bond assures that everyone your contractor is responsible for paying money to with regard to your project, i.e., suppliers and subs, are paid if your contractor should default. If your contractor has a bond other than a license or contractor's bond, you can request a copy of their bond certificate.

Ensure You're Insured

Halfway into their building project Mark and Jane recognized that they were heading down a rocky road. They had had numerous problems resulting from their builder's seeming inability to rise to the demands that their project called for. They were already experiencing heavy leakage from their ceilings at the base of all their chimneys as well as the front porch area where water was leaking into the basement from where the porch adjoined the house.

Mark was being assured by the architect/builder team that the problems were being taken care of. However, as things progressed it was becoming very clear that their hopes of having the successful home building experience they had anticipated were being dashed by the nightmarish set of circumstances they saw developing around them.

It wasn't until after they were moved into their newly built home and the "solved" problems started surfacing again, now compounded by the damage done to the drywall, trim, paint, cabinets, furniture, rugs, etc., that they began to understand the magnitude of this situation and the repercussions it could have on their finances. The building team was obviously unable to properly correct these on-going issues and the builder refused to pay for someone else to come in and assist in repairs. Mark and Jane had no other recourse but to hire an attorney.

Over a year into litigation, Mark and Jane were blindsided by the fact that their builder's general liability policy excluded covering faulty workmanship. Their contractor's policy didn't have a provision clause that would help them recoup the finances they now needed in order to repair the roof, chimneys, front porch replacement, and numerous other problems that occurred as a direct result of the contractor and his subs incompetent building practices. Mark and Jane found themselves in the difficult position of having to decide if they wanted to risk spending more money to go forward with their lawsuit and pursue their builder's assets or to settle for the less than fair amount of compensation the insurance company was offering them; to count their losses and address the corrections needed to their home using their own resources.

Mark and Jane's situation was not unique in that their builder had an inferior insurance policy. Their builder's coverage was just like the coverage currently being offered to all contractors across the country. Home Builders Associations can attest to this fact by their offerings of workshops that are specifically designed to address the "current liability insurance crisis" facing residential and commercial builders, developers, and remodeling contractors across the country.

Around the years 1995 - 2000 if you were a contractor working on numerous homes at the same time you paid a relatively low insurance premium that would cover you for virtually all that might happen on a building site. For example, it wasn't uncommon for a contractor who was working on five different projects ranging from $500,000 + to pay as little as 3, 4, $5,000 for coverage. Today, the same contractor working on the same projects has a vastly different level of coverage at a much higher premium. He could now be paying as much as 20 - 30% more for less coverage than he was receiving only seven to ten years ago. In order to keep up with these higher premiums some contractors are eliminating certain coverage clauses to "customize" their coverage to meet their monetary needs. This customizing of coverage is not necessarily done to deceive the homeowner; it is done because the contractor is doing the best he can with what the insurance companies are offering him.

This now "limited" coverage can have dire consequences to the uninformed homeowner who has hired the contractor assuming that the contractor's insurance is going to cover any unexpected problems that may arise during their building project. It will be important for you as a homeowner to adequately protect your homebuilding investment, no matter what size your budget is. To do this, you need to have a clear understanding of what is going to be covered before you sign a contract between you and your builder.

TYPES OF INSURANCE
Any reputable builder/contractor is going to carry at least two types of insurance, some possibly three. They will have Worker's Compensation, General Liability and Builder's Risk. The latter may be a policy the contractor requests that the homeowner purchases on their own.

Worker's Compensation
Worker's Compensation Insurance is insurance carried by the general contractor and/or subcontractors to protect the workers on your project who may get injured while doing their job. Whether you are building new or renovating an existing property it is imperative that your contractor have Worker's Compensation Insurance that covers everyone working on their crew. Most counties and states require proof of WCI in order to pull building permits. This will help you avoid a lawsuit resulting from an injury while the subs are working on your building site. If you were acting as the general contractor

on your project, then you would be responsible for the workers coming onto your property, so you would have to get Workers Compensation from your insurance provider.

According to Kevin Hale it is also in the homeowner's best interest to have stipulated in your contract that the contractor agrees to hire only those workers who carry their own 1 million dollar insurance coverage policy as well.

General Liability
General Liability Insurance is the second major insurance that a contractor will carry. While Worker's Compensation Insurance (worker's comp) is most important to the contractor because he is held responsible for his employees on your project, General Liability Insurance is presumably carried by the contractor to help protect the homeowner's best interest if there happens to be a problem on the building site that results in damaging the owner's home and the owner needs to seek monetary compensation.

Gary Hughes, an LLC officer/member with Gary Hughes and Associates explains it this way: "The drywall people are putting up the drywall. They miss a stud and hit a pipe. You turn your water on and there's a leak. It damages the wall or it ruins the carpet, etc. In my opinion, this should be under the 'builders warranty' to fix the resulting problem. However, if the builder does not cooperate, your only recourse for compensation is to sue him."

The monetary compensation you would be seeking would be coming from the General Liability Insurance coverage. This is why having a clear understanding of the change in the Liability coverage your contractor carries is so important to you, the homeowner. You need to know what is covered and what is not covered in your contractor's limits of Liability. To find out, you'd ask to see the insurance certificate your contractor carries for proof of insurance coverage (see page 70). Just seeing the certificate is not enough. You then need to follow up with the information provided on the certificate.

Once you have obtained a copy of the insurance certificate from your contractor you need to call the insurance provider and ask to see a copy of the coverage your contractor carries. (Your contractor may even provide you with a copy of his coverage if you ask him to.) I suggest you then follow up with the agent who handles your contractor's policy and go over any clauses that you need further explanation on or discuss the style of home you are building or renovating. Go over the materials that are going to be used on your project. Note any specialty items or applications, i.e., swimming pool, stone, stucco or slate roof tiles, an office space with specific wiring needs, etc.

You want to be aware of all the exclusions that this General Liability Coverage may have. What areas of your building project are not covered under your contractor's policy? This will help you to determine what type of added coverage you may want to get to help subsidize what your builder's insurance is not going to provide for you.

In my opinion, the area of greatest concern to the homeowner is going to be the lack of coverage or protection on your behalf from faulty workmanship. Currently, there is little, if any, protection for the homeowner from your builder's insurance policy if your contractor/builder is physically working on your project and he installs something incorrectly or incompetently. Attorney Todd Panther adds, "Neither is there going to be any compensation to the homeowner as a result of his subs installing something incorrectly or incompetently." For example, if the roof leaks because someone installed the roof incorrectly, or as your contractor or his subs policy might state, it is defective workmanship therefore it is not covered, you are not compensated for that poorly built roof. What you may be covered for is the rug or carpet or any other items that may have "consequential damage" as a result of the leaky roof but the problem itself, the leaky roof, or any other part of the roof that is now compromised or defective as a result of your contractor or his sub's poor installation, is not going to be covered by your contractor's general liability policy.

Builder's Risk Insurance

The third major insurance coverage that is essential to the homeowner is Builder's Risk. Builder's Risk insurance is going to cover your project for stolen items off your property as well as fire or weather related damage to your project or materials to be used on your project.

It is important for you, the homeowner, to ask your builder, (if he is providing the builder's risk insurance) to put your name on the policy as an additional named insured party. I recommend you do this with all your contractor's policies. Then you need to get and retain a copy of this insurance policy. The reason for this is that should you need to be compensated for a loss, you will want to have an accurate accounting of all costs involved in the rectification. More importantly, the person and only the person who is named on the Risk policy will receive payment from the insurance company. So if you are in the middle of your building project and tragedy hits, your project catches fire, you need $200,000 to rebuild what was lost, you want to be confident that the money you need is going to come to you. If you are not named as the insured you will have no recourse if the contractor were to up and walk off your project with your check in hand.

Some builders request that the homeowner take out their own Builder's Risk Insurance policy. If this is the case with your builder, ask if he has a suggestion of whom you might consider. You can also call your own homeowner's insurance provider and have them provide your coverage. Bare in mind that whatever amount is put on the policy when it is originally purchased is going to be the amount that would be worked with if something to occur on your project resulting in a claim. This means that if your policy was originally written for the $1,000,000 specified to build your home. If you make $200,000 worth of additional changes in upgrades and you have not purchased an additional policy to cover those $200,000 of changes and you had a fire that burnt your home down, you would only be covered for the original amount of $1000,000.

Note: These added changes are considered to be one of the most overlooked exposures in a homebuilding project

There may be changes in insurance coverage when you are acting as your own contractor or when you are building in a development. If you are acting as your own contractor you will want to be covered by Workers Comp as well as have proof of coverage from all the subs you may hire to do work on your property. Once you have received proof of insurance from the workers on your building site you will want to follow up with each policy and ask the agent providing the insurance to give you a copy of their coverage.

If you are building in a development it will be important for you to ask the developers what types of insurance their builders or contractors are providing if indeed they have a list of such builders. If you can pick your own builder you need to follow the information much like it is above. You might like to go a step further and ask the development if there may be any potential problems arising from your building project that could happen that your normal builder's coverage would not cover. That way you can get any supplemental insurance you may need before construction begins, protecting yourself from an unforeseen event.

This information is important to the homeowner because the homeowner needs to determine if they are going to need to supplement their contractor's insurance policy with one of their own to better protect their homebuilding investment.

New Homebuilding Warranty

The homeowner will want to ask their builder if they are going to provide them with a *new homebuilding warranty*. This is important because things can go wrong with new construction that are not going to be covered by a contractor's insurance policy.

Most homebuilders are going to provide a new homebuilding warranty for their clients. However, if the homeowners are remodeling or building a smaller project, that may be a cost that their contractor will pass on to them.

Thick arches reminiscent of older built homes frame elements in adjoining rooms, antique light fixtures and sconces throughout. PHOTO CREDIT: REED BROWN, GENERAL CONTRACTOR: CASTLE CONTRACTORS, ARCHITECT: KEVIN COFFEE

The cost of this warranty is based on a percentage of the home's estimated selling price. Most commonly builders will pay for the warranty. However, homeowner's shouldn't assume — they should confirm.

According to the *2-10 Home Buyers Warranty* company, one out of every 200 new homes built will experience a structural failure requiring repair at an average cost of $30,000.

• 25% of structural claims are due to framing problems.

• More than 50% of structural claims are caused by either soil settlement in improperly compacted fills or by expansive soil.

A new homebuilding warranty will protect the homeowner's investment once they have moved in and for years after.

When homeowners are presented a warranty brochure or booklet from their contractor, they should follow up on the type of plan that their contractor is offering to buy them. Different plans are going to provide different levels of coverage. Don't assume that because the home is a new home that it won't need to have thorough coverage. Nothing is more frustrating to a

(continued on page 74)

ACORD™ CERTIFICATE OF LIABILITY INSURANCE

DATE (MM/DD/YYYY) ④

PRODUCER ①	THIS CERTIFICATE IS ISSUED AS A MATTER OF INFORMATION ONLY AND CONFERS NO RIGHTS UPON THE CERTIFICATE HOLDER. THIS CERTIFICATE DOES NOT AMEND, EXTEND OR ALTER THE COVERAGE AFFORDED BY THE POLICIES BELOW.	
	INSURERS AFFORDING COVERAGE	**NAIC #**
INSURED ②	INSURER A: ⑥	
	INSURER B:	
	INSURER C:	
	INSURER D:	
	INSURER E:	

COVERAGES

THE POLICIES OF INSURANCE LISTED BELOW HAVE BEEN ISSUED TO THE INSURED NAMED ABOVE FOR THE POLICY PERIOD INDICATED. NOTWITHSTANDING ANY REQUIREMENT, TERM OR CONDITION OF ANY CONTRACT OR OTHER DOCUMENT WITH RESPECT TO WHICH THIS CERTIFICATE MAY BE ISSUED OR MAY PERTAIN, THE INSURANCE AFFORDED BY THE POLICIES DESCRIBED HEREIN IS SUBJECT TO ALL THE TERMS, EXCLUSIONS AND CONDITIONS OF SUCH POLICIES. AGGREGATE LIMITS SHOWN MAY HAVE BEEN REDUCED BY PAID CLAIMS.

INSR LTR	ADD'L INSRD	TYPE OF INSURANCE	POLICY NUMBER ③	POLICY EFFECTIVE DATE (MM/DD/YY) ⑤	POLICY EXPIRATION DATE (MM/DD/YY) ⑤	LIMITS	
		GENERAL LIABILITY ⑦ COMMERCIAL GENERAL LIABILITY ☐ CLAIMS MADE ☐ OCCUR				EACH OCCURRENCE	$ ⑧
						DAMAGE TO RENTED PREMISES (Ea occurence)	$
						MED EXP (Any one person)	$
						PERSONAL & ADV INJURY	$
		GEN'L AGGREGATE LIMIT APPLIES PER: ☐ POLICY ☐ PRO-JECT ☐ LOC				GENERAL AGGREGATE	$
						PRODUCTS - COMP/OP AGG	$
		AUTOMOBILE LIABILITY ☐ ANY AUTO ☐ ALL OWNED AUTOS ☐ SCHEDULED AUTOS ☐ HIRED AUTOS ☐ NON-OWNED AUTOS				COMBINED SINGLE LIMIT (Ea accident)	$
						BODILY INJURY (Per person)	$
						BODILY INJURY (Per accident)	$
						PROPERTY DAMAGE (Per accident)	$
		GARAGE LIABILITY ☐ ANY AUTO				AUTO ONLY - EA ACCIDENT	$
						OTHER THAN AUTO ONLY: EA ACC	$
						AGG	$
		EXCESS/UMBRELLA LIABILITY ☐ OCCUR ☐ CLAIMS MADE ☐ DEDUCTIBLE ☐ RETENTION $				EACH OCCURRENCE	$
						AGGREGATE	$
							$
							$
							$
		WORKERS COMPENSATION AND EMPLOYERS' LIABILITY ANY PROPRIETOR/PARTNER/EXECUTIVE OFFICER/MEMBER EXCLUDED? If yes, describe under SPECIAL PROVISIONS below				☐ WC STATU-TORY LIMITS ☐ OTH-ER	
						E.L. EACH ACCIDENT	$
						E.L. DISEASE - EA EMPLOYEE	$
		OTHER				E.L. DISEASE - POLICY LIMIT	$

DESCRIPTION OF OPERATIONS / LOCATIONS / VEHICLES / EXCLUSIONS ADDED BY ENDORSEMENT / SPECIAL PROVISIONS ⑨

CERTIFICATE HOLDER ⑩	CANCELLATION
	SHOULD ANY OF THE ABOVE DESCRIBED POLICIES BE CANCELLED BEFORE THE EXPIRATION DATE THEREOF, THE ISSUING INSURER WILL ENDEAVOR TO MAIL _____ DAYS WRITTEN NOTICE ⑪ TO THE CERTIFICATE HOLDER NAMED TO THE LEFT, BUT FAILURE TO DO SO SHALL IMPOSE NO OBLIGATION OR LIABILITY OF ANY KIND UPON THE INSURER, ITS AGENTS OR REPRESENTATIVES.
	AUTHORIZED REPRESENTATIVE

ACORD 25 (2001/08) © ACORD CORPORATION 1988

interview

Kevin Hale
Owner of Hale Insurance Agency, LLC

HOW WOULD A HOMEOWNER FOLLOW UP ON THEIR CONTRACTOR'S INSURANCE COVERAGE?

Ask to see their certificate of insurance.

Note: The following is a sample copy of a contractor's insurance certificate. This certificate was provided to me by Accord. Accord Insurance Forms are recognized and used by industry professionals. Here, Kevin provides the explanation for the information provided on the insurance certificate that you would receive from your contractor.

1. The producer (the agent who issued the insurance). This information is important to the homeowner because it is the agent that the homeowner would contact to ask specifics about the contractor's policy — most importantly, confirming that the insurance policy is indeed in force at the time of construction. The homeowner can also ask about exclusions on this policy as they may relate directly to their project. Has this contractor ever had their policy canceled? Does this agent also provide insurance for this contractor's subs?

2. The Insured's name (the contractor you are interviewing). The homeowner should have their name included on the policy. It would say "additional name insured".

WHY IS IT IMPORTANT FOR THE HOMEOWNER TO HAVE THEIR CONTRACTOR ADD THEM ON THE POLICY AS AN ADDITIONAL NAME INSURED?

If your house burns up, is blown away or something is stolen halfway through their project, whoever is *named* as the insured party will receive the claim check. If your builder has taken out the policy and it's in their name, the claim check will be written to that builder only. If the homeowner requests to be added on as a *name* insured, then the claim check will be written to them and their builder. This should be done at the very beginning of their project.

Note: Once the homeowner has decided on a contractor to hire, they would want to have this insurance information in place before they sign any contract to hire the contractor. If they have any questions regarding how this policy does or does not protect them and their property, they should call the contractor's insurance agent.

I suggest that the homeowner take the insurance information to their insurance provider. If their insurance providers aren't specialized in construction coverage, ask them to direct them to an agent in their company who is. Then go over the insurance coverage with these agents to determine whether or not the homeowner needs to purchase any supplemental insurance of their own. Sometimes, homeowners don't recognize the value of insurance until they need it. They need to know how they are and are not covered before beginning their project.

HOW COMMON IS IT FOR A HOMEOWNER TO INQUIRE ABOUT THE INSURANCE COVERAGE OF A CONTRACTOR AS TO HOW IT APPLIES TO THE HOMEOWNER?

Never. And I never use never. I don't get homeowners calling me except on builder's risk coverage.

WOULD YOU SUGGEST A HOMEOWNER ASK TO SEE THESE DOCUMENTS WHEN CONSIDERING HIRING A CONTRACTOR?

Yes. The homeowner would ask for a copy of the certificate that shows both parties listed as the insured. This certificate provides the homeowner with the following:

3. The policy number (for the homeowner to reference when asking about the policy)

4. The date the insurance policy was issued

5. Policy effective and expiration dates

6. The insurers affording coverage (the insurance company who provides the coverage)

7. The type of insurance coverage (general liability, workers compensation, builders risk, etc.)

8. The amount of coverage for each type of insurance

9. Description of operation's, location's, vehicle's exclusions added by endorsement or special provisions (this area will have the lot number or address, a deductible amount and any additional names of insured people — which is where the homeowner's name would be)

10. Certificate holder

11. Cancellation section.

Kevin Hale of Hale Insurance suggests that the homeowner have included in their contract that their contractor agrees to pay all insurance premiums due throughout the duration of the project or they will be held liable.

Joel Volker, staff counsel for *P&C Acord* forms, suggests that a homeowner ask for a new copy of the contractor's insurance certificate numerous times throughout the life of the project. They could also keep up with the agent that issued the policy.

It's important that the homeowner understand what this section is communicating to them. If their contractor does not pay their monthly premiums throughout the duration of the project this policy can be canceled and the insurance provider is not responsible to let the homeowner know about it! If an accident occurs on the property, even though it may be within the specified dates shown on the insurance certificate, the home-owner can be held liable if their contractor's insurance policy has been canceled — unbeknownst to the homeowner.

Kevin Hale suggests that you have included in your contract that your contractor agrees to pay all premiums due throughout the duration of your project or he / she will be held liable. Joel Volker, staff counsel for P&C Acord forms, suggests that a homeowner ask for a new copy of the contractor's insurance certificate numerous times throughout the life of the project. You can also keep up with the agent that issued the policy.

(continued from page 71)

homeowner than to start paying thousands of dollars to correct, repair or replace something in a home that they just spent hundreds of thousands of dollars building a year or two ago.

To get an idea as to what a new home warranty will provide, check out the *2-10 Home Buyers Warranty Corporation.* Go to 2-10.com, click on *home buyers' warranty corporation* and click on *new home builders* or call: 1.800.488.8844 and ask for your local representative. Another company you can look into is *Old Republic Home Protection, www.orhp.com.* This will provide you with a good source of information with which to assess new home warranties.

Be sure to confirm that the warranty you receive is fully transferable if you decide to sell your home.

Contract

There are as many different building contracts as there are builders. Some are pages long and others are a couple of paragraphs. I mentioned that the AIA (American Institute of Architects) creates professional documents that the architect often uses with their clients. The AIA also provides construction documents for contractors. Do not sign a contract without seeking legal counsel from an attorney who is well-versed in residential construction law. (See chapter 3 for info on finding such an attorney.)

Note: Do not sign a contract with an indemnity clause in it until you have reviewed it with your attorney. You could be signing away your rights to receive compensation from your contractor if something were to go wrong while they were working on your project.

The following is an example of a contract that was presented to a homeowner by a prospective contractor. It's an example of a contract that you do not want to sign. This contract is more like a letter of agreement. While generally encompassing the construction process, it is vague and does not provide enough detail as to what the homeowner can expect throughout the months of the project.

Dear John and Susann,

We propose to furnish all labor, materials, tools, equipment, workman's compensation insurance and general liability insurance to build your home, as per Johnston's Design plans and dated 3/15/07, on your lot at Lot 11, Summerset Drive in Townsend, WA. This revised price is based on the plans dated 3/15/07, with the following exceptions: 1) the rear deck is not included; 2) the exercise room in the basement is left unfinished; and 3) the front walkway is now brick. The job shall be done on a management fee basis, with Jackson Builders receiving a flat fee of $74,000 for acting as general contractor on this project.

In consideration of this fee, Joe Builders agrees to construct the house, including negotiating all contracts with subcontractor, help with material selection, arrange for all materials, labor, equipment and subcontractors, etc. And all other functions of a general contractor. Joe Builders shall build the house in accordance with all current codes, rules and regulations pertaining to domestic construction.

Joe Builder's fee of $74,000 shall be paid out based on work completed to date as follows:
1. Beginning of framing $12,000.
2. Beginning of second floor framing $12,000.
3. Completion of all framing $12,000.
4. Drywall is delivered to site $12,000.
5. Beginning of painting $12,000.
6. Move in $10,000.
7. Completion of initial punch list $4000.

Our approximate total price as of now is broken down on the attached budget sheet. This price does not include any cost of plans, builder's risk insurance (furnished by owner), window treatments and any other finishes not specified on the plans or on our budget sheet, or any requirements that the county codes department may require.

Example of the Budget/ Accounting Summary to be Used on Your Project

This is the most important aspect of your homebuilding investment that you need to understand. You need to know how your contractor is going to spend your money to build or remodel your home. Most homeowners enter into their homebuilding project with little or no understanding of how to be responsible for the managing of these funds. I am the first to admit, this was one of our downfalls.

It is common for a homeowner to abdicate this responsibility to their contractor when it comes to managing the building budget. I know of homeowners who have given their entire building budget over to the contractor at the onset of their project. Ask yourself, as great as your contractor is, would you provide them access to your checking and savings accounts, permitting them to spend your money as they deem fit? Would you allow them access to your retirement account and trust them to make the investment decisions for your future? How easy would it be for you to lend a family member or relative $40,000 out of any of these accounts? Not likely. It's taken you a long time to get into the financial position you're currently in that affords you the opportunity to build or remodel your home.

As I mentioned in chapter 3, you can secure a homebuilding or remodeling loan within a week or two, the emotional connection you have with money that has taken you years to establish is absent when it comes to identifying the same protective energy to these newly found homebuilding funds.

What you want to determine is that you understand the way in which your money is going to be applied to your project. How is your contractor going to give account to you for what they are spending? How often are you going to meet to go over the budget? Who is going to be responsible for managing your funds? It's common for the homeowner to assume that the contractor is going to manage their funds. While the typical homeowner might make that assumption, the proactive homeowner is going to recognize their responsibility to their investment and manage their funds with the assistance of their contractor and their loan officer. A homeowner who is using the services of an architect for construction management can also ask the architect to assist them in reviewing their contractor's draw requests.

Fee

Most likely, a builder is going to charge you one of two ways to build your house. They are either going to give you a fixed rate, meaning that they will take all the information from your project, determine the cost to build it, factor in their fee and if experienced, a contingency amount as well. Then they will agree to build your home for this set price. Or they will offer you a cost-plus-time-and-materials contract. Cost-plus is just that. It's the cost of your project plus the builder's fee added on. If your project changes in scope so can this builder's fee.

Cost-Plus

The cost-plus method of payment is the most common in custom homebuilding. In the cost-plus contract, your design is estimated to cost a certain amount of money to build and your contractor then adds their fee to manage the construction process. If you are agreeing to a cost-plus contract, consider adding a clause that puts a cap or maximum-not-to-exceed clause in your contract. A homeowner needs to be familiar with the PHM™ on the front-end of their project if they are going to work with a contractor on a cost-plus contract. If you are considering working with a contractor that is going to use a cost-plus contract, you want to make sure that the contractor you are working with is very experienced in bidding their projects. You need to follow up with the references of this contractor and ask the homeowners if they went over budget or over schedule. If they say yes, you need to ask by what percentage and what types of things caused them to go over budget or over schedule. Did they find that their allowances were too low for what they wanted in their home? Did they get many change orders? Were there areas of the budget that went over that they were not responsible for — such as framing, foundation, etc.? Did they think that this contractor was as experienced in

pricing as they led them to believe on the front-end of their project?

Because it is a given that homeowners tend to come into the homebuilding process with unrealistic expectations as to what it actually costs to build or remodel a home, contractors are often caught in a catch twenty-two. They want to win your project because they want to have a job to make money. However, they know from experience that a homeowner, new to the homebuilding process, cringes upon first hearing a realistic bid for the work they want done. So the honest contractor risks losing you to the contractor who shoots lower than what they know the project will actually cost to get you to hire them.

A Low Bid Isn't Always the Best

The majority of the time, the homeowner indeed hires the contractor who bids lower in hopes of saving money. Unfortunately, once into the project, the contractor who bid low to land the job now has to make up for their hidden costs and the homeowner can end up spending more with this contractor then they would have accepting the higher, more realistic bid from the other contractor.

The most common scenario when a homeowner hires a contractor based on a lower bid in hopes of saving money is that the contractor has provided the homeowner with allowances that are not going to meet their project's needs. This is done for one of two reasons: a) the contractor is not experienced enough with the homebuilding process to know how to accurately set allowances in place or b) the contractor is fully aware of how much your home will actually cost but comes in lower to win the project. Then, once into the building process, when you start shopping for product, what should be the most fun part of your process quickly becomes frustrating and sometimes heartbreaking because you are hit with the realization that the tile you had counted on putting into your home costs twice as much as this contractor provided for in your allowance. This is the case with your lighting, your appliances, your carpet and every other allowance that the contractor provided.

This was the case on our project. The lighting allowance for our entire home was $5,000. If you know nothing about building or remodeling a home, $5,000 may sound like it will buy a lot of light fixtures. The reality is that that amount covered our entry-way light and some recessed lights. We still had over 75% of our home without lights. It was either string flashlights from the ceilings or substantially increase that lighting amount to buy the lights we needed throughout our house.

Multiply this budget increase times every other item you were given allowances for and you can see how easy it is for a homeowner, who doesn't have a proactive mindset and doesn't know how to assess their bids and allowances, to go over budget. When this happens, the homeowner begins making sacrifices.

There is no risk to the contractor when they do a cost-plus contract with you — unless they have signed the maximum not to exceed clause in your contract — and most homeowners don't know to include this and most cost-plus contractors don't offer it. So, in a more common cost-plus agreement, no matter what price your project turns out to be, the contractor is going to make their fee. The risk you run with a cost-plus contract is you not knowing enough about the actual cost of things before you begin building. A typical homeowner's experience on a cost-plus project is likely to be something like this.

You are three to four months into the project and the contractor tells you they need the plumbing fixtures. You go out to make your selection only to find that the allowance that you were given is much lower than the actual cost of the plumbing fixtures you want to put into your home. When you bring this up to your contractor, they say, "Well, if you want to make that change I will issue you a change order and we will put the more expensive faucets in your home." In your mind, these have been the faucets you had always wanted, not an upgrade. However, because you are exceeding the allowance that was allotted in your original budget, you are in fact upgrading.

Cost-plus Analogy

A simple analogy to help explain what commonly happens to the typical homeowner who enters into a cost-plus contract with their builder.

You are having a dinner party for 20 people and you needed to hire a party planner (contractor) to help you manage this event. You decide to interview two different party planners (contractors) to manage your party. You tell them that you want to serve a shrimp salad, bread and some chilled white wine. Your budget has to stay around $500. The party planners know that it is not likely that you are going to be able to put this party on for $500. (In fact, it is going to cost you more like $700.) You get a bid from one party planner for $700 and another bid for $500. Since $500 is what you were thinking of spending, you hire the party planner who bid $500. This party planner wants this job so they agree to do the job within your budget, which you have set at $500 plus their fee, which is 10%. So you sign a contract, assuming your grand total is going to be $550. It's a little higher than what you wanted but at least it's not $700.

To make this party happen this party planner has to:

Rent tables $100
Rent plates, glasses, flatware $100
Rent chairs $100
Rent Hall $125
Total $425.

You are responsible for the food and drink. To stay within your budget of $500 your party planner provides you with the following allowances:

Food allowance $35
Drink allowance $40

You know nothing about throwing a dinner party, so you assume that these allowances are sufficient to buy the food and drink for your 20 guests. On Thursday you get a call from the party planner (contractor) who says you have to buy the food and have it to them by Friday so they can put it together for your party on Saturday. So Friday morning you go to the wholesale food store to buy the food. You meet with a salesperson and tell them that you are there to buy food and drink for your dinner party. They ask what your budget is. You say, "I have $35 for food." The salesperson takes you to the cracker isle and says, "You can pick from one of these three boxes of crackers." You say, "But I wanted something more substantial, like a shrimp salad and bread." The salesperson says, "OK, but that will cost you $135." You think gosh, I had no idea it would cost this much. Now you have a problem. The party is tomorrow. You have to decide, do you buy the crackers knowing you will not be happy with that choice but it is what your allowance provides for, or do you pay the extra $100 for the shrimp salad and bread which is what you assumed your allowances were going to cover and really more representative of what you were thinking of doing when you first decided to do the party? You have no other choice but to pay the extra $100. The same thing happens with the drinks. Instead of paying $40, which was your allowance, you end up having to pay $140. Now you are $200 over your $500 budget for your party.

You bring the food to the party planner and tell them how much you had to go over budget to do your party. The party planner says, "Well, if you would have stayed within the allowances you were given you wouldn't have gone over your budget," which is true. The party planner gives you a change order for the additional $200 plus their 10% fee charge of $20 for a total of $220. And to make matters worse, this party planner has informed you that you are not going to be able to start the party at the time you had originally decided upon. It's going to take a few extra hours for their people to finish up before your guests can be let in. So when all is said and done, you are looking at $200 dollars extra for your food and drink and $75 extra for the three additional hours you are renting the hall (your second change order). Your party planner is expecting the change-order fees to be paid in full before your party begins.

So all totaled, you exceeded your budget by $295 to get the party you thought you were going to get in the first place. In a homebuilding scenario, this is what can easily happen on a cost-plus contract because a homeowner does not know the cost of the items they are going to be responsible for (to confirm their allowances are sufficient) when they begin their project.

The proactive mindset would be very different for that party giver. First off, the proactive homeowner would have sought more bids from other party planners. That way she will give herself a better source of information to base her numbers on versus one high and one low. Then, once receiving the bids for her party, she would have gone over each bid and asked each party planner to provide a breakdown of everything on their bid. She would have asked these planners to explain why there was a difference between the numbers that they were providing. She could also have asked the party planner, the one whose bid was $700, how she might substitute things to bring the price down a bit. On the lower bid, the PHM™ teaches the homeowner to ask this party planner to give account for the items they cut back on to provide a bid of $500. Most importantly, upon receiving the bids, she would have taken them to her loan officer who specializes in party planning financial matters (construction finance) to review these bids with her.

Go over the allowances with someone who indeed has a history with and specializes in party (construction) finance. A PHM™ party planner would have visited other parties to get an idea of what they cost to confirm that what they would be able to get for $500 is the type of party they want. This hostess, by doing her homework on the front-end of her party, in her own time, relaxed and in control of her situation, may have learned that she could have substituted salmon for the shrimp and made citrus wine spritzers instead of serving wine, to bring her price down and closer to her budget, and still have a party she loved. She'd know all of this before signing a contract.

This is why some contractors do not do competitive bidding on projects. It takes them too much time to put together a realistic bid, only to risk having a homeowner who is not familiar with the high cost of building or remodeling turn them down for someone who provides that homeowner with a number that is closer to what they want to hear.

Some contractors come in low to get the job and can take advantage of the unsuspecting homeowner. Once you have signed a contract with this builder, it will be much more difficult for you to get out of using them, especially if you are months into the project when you become aware of the problems with their bid. Typically, if a contractor has lowballed a bid, they are going to have to make-up for the cost at some point in your project. I had one woman tell me that her contractor started to overwhelming change-order them halfway into the project. He was coming up with all kinds of charges on his change orders. I had another homeowner tell me that her contractor waited until the end of her project to issue the change orders. This surprise cost put a huge strain on their reserve finances and they had to take money out of their IRA to pay for them.

My suggestion for a homeowner who is going to use a contractor that works from a cost-plus contract is to do all the review work I suggest in the interview with Will Forte. If this contractor holds up and their references are strong, you know that they are a team player. You'll know that you will be receiving receipts and that they have a good accounting system and all the other benefits that go along with an up-and-up experienced builder. If all this is in place, hire them. Let them know upfront that you are going to be expecting their help in the design process. Get a pre-construction services contract that both you and this contractor feel good about. Have it reviewed by your attorney before you sign it. Now you will be able to use this contractor's expertise on the front-end of your design process to get all your specifications laid out within budget before you begin your project.

(continued on page 81)

interview

Will Forte
Forte Building Group

Will is one of the first contractors that I interviewed for this book. He understands the importance of a proactive team mentality and encourages it from the beginning of the design phase through completion of the project.

HOW IMPORTANT IS IT FOR THE HOMEOWNER TO INCLUDE A CONTRACTOR'S EXPERTISE WHEN IT COMES TO DESIGNING A CUSTOM-BUILT HOME?

I feel like it's a requirement if they really want to be successful.

HOW MIGHT INCLUDING THE BUILDER'S EXPERTISE DURING THE DESIGN PHASE BENEFIT THE HOMEOWNER?

The contractor will help with accurate cost estimating and engineering analyses in the design process. They can offer alternative construction methods to help keep the design in check relative to the homeowner's budget. The contractor can have a lot of knowledge about working with the architect. It adds a different level of expertise that architects often don't have about cost estimating and assessing the impact that different design features will have on cost.

HOW MIGHT INCLUDING YOUR EXPERTISE DURING THE DESIGN PHASE BENEFIT YOU THE CONTRACTOR?

It's a great benefit to the contractor. By the time the house is designed and the homeowner is ready to start construction, there's no learning curve for the builder to catch up with. He's already up to speed, he's well educated about the project, knows it inside and out, and, by then, he has developed a good working relationship with the homeowner. The benefits are tremendous in that regard. It facilitates a much smoother process.

HOW MIGHT A HOMEOWNER EXPECT TO COMPENSATE THE CONTRACTOR FOR THIS CONSULTATION TIME?

If they've chosen me to build the home, I work for them during the design phase on an hourly-rate basis, to the point where we actually establish the cost of the project and get the design finished. When we move on to construction we develop a construction services contract.

DO YOU FIND HOMEOWNERS HAVE A GOOD GRASP OF WHAT IT COSTS TO BUILD A HOME WHEN THEY FIRST DECIDE TO DO SO?

The rear step of an old cottage found on property was used for the ledge of this stone fireplace, rustic look and feel achieved by using structural timber for columns and beams. PHOTO CREDIT: SANFORD MEYERS, GENERAL CONTRACTOR: FORTE BUILDING GROUP, ARCHITECT: SCOTT WILSON

No. No one ever expects it to cost as much as it does and everyone wants more but wants to spend less.

WHAT IS THE MOST COMMON MISCONCEPTIONS A HOMEOWNER HAS UPON FIRST VIEWING THE BUDGET YOU'VE DEVELOPED FOR BUILDING THEIR HOME?

That everything they would want is included in this price and that they wouldn't need to upgrade. They might assume they can get anything they want for this price. It's never unlimited and it's always a challenge to meet their expectations budget-wise.

WHAT PERCENTAGE OF HOMEOWNERS MAKE CHANGES TO THE HOUSE PLANS DURING THE CONSTRUCTION PERIOD?

100%.

WHAT DO YOU CONSIDER TO BE THE MOST COMMON REASON FOR HOMEOWNERS TO MAKE CHANGES DURING THE CONSTRUCTION OF THEIR PROJECT?

Upgrades would be the first reason. They didn't have a clear understanding of what their finishes were or what they could buy with the allowances that they have. As they get into a more detailed kind of process and actually start visiting places and looking at all the great options and, of course, updates and new products, they upgrade, whether it be in appliances, light fixtures, finishes or whatever. Also, I would say the homeowner's lack of vision or their inability to understand the plans, so once the project is underway they say, "this doesn't look the way I thought it was going to look," or "this room is not as big as I thought it would be." So they make a change.

Author's note: This is an excellent example as to why it is so important for you to ask your architect, home designer or interior designer to help you envision what your home is going to look like during the design phase. You do not move on in your process until you are confident you know what you are getting.

WHAT ADVICE WOULD YOU OFFER A HOMEOWNER BUILDING THEIR FIRST HOME TO HELP THEM AVOID MAKING A LOT OF CHANGES DURING THE CONSTRUCTION PHASE?

Do your homework up front. Study the plans and spend as much time as possible with them. If you don't understand something, ask. Try to envision as much as possible by visiting a newly completed home or homes under construction that are currently on the market and of the same caliber that they anticipate building. Walk around in the rooms that are spec'd with the same sizes that they plan to build. See how that space feels. Anything that they can do to make themselves more familiar with the process, i.e., investigate products and specify products as accurately as they can up front.

HOW CAN A HOMEOWNER USE THE SALE PRICE ON A HOME AS AN ESTIMATE AND EQUATE THAT TO HOW MUCH IT WOULD COST THEM TO BUILD SOMETHING COMPARABLE?

Actually that's my favorite way to answer someone's question when they want to know how much it will cost to build a home. I can say, "Let me take you to a home that is similar in size to what you might want and I'll tell you what that home costs." Then they can equate that to how it compares to what they really want in their home. I think that when you can see a home that's been built, touch it and feel it and walk through it and see the finishes and things like that, then I can say this home costs this much or this costs this much per square foot to build. They get a good handle on what they can get or how much something that they want may cost. I think it's the responsibility of the contractor to help the homeowner understand how much it's going to cost.

(continued from page 79)

Turnkey and Fixed Rate

A builder who works from a fixed rate means that they will take all the information from your project, determine the cost to build it, factor in their fee and, if they're experienced, add a contingency. They combine those numbers and agree to build your home for that price. If costs of materials go up or down, the building cost remains the same. The builder hedges the risk of these market changes in their bid. That's where the contingency comes in if needed. If you are getting bids from numerous contractors who are adding a contingency, ask how much they are adding. If this contractor is experienced at pricing this fee should be very low. Alan Looney's, Owner/Chief manager of Castle Contractors, is $1^1/_2$-2%. This final cost changes only if you make changes that increase the cost from what you originally agreed upon.

A number of the contractors that I've interviewed for this book use a turnkey contract agreement. Turnkey is essentially a fixed-fee agreement. I do want to clarify that fixed fee can refer to a project or home that a builder or developer is offering in a development at a fixed rate. This would be a home that would be built from a set of plans specific to that builder or developer's offering. The homeowner would then choose from a specified set of materials, i.e., cabinets, flooring, carpet, appliances, etc. that the builder or developer provides.

That is not the type of homebuilding experience I am referring to when I talk about the turnkey process. The turnkey contractors that I am referring to, and suggest that you hire, are contractors who build custom homes. These homes range in price from $700,000 to $10,000,000. So when you interview a contractor who works from a turnkey contract, it's important that you determine that they are experienced in building custom homes.

Also, you want to make sure that the turnkey contractor you interview has a PHM™ perspective and welcomes working with a team of other professionals. You do not want to hire a contractor who does not walk you through making all your selections up front to confirm that you are within your budget parameters before you begin construction. There are some fixed-fee contractors who will take a set of plans and give you a bid with allowances. If you agree to this without first specifying your selections, you could end up in an agreement similar to the example I provided in the first cost-plus scenario.

Alan Looney and Jim Catlin (both interviewed in this chapter) are turnkey contractors.

The architects and contractors who work with this type of turnkey process are proactive professionals who make it their business practice to enable you to be in charge of your choices and protecting your money. I suggest you try to find an architect or contractor who practice this process in your area. If you cannot, go to my web site and see if we have any listed for you. The best thing about my Proactive Homebuilding Method™ is that by following my interview process, and using the PHM™ lessons you've learned in this book, you can assemble the right professionals to create a like-minded team of people that will help you achieve the homebuilding experience that you deserve. You will have the added bonus of my web site and homebuilding tools to round out your experience.

The Value Analysis or Value–Engineered Bid

This is a bidding procedure that your contractor can use to break down their estimates into line items versus the usual lump sum. It allows you more control over your budget requirements. If your contractor provides you with this type of bid, you can then bring this to your architect and your architect can design your home to better fit your budget. You will be able to choose between different materials, if need be, at the front-end of your project — while having the advantage of your architect or home designer design these items into your project.

This is a PHM™ move; to combine both your contractor's expertise in market pricing

(continued on page 84)

interview

Alan Looney
Owner / Chief Manager of Castle Contractors

Turnkey

Alan was the first contractor I had interviewed that worked with a turnkey contract. Alan was first recommended to me by my loan office. Alan is, without a doubt, one of the most proactive homebuilders I've met.

EXPLAIN THE DIFFERENCE BETWEEN A COST-PLUS CONTRACT AND A TURNKEY CONTRACT AND HOW IT CAN BE BENEFICIAL TO THE HOMEOWNER.

Cost-plus is a contract someone enters into with the builder stating that the homeowner is responsible for the cost and all related expenses of building the house plus a percentage of the total project as the fee for the builder. There is no accountability and no risk to the builder. The risk is carried by the homeowner.

Turnkey is a guaranteed contract for the homeowner, which is signed at the beginning of the project. When the owner signs the contract, all costs are in the contract, including architectural design, interior design and the builder's profit. This is more beneficial to the home owner because it guarantees a price and the only additional costs are for any homeowner change orders.

HOW DO YOU CREATE A TURNKEY BUDGET?

First, establish a realistic budget. You have to work with the homeowner to design a comprehensive plan that respects the homeowner's budget. We have to know lot cost, desired square footage, design style and entire finish selections. Our designers work with the homeowner to accomplish this. For example, all finishes from exterior façade like brick, stucco, stone, windows, paint to interior finishes, floors, appliances, fixtures prior to the contract being finalized. Our designers guide the homeowner through the process to create the home they desire while staying within a budget. It is an educational process for the homeowner and it can be overwhelming. Over the years, we have perfected this process and excelled at this as a builder. Homeowners are provided assurance, a good comfort level and are able to sleep at

night. This is a trust issue. We take it very seriously and know it is a big financial commitment for our clients.

HOW DOES THE HOMEOWNER COMPENSATE YOU FOR THAT TIME BEFORE YOU'VE ACTUALLY STARTED BUILDING?

When a homeowner approaches us to build a house, before we start the building phase, I enter into a professional services contract or a pre-construction contract. This contract includes the costs associated with the pre-build phase, architectural design, landscape plan, lighting plan, kitchen design, interior design, etc. If the homeowner elects to not build with Castle Contractors, it covers my costs.

WOULD A LENDER CONSIDER THIS PART OF A HOMEBUILDING PACKAGE TO BE INCLUDED IN A MORTGAGE?

It can be. It can be included as part of your 10 to 20 % downpayment on the house.

WHEN I FIRST BEGIN THIS UPFRONT PROCESS, I SHOULD BE READY TO PAY THIS FEE OUT OF POCKET?

Definitely out of pocket. For example, the money could come from a savings account.

IDO YOU THINK HOMEOWNERS COME TO YOU WITH REALISTIC EXPECTATIONS WHEN THEY WANT TO BUILD THEIR HOMES?

I would say most of the time they don't. They think they will get more than their budget actually allows. We had a recent client that built a two-story house with an unfinished basement. During the middle of the estimating process, he asked us to give him a price for finishing the basement. I let him know the finished basement would put him over the budget and he didn't believe me. When he saw it in black and white, he understood the impact to his bottom line and it helped him make an educated decision. I like the way this process serves our clients' best interests.

WHAT I LIKE ABOUT THIS PROCESS IS THAT IT'S DONE IN A RELAXED STATE AND THE HOMEOWNER IS IN CONTROL VERSUS THE HOMEOWNER COMING ON SITE AND THE CONTRACTOR SAYING, "WE NEED THIS BY TOMORROW" OR "WE NEED THIS NEXT WEEK." WHEN THAT HAPPENS THE HOMEOWNER'S RUSHED AND OFTEN TIMES WILL MAKE DECISIONS THAT THEY'RE UNHAPPY WITH. THEY WILL EITHER LOOK AT IT EVERY DAY AND NOT

BE HAPPY WITH IT OR CHANGE IT OUT, WHICH RESULTS IN A
CHANGE ORDER THAT COSTS MORE.

Everything is pre-selected, pre-designed and a
realistic budget is set. It isn't a generic, cookie-
cutter budget used for anyone building a 5,000
square-foot home. It is a real budget from real
selections and you can't believe how much hap-
pier the entire process is for the client and our
building team.

HOW WOULD YOU RESPOND TO A HOMEOWNER WHO THINKS
THAT THEY MIGHT HAVE A DIFFICULT TIME KNOWING WHAT
EVERYTHING IS GOING TO LOOK LIKE IF THEY PICK IT OUT ON THE
FRONT-END OF THEIR PROJECT VERSUS PICKING IT OUT WHEN
THEY ARE ACTUALLY IN THE SPACE UP ON THE SITE?

It's our job to help them visualize. We have
been in business over a decade and have so
many customers who are happy to have folks
take a look at their masterpieces. In addition,
we work with excellent suppliers who also
afford the homeowner this same opportunity
through their customers or a full-service showroom. Our staff designers also have a wealth of
product samples and present detailed information to help make this process easier.

HOW IMPORTANT IS IT TO PERFORM AN ENGINEERING
SITE-PLAN?

This is a critical step, and, as a builder of integ-
rity, I wouldn't consider a project without one.
It is important to know the site conditions that
will impact construction costs. The lot the homeowner selects may have significant slope on
it and would require a basement. What if the
customer didn't want a basement or the cost it
would entail?

THAT'S ONE OF THE THINGS I THINK IS MOST DIFFICULT FOR A
HOMEOWNER. THEY HAVE NO WAY OF KNOWING ABOUT LOTS
AND IT IS LIKE THEIR HANDS ARE TIED.

For the majority of people, it is difficult for
them to look at a lot and determine the amount
of grade changes along with the additional costs
involved in putting in a retaining wall or how a
driveway will need to be laid out.

I THINK THAT'S AN IMPORTANT POINT. I CAN GO TO A CONTRAC-
TOR AND ASK IF THEY CAN BUILD ME A HOME FOR $750,000. IF
THEY SAY YES, WHICH WAS OUR CASE, AND OUR BUDGET WAS
$5,000 FOR SITE WORK, THAT AMOUNT WON'T COVER THE COST.
Yes, you are correct.

Chocolate, pumpkin, and umber combed faux-finished walls, Blue Jade ceiling,
scagliano stone mantle, custom wrought ironwork, Steinway piano in this Castle-
built music room. PHOTO CREDIT: REED BROWN, ARCHITECT: KEVIN COFFEE

OFTEN, THAT'S NOT WHAT IS DONE. BUT THE HOMEOWNER TAKES
THAT BID, ASSUMING THAT WHAT IS IN THEIR MIND IS WHAT THIS
BUILDER IS GOING TO BUILD FOR THAT AMOUNT OF MONEY.
THEY DON'T KNOW ENOUGH ABOUT THE PROCESS.

Right.

THE HOMEOWNER IS UNEDUCATED AND A LOT OF CONTRAC-
TORS — THIS IS KIMBERLY'S POINT TOO — WILL SAY, "WE'RE
GOING OVER BECAUSE YOU'RE GOING OVER YOUR ALLOWANCE."

To me that's dishonest of the builder. He's a con
guy who wants to get them locked into their
contract quickly before they walk away. We
don't pressure anybody to sign a contract. We
have a great name in the city and we stay busy.
We'll work within your timetable.

IF A HOMEOWNER HAS DONE ALL OF THIS WITH YOU ON THE
FRONT-END, THEN, ONCE YOU START TO BUILD, THE WORK ON
THE HOMEOWNER'S SIDE, FOR THE MOST PART, IS DONE.

Yes, for the most part. We have a breakdown of
the sequence — what's first, what's second and
what's third. Once it's all done and we agree to
that number, then we sign a contract and they
close on their construction loan. Then, they'll pay
me a deposit and we'll start building the house.
We draw monthly payments until the work's
done. Now the fun part is to see the project go
up, to see your hard work come into play. The client visits the work site and is excited. The house
is framed and they can see the flow of the home.
It's great to see the expression on their faces.
When you're doing the finishes, you still give
them a chance to change their minds. Typically,
for Castle Contractors' clients, this is minimal.

(continued from page 81)

with your architect's expertise in design. You have all the prices laid out so you can see the breakdown and make educated choices. You can say no to something you thought you originally wanted but after reviewing the cost from your contractor's value analysis, you have the option of making another choice. Guided by both your contractor and your architect, you are in a position to make an executive-level decision because you have the information and the expertise of the team you hired.

You may find that contractors are reluctant to put in the amount of time it will take for them to compile this type of bid for you if you have not committed to hiring them. Make your decision as to what contractor you are going to hire. When interviewing them, ask if they have done this type of bid for a client before. Ask them if they would be willing to do this for you if you were to hire them for your project.

CHANGE ORDERS

Once construction has begun on your project, if you make a change that causes an increase or credit to the cost of your project, your contractor would issue you a change order. Confirm that this is the procedure of each contractor that you interview. The change order is a way of creating a paper trail of accountability for both the homeowner and the contractor with regard to any changes that affect the original cost of the budget.

Ask the contractors you meet with to provide you an example of the change order that they use. You want to see the type of information that they provide on their change orders. You will be looking for a description as to the type of change that is going to take place. The scope of work needed to make the change. What materials will be included? Ask the contractor you are interviewing to define for you what would constitute a change that would result in them issuing you a change order on your project. Ask them to define a costly change and what might be construed an incidental change.

You will want to request that you receive a change order for all the changes that you make on your project. It is important that you and your contractor sign the change order before the change is made. This should be in your contract. If you are using an architect for construction administrative services on your project, then it is most likely that your architect will want to be included in any changes as well. That way, everyone is aware of any change and in agreement as to how it is to be carried out and at what cost, if any, to you.

What might seem like a simple change to you could actually have a significant impact on cost, schedule or the design of your project. You do not want to find yourself in a dispute over thousands of dollars because you did not have a clear understanding of what the change you requested would entail.

By requesting to see and sign the change order before work commences, you proactively involve yourself in understanding how your decision is going to affect your budget. If you decide that the change you want to make is not worth the amount of money it would cost to make this change, i.e., *defend what you spend*, you can decline the change before it is carried out.

I have heard of homeowners who did not receive a change order until the very end of their project. Then, all at once they were handed a number of change orders totaling tens of thousands of dollars! These homeowners couldn't remember half of what these change orders were for or even if they had actually taken place. I have also heard of homeowners who were change-ordered to death, nickel-and-dimed, so to speak. If they wanted to move an electrical outlet over six inches, they were charged the same amount as if they were asking to move it ten feet. Ask your contractor how they handle this type of thing. Some contractors will let you make a few of these types of incidental changes. Other contractors will charge you extra for everything that you do that is not on the set of plans.

The other side of the coin is the homeowner who starts making change after change. This is

By implementing Green building philosophy, this Woodmeister built kitchen was conscientiously designed and built to minimize the use of chemicals for a family highly sensitive to allergens. Only solid materials were used along with open shelving for easily cleaned surfaces. PHOTO CREDIT: GARY SLOAN, GENERAL CONTRACTOR: WOODMEISTER MASTER BUILDERS, ARCHITECT: BENTLEY AND CHURCHILL ARCHITECTS

very disruptive for a contractor who is tying to keep his crew on a work schedule. That contractor now has to pull subs from other jobs, delaying work on those projects to come and redo what this homeowner is changing.

When used properly, change orders can prove to be a valuable tool of documentation on any given project.

Business Procedures or Company Overview

Depending on the size of your contractor's business, they will have several employees that work for them. Ask the contractor during your interview about the subs that they will have working on your project.

Questions to ask contractor, about subs:

• How long have these subs been with this contractor?

• Will all the subs working on your project speak English?

• Will all the subs that are going to be working on your project be insured? This is something that you will require in your contract, so it is good to have it discussed on the front-end in your interview.

• Will you be able to receive warranty and contact information from the subs on your project that you may need to contact in the coming years to provide additional services to your project if need be? Contractors are going to provide you with a year of follow-up on the work they did on your house. What you want to have is warranty information from the subs that would allow you to contact them just in case this contractor moves. Or, when the year is over and you may need something changed, added, or repaired. It is always helpful to have an electri-

Cherry cabinetry by Woodmeister add to the warm tones of this kitchen, curved design helps to soften open space and provides ample storage for homeowners. PHOTOGRAPHER: GARY SLOAN, ARCHITECTURAL MILLWORK: WOODMEISTER MASTER BUILDERS, GENERAL CONTRACTOR: CONRAD & SULIVAN

cian, a plumber, a HVAC specialist, etc. who has a history with your project be able to come back to do the work needed versus bringing someone in who is going to have to take the added time to catch up.

PROJECT MANAGERS

If this contractor will have a project manager on your job, this will be the employee or worker that would manage your project. Apart from your contractor, this is the person you will be interacting with the most. If your contractor were not on the site when you needed to address something, it would be this employee that you would communicate with. Usually, if a contractor has a number of projects going at one time, they will have a project manager help-

ing to supervise numerous projects for them. If this contractor that you are interviewing is planning on assigning a project manager to your project, there are some questions you will want to have answered about this project manager before you agree to hire this contractor.

First and foremost, you want to know if this project manager is going to take the place of your contractor on your project. Contrary to what homeowners may assume, most contractors don't actually build homes. Rather, they are contracted to oversee the building of your home. A lot of contractors have engineering backgrounds versus construction backgrounds and they have decided to go into the business of homebuilding. If their business grows it's because they are successful in overseeing construction projects. They hire the right people to do the work needed on these projects in order to produce the end product that the homeowner wants.

Ask your contractor if they will be the dominant person on your project that you are going to interact with or if it will be this project manager. If a contractor uses project managers, it is a good sign that this contractor is placing the proper importance on the needs of your project; especially if you are building a custom home. There may be some remodeling projects that will only require one sub's attention at a time. This is information you will want to have clearly defined before you sign your contract.

Our contractor had numerous projects going at the same time. He was not a builder. He contracted to oversee the construction process on any given project. When we inquired about having a project manager on our job, the contractor said it was unusual that any project would need the constant services of a project manager. If we desired to have a project manager on our project we would have to pay for that worker's services in addition to the builder's fee. Being new to the homebuilding process, we did not identify this as a red flag with this contractor.

Looking back through the eyes of our experience, his stance clearly indicated a lack of understanding of what building a custom home would entail. The sub that he put in control of our project was not experienced in managing a building site. He was overwhelmed and often frustrated. He was unable to properly assist the subcontractors who came to our project to install granite, cabinets, masonry, etc. When a contractor chooses to place an inexperienced sub in the position of managing a large construction project, it is not only unfair to that sub and everyone who they are working with, it also puts your project as risk.

I had ordered a wood-burning pizza oven for our backyard patio. I came up to our site one day to see the sub, that our contractor designated as the project manager, cutting into the faceplate that covered the opening of the pizza oven. I inquired as to what he was doing.

He said that this piece of my oven (which was purchased and shipped out from Los Angeles) was the wrong size and he was going to make it fit by cutting off the sides. This sub was unable to address this problem with our contractor because the contractor was out of town and not receiving calls. Knowing this, I asked if he had called the company in LA to confirm his theory. He said no, he didn't have to. He was figuring it out as he went along. I knew that this sub had not assembled this type of oven before and, more importantly, I knew how much the pizza oven had cost us. I was concerned with what he was doing. This is a great example as to why you want to hire professionals that have a PHM™ perspective. A PHM™ homebuilding contractor would not have put this level of sub in a project management position. They would not leave town without covering their project's needs beforehand and wouldn't have cut off communication with their subs while projects are ongoing.

I called the oven providers in Los Angeles and explained the situation. It turned out that the faceplate was exactly the correct size but that this project manager had instructed the mason to brick the front of the oven incorrectly. He was now trying to compensate for his mistake.

If you are building a sizeable project and, upon interviewing a contractor, you find yourself in a similar scenario, where the contractor doesn't have the knowledge or experience to provide proper management for your project, I suggest you pass on this contractor. Give yourself the opportunity to meet with other contractors who have the level of business expertise to adequately provide the services that your project will need.

Project Manager Questions to Ask a Contractor

• First off, you will want to meet this project manager along with this contractor to see how comfortable you are with them.

• How long have they been a project manager for this contractor?

• What are their responsibilities going to be on your project?

• What experience did they have to qualify for this position? (Alan Looney's project managers have graduated from colleges and universities that offer construction management majors.) Other contractors assign the position to someone that has been working with them over a period of time and has achieved a level of knowledge and expertise in the construction process to be able to manage a project. It is important that you know why this person is someone you can entrust your project to.

• How will this person be relating to you throughout the project?

• Ask this contractor to include clients in your reference list that had this project manager work on their project.

• Follow up with these clients and ask them how they thought this person handled their job.

• Did they maintain a productive work environment?

• Were they helpful when the homeowner needed assistance and could not talk with the contractor?

• Did they communicate the homeowner's needs accurately and in a timely manner?

• If this homeowner were to build again, would they ask for this project manager to mange this project as well?

Read through any written information that this contractor provides for you about their business. If they have taken the time to put this material together for their potential clients, they obviously feel that they have something of value to offer you. I received the written material that Alan Looney, one of the contractors I feature in this book, gives to his clients. It was very helpful in defining what a homeowner would expect when working with Alan. He includes everything from examples of change orders, contract information, the schedule that his projects follow, to advice on how you can best prepare for the process. This is not only helpful for the client; it is also a great example of good business practice. Alan knows the value of working with a client that is well-versed in his company's procedures before they begin working together. A builder

who adopts the PHM™ to his business practice is going to make a great team player for your homebuilding team. He has already demonstrated that he will Proactively assist you in your efforts as CEO to achieve a successful homebuilding experience.

Green Homebuilding

If you are interested in building or remodeling with green homebuilding materials, ask this contractor to have examples ready for you that represent work they've already done on other projects. Some of these projects may not be LEED certified. However, they met the homeowner's requirements or needs for their lifestyle. If this is the case in any project that your contractor shows you, ask them to go through the work that was done with you. What you want to confirm at your first meeting is that this contractor has experience with and understands how to incorporate green building product into a home design. Ask for references from this contractor to follow up with the clients that this contractor did the work for.

Sustainable Housing

If you are interested in building a sustainable home, you will need to hire a contractor who is well versed in implementing the design requirements beginning with the initial design phases — no on the job training with your project.

Portfolio

I know a number of great contractors who are excellent builders and just have not taken the time to hire someone to put together a portfolio or web site to show the work they have done. If a contractor does not have a portfolio put together of their work, but comes highly recommended, ask to see the some of the client's homes that they have built or remodeled that represent the type of craftsmanship you are requiring. If the contractor is with you during your visit, ask the homeowner if you can have their number to follow up this visit with a phone call. Then, when you get into the privacy of your home, call and ask some of the reference questions that I have provided to help evaluate this contractor for your project.

If the contractor does have a portfolio, it will give you valuable information as to whether or not this contractor has worked on projects similar to yours. If not, you risk hiring a team of people who are learning on your project. As I've said before, no on-the-job training on your project. You do not want to make the assumption that because a contractor has built homes before, that they will be able to meet the needs of your project. If you do not see the level of quality and skill represented in the contractor's work that you know your project will require, pass on hiring this contractor.

Purchasing from Home Stores

I was talking with a contractor the other day about this book. As we were discussing some of the details, he mentioned a source of contention with he and his clients of late. Some of his clients have opted to purchase home product and décor from a large home store that advertises discount prices for those who shop there for their homebuilding and remodeling projects. His point is that when a client decides to go with this option, they are asked to sign a contract with this company. This agreement now puts this company in control of the delivery schedule. This wreaks havoc on the contractor's ability to run the project. If the homeowner orders an appliance from this company, it is not delivered to the building site. It is delivered to the homeowner's home. Then the homeowner is responsible to get it to the site. If your contractor has scheduled his subs to be on the site at a specific time to do their work and you do not have your cabinets or your range or your light fixtures at the site when those sub-contractors are there to do the work, it costs your contractor money. If your contractor has numerous projects going at one time, and has to pull one sub off a project to piecemeal your project, he is now losing money on both projects.

This contractor proceeded to tell me that one day he arrived at the building site to find a refrigerator sitting on the front steps. Whoever

the homeowner had deliver it had left it there. Now the contractor has to have his subs move this heavy appliance on into the house and put it in place. They didn't have the proper equipment. The men that had to do this were taken away from the work they were to focus on, and if something were to happen to this expensive appliance, who is responsible? It is unfair to hold the contractor responsible. The homeowner needs to assume responsibility. The contractor cannot be expected to warranty this appliance because he had nothing to do with ordering it. It was not purchased through a source that the contractor can depend on.

If you are considering purchasing product for your homebuilding project from a discount service like this, talk with your contractor upfront about it first. Make your intentions known so that the contractor can prepare accordingly. Discuss it at your interviews and ask the contractor how they may or may not work with this situation. Take the time to work out the amount of money that you are saving and compare it to the amount of money that you would save with your contractor's discount. This contractor said that his discounted prices are very comparable to what this company is offering. Factor in the transporting of all the materials that you are going to be responsible for getting to your building site. Are you going to have to pay delivery fees on top of the savings you are getting? Is voiding out your builder's warranty worth the savings? Review the contract before signing to help you understand what position you may be putting your contractor in. If you are causing more work for your contractor than what was originally agreed upon, you should be open to compensating them for these extra add-ons.

I am the first in line for a good sale. I am very familiar with the adrenalin rush that you get when you walk into a store with discounted items. Just choose your items wisely. You may not want to purchase things that are related to the actual construction of your home unless the place you are purchasing them from is going to work with your contractor's stipulations.

to do list

PRELIMINARY REVIEW AND FIRST INTERVIEW LIST

- ☐ Current License information
- ☐ Credentials
- ☐ Bond information
- ☐ Copy of Insurance certificate
- ☐ Example copy of contract
- ☐ Example of their Budget / Accounting summary to be used on your project
- ☐ Example of value analysis or value-engineered bid
- ☐ Example copy of Change Order to be used
- ☐ Business procedures or company overview information
- ☐ Portfolio
- ☐ Building Green or Sustainable Housing experience information

CONTRACTOR INTERVIEW QUESTIONS

- ☐ How long have you been in the construction business?
- ☐ What made you decide to be a contractor?
- ☐ What is one of the biggest challenges you face when you work with a new client?
- ☐ This is my first time building/remodeling a home. Given your experience and expertise, what are some of the assumptions or misconceptions you have found that homeowners who are new to the homebuilding experience bring to their project?
- ☐ What might a homeowner new to the homebuilding process assume you would be responsible for, but in fact you are not?
- ☐ How will you be communicating the process with me as we go along?
- ☐ How long do you think this project will take?
- ☐ What do you estimate this project will cost?
- ☐ How close to budget are you with your estimates?
- ☐ What percentage of your work includes working with architects?
- ☐ Do you mind working with architects?
- ☐ How might working with an architect benefit a project that you are working on?
- ☐ Have you assisted an architect with cost projections on the front-end of the design process?
- ☐ Have you ever had difficulty working with an architect? If so, please explain, and explain how you worked it out.
- ☐ What percentage of your work includes working with interior designers?
- ☐ Do you mind working with interior designers?
- ☐ Do you consider yourself a team player? Explain.
- ☐ If I hire you to build/remodel my house I will want you to be involved in the design phase. Is this something that you have done before?
- ☐ Have you provided your clients with a value analysis or value-engineered bid before?
- ☐ What will your fee be for this project?
- ☐ How often do homeowners who work with you go over budget?
- ☐ What would you say is the largest contributing factor to the homeowner going over budget on their project?
- ☐ How might you help me or advise me as to how I might arrive at a realistic budget before I begin construction on my project?
- ☐ If I hire you to build my home, how will you be compensated for this assistance with the design phase of my building project?
- ☐ How often do your projects run over the due date you specify on the front-end of the building project?
- ☐ If you run over schedule on my project and my loan closes before you are finished, how will you handle that situation?
- ☐ Give me an example of what might constitute a change order on one of your projects?
- ☐ How do you handle the change orders on your projects?
- ☐ I would like to have all my choices made by the time we start construction so I have a good idea as to what the cost will be. How will you help me do that?
- ☐ Who do you do your business banking with?
- ☐ Do you offer your homeowners a new home warranty product like the 2-10?
- ☐ What types of insurance do you carry and what is the amount of your coverage?
- ☐ Are you bonded? What is the amount of your bond?

☐ Tell me how you will include me as an insured party on your insurance policy.

☐ Are you going to be providing me with the builder's risk insurance policy or will I be responsible for that?

☐ Will you provide me copies of the certificates once my name is on them before we sign a contract?

☐ I am interested in receiving copies of receipts for my project; can you provide me with these along with your draw requests?

☐ How often are you going to submit a draw?

☐ How often will we meet to go over the project schedule and building budget?

☐ How often will we be meeting for progress schedule reports throughout my project?

☐ Who will be attending these meetings?

☐ Do you usually manage the building budget for your clients?

☐ I would like you to go over your accounting procedure with me

☐ How often will you be going over the budget status on my project with me?

☐ How do you handle correspondence between you and a homeowner on your projects?

☐ Is there any protocol in talking with subs that you would like to go over with me?

☐ What is the best way for me to handle communicating with you if I have a concern as to how something is going on the project and you are not on the building site at the time?

☐ Are there any exclusions on your current insurance policy that may apply to my project that I should be made aware of at the beginning of our project?

☐ If a situation arose during project construction that you hadn't dealt with before, how would you choose to handle it?

☐ Do you guarantee you and or your subs work?

☐ How do you follow up on a project for a client after the home is built?

ADDITIONAL QUESTIONS FOR REMODELING CONTRACTOR

☐ How long have you been in the remodeling business?

☐ Have you worked on other projects that were similar to mine?

☐ Do you see any special challenges with my project? If so, how will you handle them?

☐ Do you have a regular crew of subs that you work with?

☐ Are you able to ascertain if there might be anything that would cause my building cost to change?

☐ What percentage of contingency funds do you suggest I add to the overall budget?

☐ We are planning on living in the house during construction, how will you help me prepare my home for this project before it begins? Are there any special precautions that you can see that I should consider taking before you and your workers begin work?

☐ Can you erect a temporary wall to divide the workspace from our living space (if this is feasible for your project)? If not, do you have any other suggestions for us to create a separate family zone?

CONTRACTOR FOLLOW-UP REVIEW CHECKLIST

☐ Follow up on contractor's license

☐ Ensure the license is up-to-date

☐ Ensure that there are no complaints, liens or suspensions

☐ Confirm contractor is licensed to build your price of home

☐ Follow up with local Better Business Bureau, www.bbb.org

CREDENTIALS

☐ Check online for credentials and see what they represent.

BOND

☐ Determine the amount of the bond and determine if you will require an additional amount for your project.

INSURANCE CERTIFICATE

☐ Call insurance agent and ask if this contractor is currently insured.

☐ Do they pay their premiums on time and consistently?

□ Has this contractor ever had their insurance cancelled?

□ Is this contractor known to work with insured subs?

BUDGET

□ I have gone over the budget and accounting procedures my contractor is going to use on my project.

□ I have reviewed this contractor's accounting procedure with my loan officer.

□ I have a clear understanding as to how my budget is going to be managed throughout my project if I work with this contractor.

□ I know who is going to be assisting me in managing my homebuilding budget before my project begins.

□ I understand the fee that is going to be charged from this contractor when our project begins.

□ I understand how a cost-plus arrangement is going to be financed throughout my project.

□ I understand how working on a cost-plus contract is going to mean that I have to be more proactive on the front-end of this project to determine if my allowances are sufficient to pay for the product I want to put in my house before we begin building.

□ I have all the information from this contractor that I need to begin making my choices for this project on the front-end of the project.

□ I understand how any changes that I make to my project that result additional costs may also cause this contractor's fee to increase.

FIXED FEE, TURNKEY

□ I understand that I will be expected to make all of my decisions on the front-end of my project before I begin construction.

□ I am confident of the team of people I will be working with on this Turnkey project to help me successfully make my choices before this project begins.

CHANGE ORDER

□ I have a clear understanding as to what a change order represents on my project.

□ I see where the signatures are required on this change order before it can be carried out.

□ I understand when I am to pay for this change order upcharge on my project.

□ I understand why this change order is going to be issued to me when I make a change on my project.

□ I understand that the contractor who I hire will write out everything that is going to be involved in this change on this change order before carrying it out.

□ I understand the importance of including my architect on any change I make to my original design before the change takes place.

BUSINESS PROCEDURES/COMPANY OVERVIEW

□ I understand if my project is or is not going to have a project manager and if there is an additional cost for these services.

□ I have followed up with other clients who have used this project manager.

□ I have read any information the contractor has provided for me regarding information as to how their business is run.

□ I know if my contractor is going to have anyone on my project as superintendent and I have references that I am going to follow up on as to other clients that this superintendent has worked with.

□ I understand all procedures that this contractor has laid out in his manual and I am comfortable with their procedures and homebuilding process.

PORTFOLIO

□ I have reviewed this contractor's portfolio and I am confident that the work I saw is representative of work that I will be requiring on my project.

□ The work in this portfolio inspired me.

□ After reviewing this portfolio, I am confident that this contractor can produce the quality of craftsmanship that I desire.

BUILDING GREEN/SUSTAINABLE HOUSING

□ I understand what it means for this contractor to be Leed certified.

☐ This contractor is not Leed however, I am confident in this contractor's knowledge and experience in building with Green product.

☐ I understand how building with Green materials will be more expensive than with regular product and the cost is worth it to me.

☐ I am confident in this contractor's knowledge and experience in building sustainable housing.

CONTRACT REVIEW

☐ After reviewing the contract with a construction attorney. I have a clear understanding of what it says with regard to the services the contractor is going to perform on my project.

☐ I have a clear understanding as to how this contract does or does not protect my interests with regard to this project.

☐ I've made any additional changes to this contract with the help of my attorney. I'll provide the contractor with these changes so they can review them.

CONTRACTOR REFERENCE QUESTIONS

☐ Name of client

☐ What type of project did this contractor work on for you?

☐ Did this contractor provide you with copies of their insurance certificates? Were you listed as additional insured?

☐ Did this contractor help you begin your project with realistic expectations?

☐ Did this contractor provide you with a realistic building budget at the beginning of your project?

☐ Did this contractor help you manage your building budget throughout the project?

☐ Did you have an architect work on this project too? If so, how did your contractor and the architect get along on your project?

☐ Would you say that this contractor is a team player?

☐ Were the subs that this contractor had working on your project professional in their behavior and quality of workmanship?

☐ Did this project run on schedule and within budget?

Architect Nancy Hayden custom designed this vanity piece of furniture in keeping with historic architecture of client's home. PHOTO CREDIT: DONNA YANCEY, ARCHITECT: NANCY HAYDEN

☐ Were you pleased with the way this contractor ran your project?

☐ Would you ever build again?

☐ If you were able to build again, would you use this contractor on that project as well?

☐ Would you recommend this contractor?

☐ If any questions arise after their review, I will consult with my attorney before signing.

CHAPTER SEVEN

YOUR PHM™ HOMEBUILDING TEAM

your interior designer

If I were to provide you with a title that I thought best described the services of an interior designer or specialty designer, it would be "the homebuilding angel of mercy."

The amount of time, money, energy and stress you will save yourself by enlisting the services of an interior designer cannot be overestimated. I am a very hands-on person, I research everything and weigh all my options before making a decision. In homebuilding, your choices are vast, varied and need to be made in a relatively short period of time. It's easy to get overwhelmed.

Interior designers will have different levels of experience and expertise, depending upon their training and experience. Homeowners may not understand the extensive training that goes into receiving a four-year degree in interior design. Some designers come to the process naturally; they may have a knack with space and décor. It's up to you to determine what you need for your project and the degree of expertise that will be needed from the professional you hire. Some construction firms retain the services of a licensed interior designer to help with the actual drafting of home designs or renovation plans. Personally, I recommend using an architect for these services, however, if using an interior designer is an option that you are considering, do the follow-up necessary to confirm that this person is experienced with the type of work that your project calls for. An interior designer or home designer is not going to have the level of training and expertise that an architect does. So if you are working with a construction firm that uses an interior designer or home designer to draft a home plan, know that you are going to be dependent on this construction firm to be expert in their knowledge of homebuilding because they will be the dominant player on your project. You will want to follow up with other clients who have used their services in the same manner that you are considering. Visit a number of these homes. You will need to confirm that the construction firm who is using the interior designer for home design purposes has a good reputation and experienced builders who can address any concerns that may come up during the construction process, this may be a good choice for you.

CERTIFICATION

At least twenty-five states across the country have adopted the Interior Designer Title Act. This is a law that is enforced by the state that recognizes the professional status of a Registered Interior Designer. For an interior designer to use the title of Registered Interior Designer, they would have to meet the requirements set by the law in that state, which would consist of six years of both education and industry experience. Two sites that I suggest you visit to read more about the training and expertise that an interior designer can bring to your project, are: American Society of Interior Designers, ASID, asid.org, and the National Council for Interior Design Qualification, NCIDQ, ncidq.org.

INVOLVE THE DESIGNER FROM THE BEGINNING

When we were building our home, I became overwhelmed with all the decisions I had to make to pull the house together. We forget that it has taken us years of experiences to have gathered and collected the items that make up our current living space. Trying to keep a semblance of the emotional richness (that we had in our old space) in this new and improved space that we're creating in such a short amount of time can be a daunting task even for the most ambitious homeowner. I found that you are so *inside* the process, focusing on details, that it's difficult to step *outside* of it and envision the bigger picture. A designer, on the other hand, is expert at doing just that on your behalf. While you're looking at a blueprint and trying to decipher your entryway from your master bedroom porch, a designer is able to look at the same flat sheet of paper and see whether or not you'll bump your hip when coming around the kitchen counter due to the chair that your son is sitting in while eating his afternoon snack. They have this uncanny ability to visually move your things around within the spaces of your house plan like a Rubik's cube.

The homeowner, new to the homebuilding process, can easily underestimate the value of having a designer on the front-end of the design process of their project. The assumption is that you wouldn't need their services until later when you start adding more of the esthetic touches. This compartmentalizing of your key people minimizes your potential for achieving the best home design. By not including them in the beginning developmental stages, you miss out on establishing a communicative foundation that can provide your architect or home designer with the essential information necessary to establish a cohesive custom design from the get-go.

Oftentimes, the interior designer is left out of the design process all together and asked for their services only when the homeowner is ready to begin purchasing furniture or deciding on paint colors. By taking this approach, you will spend more time and money with your interior designer because they now have to take the time to get familiar with your home.

And, if things have been designed and built a certain way, you may have to pay extra to have them moved or adjusted. For example, you may have planned on putting a table with a lamp next to a chair in your living room that calls for an additional outlet. This is the type of information that your designer can bring to your architect so the architect can better customize your home plans, otherwise, this outlet may be left out all together because it's not in running with the normal placement of outlets. You can use an unattractive extension cord or change it out now for an additional cost. An outlet may be a small change to make but a window that was designed and installed without consideration for your buffet table because your architect didn't have this information will have a bigger impact on your project. Having the insight in the beginning of the project to include details like that little outlet is going to make such a difference on the overall quality of your design in the long run. An interior designer can help you design around your needs versus having to design around your home's limitations.

You will save money on the front-end if your interior designer assists your architect with these details.

Your interior designer will also be of benefit on the building site if they have been able to walk through your home and conceptualize your space through the design phase. When an experienced interior designer walks into your home they can visualize the space filled with your items. They can mentally move furniture around and add pieces here or there within the confines of framed walls and plywood floors. This ability to conceptualize your space with your belongings in it can also save you from purchasing furniture that will not work in your home. This is going to save you a lot of time and effort.

How frustrating would it be if you had a piece of furniture that was very important to you and the area where you wanted to put it is not large enough to accommodate it? Now you either have to pay to have the wall changed or you are going to have to put that piece of furniture somewhere else.

Some interior designers can help you manage your responsibilities on your building site as well. They can set up appointments for you with vendors that need to come onto your site. Or they can meet with the vendor at the showroom and make the choices that you have gone over. This can be of great service if you have other commitments or work obligations throughout the week.

Once, when I was building, I walked into a millwork shop to pick out my crown molding for our main floor and stair railing for our entryway. How difficult can it be? I walked into the showroom confident that I would be out of there with samples in hand in less then thirty minutes. Three hours later, the sales rep came over to the area of the showroom floor I was now occupying to once again ask me if I needed any assistance. I looked up at her and said I think I have narrowed it down. She glanced over the dozens of selections I still had spread out within a ten-foot radius around me, smiled and said, "Well, I'll be up front when you're ready." I scooted back up against the wall to gain some support for my back. I don't know how much longer I sat there; I just know it was dark by the time I left empty-handed. The next morning, I called my interior designer, Evy, and relayed my story. Later that afternoon we met up at the lot and she brought in the samples I needed to show the finish carpenter. It was perfect. I loved her choices.

The best time to bring an interior designer in on your project is at the beginning. They can be very helpful with the design process. An interior designer approaches your design from a different perspective than your architect or contractor. They are able to conceptualize your personal belongings in the spaces that the architect is designing. For example, if you are planning on having a sitting area in your bedroom, your designer is going to be able to help the architect design around your furniture to provide enough space for everything you are going to want to include. If you have art that is going to be showcased with lighting, or if you have a grand piano that is an important element to your family's functions, the interior designer's expertise will help make sure that your interior needs are adequately provided for.

Two Scenarios

The two scenarios below will illustrate the importance of including the team players such as your contractor, interior designer or specialty designer along with your architect at the beginning stages of design development.

Let's assume that you are going to be responsible for heading up a fundraiser. You are asked to raise money for the children's hospital in your community. You have eight months before the big event. You are somewhat familiar with the process because you have attended numerous fundraisers for this cause in the past. The first thing you do is set up a meeting with last year's chairperson, Jennifer, who headed up the event to take notes on how best to approach this. Jennifer tells you that you need to get all of your co-chairs together to discuss everyone's roles and responsibilities. Then you need to

build a timeline as to what needs to get done and when.

Your co-chairs are John, who is responsible for publicity, Michelle, who is responsible for creating the menu and hiring the caterer, Stephanie, who will be heading up the silent auction, and Kevin, who has agreed to do the invitations and door prizes. You will be the MC for the evening's events.

SCENARIO ONE:
You set up your first meeting. You call the people you think are most important to have attend: John, Michelle and Kevin. You decide that Stephanie does not need to be at the initial meetings because she is in charge of the silent auction and preparation for that doesn't need to take place for a few more months. Fast forward. You are well on your way to pulling this together and though your budget is tight, you are confident that you will remain in the black once the night is over. The ads are placed, the hall is rented, the menu planned, food ordered and now it's time to start talking with Stephanie about the auction.

You ask Stephanie to meet you at the building where the event is to take place. Once inside, you both start walking around the room and you show Stephanie where the tables are going to be set up and how the food is going to be served. Stephanie starts telling you about some of the prizes she has gathered and how she would like to display them. She also mentions the fact that a number of the sponsors who have donated substantial gifts want to have specific information included in the program regarding their company. You agree to pass on the information to John so he can include it in the programs and the ads that he has put together. You thank Stephanie and tell her you will be in touch with regard to setting things up.

When you call John and tell him about including this information from Stephanie, he says that the program is already designed and he isn't sure if anything else can be added at this point. He will let you know once he hears back from the printer. He also tells you that his budget for advertising is spent and he would need more money to include this added information from Stephanie about the sponsors.

A week before the event you schedule a meeting to have everyone at the hall for the initial walkthrough. When you arrive, Stephanie and Michelle are already going over the plans. The table and chairs are set up and the stage is being assembled. Stephanie greets you with, "I think we have a problem!" You ask, "What?" She then proceeds to explain that there is not enough space in this hall for her to set up the auction items while the food is being served. You ask Michelle if she agrees and both of the women begin telling you why they don't think the space will accommodate what they need to have happen simultaneously.

To further complicate things, John shows up with the programs and Stephanie realizes that some key information regarding a number of the sponsors who donated items for the auction have been left out. When she points this out to John he produces a single sheet with the added information and says that you all are going to have to manually insert this sheet into the programs. He says that he had to do it this way because the cost to redesign and reprint the entire program was too high. You receive a call from Kevin who is stuck in traffic but just wanted to let you know that the last of the door prizes came in today and so far only fifteen people out of the two hundred and fifty you've invited will not be able to attend.

SCENARIO TWO:
You call your first meeting and include every one of your co-chairs. John, Michelle, Stephanie and Kevin. Even though Stephanie's responsibilities won't come into play for a few months, you realize that she is a key contributor to the overall project and what decisions are made now can affect what she is able to do later. While John is discussing the program, Stephanie brings up the option to include sponsors and any other information that might be added before the final print. John agrees to let Stephanie know when

he is going to hand in the program details to the printer so they can make sure that everything is accounted for. Michelle and Stephanie agree to meet up in the next week or so to look at different rooms to rent for the event.

The first hall that they look at will not provide Stephanie the space she would need to set up her auction items if food is going to be served at the same time. Stephanie remembers that one of the sponsors, who is donating a gift for the auction, mentioned that he had a connection with a hotel in town that had a wonderful banquet room. Stephanie calls the sponsor and he arranges for Stephanie and Michelle to meet with the event planner at the hotel. It turns out that the banquet room is going to work out much better for this charity event and the hotel will donate the space for free. The event planner from the hotel suggests that they consider using the hotel's chef to help create the menu and prepare the food. Michelle is happy with that because it would be convenient for her to have everything prepared on site. Stephanie says goodbye to Michelle and heads over to John's office to drop off the information she wants included in the programs because he is sending them to the printer in the morning.

A week before the event you schedule a meeting to have everyone at the hall for the initial walkthrough. When you arrive, Stephanie and Michelle are already going over the plans. The tables and chairs are set up and the stage is being assembled. Stephanie greets you with, "I am so excited! Everything is coming together great!" Michelle says, "This is a perfect space to host the event in." John arrives with the programs that include all of the information Stephanie wanted about the sponsors. You receive a call from Kevin who is stuck in traffic but just wanted to let you know that the last of the door prizes came in today and so far only fifteen people out of the two hundred and fifty you've invited will not be able to attend.

In the first scenario, by not including Stephanie on the front-end you missed out on her ability to contribute to your event in the beginning stages. She had valuable information that needed to be included in the printed program. Having to add that information after the program was designed cost you time and money. It also created more work for you and your team to have to add the single page. It added stress and produced a program that was piecemealed together versus being one cohesive unit. Had you included Stephanie when you and Michelle chose the hall to host the event, she could have told you right off that that space was not large enough to accommodate both the auction and food needs for the evening and you would have had the opportunity to make the change. As it was, you now had to make due with what you planned and the quality of your event was not what you had hoped for.

The head of any successful company knows the benefits of including all their key players in the communicative process and letting them contribute their expertise in the beginning of establishing a project. It makes your job much easier and the overall results more likely to succeed. You, being the PHM™ CEO of this home-building venture, will be applying the same strategies they use.

Finding the Designer For You

The personalities and business acumen among interior and specialty designers will vary as much as every building project does. Evy, my interior designer, was a delight. I would walk away from our meetings refreshed and inspired. The stress I had built up in the process of making my decisions would melt away as she began eliminating all the excess options and helped me to focus in on the few that most resembled the look I was trying to achieve. Her ability to judge the size and scale of trim pieces and focal points of our home was a great contribution to the architect and contractor. This helped me save money while adding lots of unique elements to our home.

When I decided to work with an interior designer, it was important to me to find someone who would build upon the things that my family enjoyed and embraced in our lives.

I have a quirky family, so I needed a quirky designer. I arrived at our lot late for our meeting and found Evy entertaining the subs with her accordion. Apparently, it started out as a simple happy birthday tribute to one of the framers, then it quickly became a per request concert that lifted everybody's spirits. Evy's sense of humor and "outside the box" personality, combined with her immense talent in helping her clients, create home environments that are truly unique extensions of themselves. She was a great match for us. When looking for an interior designer or specialty designer, feeling comfortable with their personality and expression of style is vital to your ability to explore and discover the intimate detailing you'll come to cherish in the new home you've created.

Your designer should make it easy to involve your kids in the design process as well. Depending on their age and their tastes, a designer can assist them in personalizing their rooms. Your child can bring samples or items that are important to them to one of your meetings. Then, let the designer come up with ways of incorporating these elements into their space in a manner that everyone can live with. Evy did a great job with both our kids. She was able to include them in a manner that graciously integrated their personalities into our home.

I suggest that you use a designer's services to whatever extent your budget allows. Don't let a tight or limited budget prevent you from working with an interior designer. You may be able to hire an interior designer for consultation only. If that's the case, you can still gain from their insight. Prioritize your needs and make sure you are using the time you can afford to your advantage. Be prepared on the front-end of your meeting. Make a list of what you want to go over. Have your pictures, fabric swatches, measurements, room layouts and anything else that will help your designer have a better understanding of what you want to achieve.

If you are not able to get all your furnishing completed now, relax and let things evolve over time. Your interior designer can help you set long term goals that are easier on your budget.

interview

Evy McPherson
Interior Designer (my interior designer while I built my home)

WHEN WOULD BE THE BEST TIME TO INCLUDE THE SERVICES OF AN INTERIOR DESIGNER ON A BUILDING PROJECT?

Bring them in on the initial meeting with the architect and the builder. The projects that I have been brought in on at the beginning of the process all seem to go smoother. Everyone has a clear understanding as to what is going on.

HOW DO YOU HELP SOMEONE UNDERSTAND WHAT'S AHEAD OF THEM WHEN THEY COME TO YOU AT YOUR FIRST MEETING?

You begin to walk them through the process. It's best if they can begin making their decisions on the front-end of their project. For some, it may be harder because they're not working in the actual space. But it's going to be more accurate and they will get what they want. It will also give them enough time to live with their decision. Otherwise, if they wait until the project is underway, they are going to be rushed into picking out plumbing fixtures the day they need them and they have to choose from what's available versus what they really want.

WHAT TYPE OF THINGS DO YOU LIKE A HOMEOWNER TO BRING TO YOU ON THE FRONT-END OF THEIR PROJECT TO HELP YOU DETERMINE WHAT THEY WANT IN THEIR HOME?

If the client can provide me with as much detail and descriptive information as possible, like magazine pictures, or a notebook they've compiled to help communicate what it is that they want to accomplish, the better the project is going to be. I can use that information and build from it.

DO PEOPLE HAVE A GOOD GRASP ON BUDGETING FOR THEIR INTERIOR DESIGN FEE ON THEIR HOMEBUILDING PROJECTS?

If the homeowner doesn't know to plan ahead for these expenses up-front, oftentimes you get what I call the pyramid effect. The builder is the one who gets the largest chunk of money. Then, depending on how the homeowner's budget is holding up, what's left over starts to trickle down to the bottom, usually to the designer, then to the landscape architect.

WHAT ADVICE WOULD YOU GIVE A HOMEOWNER ONCE THEY GET THE BUILDER'S BID TO HELP THEM UNDERSTAND WHAT ACTUALLY IS IN THAT BID?

They need to go and see how much things cost and if this contractor's bid is going to provide for what they want before they accept it.

HOW DO YOU CHARGE FOR YOUR SERVICES?

Sometimes I charge by the hour and sometimes I charge a flat-fee for the entire project. Doing a flat-fee gives me more control over the whole project, so when it's nearing the end, I get to go pick out lamps and other finishing touches that make the whole project look cohesive. To determine the flat-fee, we would go through the entire project. Specify what the client wants, such as furniture, lamps, etc. Then I would put my fee on top of that. If a client has a difficult time defining what exactly they want, then we would get a general idea and I would give them an estimate. Doing it on an hourly basis can create a problem if the client runs out of money before the project is completed. Then aunt Sarah picks out the lamps and misses the whole concept.

WHAT IS THE MOST COMMON MISCONCEPTION THAT PEOPLE MAY HAVE WHEN IT COMES TO HIRING AN INTERIOR DESIGNER?

The fear that hiring an interior designer is going to cost more than if they didn't hire one, and that's not necessarily the case. There are a lot of ways for me to actually save people money. I offer my clients design ideas that will allow a client to use materials in creative ways so they don't have to buy the most expensive to achieve a great look. Designers are trained to do that with many applications.

WHAT DIFFERENT LEVELS OF SERVICES CAN AN INTERIOR DESIGNER OFFER A CLIENT WHO IS GOING TO BUILD OR REMODEL THEIR OWN HOME?

A designer can give consultation services or be very involved throughout the project. I have great resources for my clients, which include contractors and subs. If you're remodeling or renovating your home and you need a builder, I can suggest one that I trust. I can help bring in different trade people like wallpaper hangers, painters, faux finishers, trim carpenters, etc.

WHAT SHOULD A HOMEOWNER LOOK FOR IN AN INTERIOR DESIGNER THAT THEY ARE CONSIDERING HIRING?

Dori and Interior Designer Evy McPherson in Evy's home office.
PHOTO CREDIT: LOREN BALMAN

• That they are stylistically appropriate for your taste. There are two types of designers: one that does one style, and, the client will go to that designer for that specific look, and the other is the designer that does all types of styles. It's important that when the client is choosing a designer that they choose someone who is going to do what that client wants done in their home.

• That they are going to devote the time needed to the project. You don't want to hire someone who's in the middle of a large project and they are not going to be able to give you the time you need, especially if you are working on a schedule with a builder.

• That they understand how long the project is going to take and that they will be available for that amount of time.

• That they have access to resources that are job appropriate. I think that's a big one. It's important that the designer you hire is able to get the required work done on your project. You may want something that is not done locally. For example, if you want something contemporary, make sure that your designer can get things like that done.

• When they see your pictures, how do they react? Do they react negatively? Even if they think they are giving you constructive criticism, if you don't agree with them, then you probably don't want to work with them.

• Once you show them your pictures, ask them if they are comfortable with this style.

• Ask them to give you references and follow up with those references. Ask the clients if they had a good experience. How was everything handled? Were there any problems with deliveries or installations? If so, how were they handled?

• A lot of things can happen after the client moves in. For example, I had a lantern break. Who does the client call? Or a drapery falls down. Does the designer say, "Well, spread it out and use it as a rug"? Or, "I'll call someone to take care of that for you." It's important that the client hires a designer that they can depend on to follow up on things, even when the checks stop coming in. I don't get paid for that type

of follow-up and sometimes it's a pain to deal with, but it's why you get return clients.

WHAT IS THE MAIN OBJECTIVE OR GOAL OF A DESIGNER ON A GIVEN PROJECT?

At the end of the project, if my client says that they had a great experience, I feel like I have accomplished my goal. I delivered an end result that they are happy with and if something went wrong, or there was a change in the budget, I took care of it to their satisfaction and they felt like they received the results they wanted.

AT WHAT POINT IN A PROJECT SHOULD A HOMEOWNER AND DESIGNER PART WAYS?

Hopefully, after the designer gives the homeowner a nice thank you gift for the opportunity to work with them!

(A note about when to part ways with a member of your team. One of the things that we learned on our project is, when things begin to go wrong, stop and determine the source of the problem. If you have lost trust in this employee, and you don't feel like you can easily and confidently express your needs and desires to them, then you need to dismiss them from your project. We continued to give our contractor the benefit of the doubt for too long. Keeping him on our project as long as we did negatively affected the outcome of our homebuilding experience. If you have hired a good building team, it's unlikely that you'll run into this problem. If you do, your team members will affirm your concerns.)

HOW COMMON IS IT FOR A HOMEOWNER TO EXCEED THEIR ORIGINAL BUDGET BY THE END OF THE PROJECT?

Probably as common as people overeat.

SO 100%

Yes.

to do list

Interior Designer Interview

☐ How long have you been an interior designer?

☐ What type of training have you received in your field?

☐ Have you worked on other projects similar to mine?

☐ Are you confident that you have the resources to provide me with all that I will need for this project? Please elaborate.

☐ Do you carry insurance?

☐ Is your work schedule going to provide you enough time to devote to my project from beginning to completion?

☐ Describe all the services that you are experienced with and able to provide for me on my project.

☐ Do you have experience in assisting a homeowner manage their responsibilities throughout a homebuilding project?

☐ Have you ever helped a homeowner manage a building budget between the contractor and the homeowner on any of your homebuilding projects?

☐ Do you see any specific challenges to my project?

☐ How is a change in the product that we ordered handled?

☐ Give me an example as to when a change can be made and when a change cannot be made.

☐ Have you worked with an architect and or a contractor on a project before?

☐ Give me an idea as to how that process would go?

☐ Have you been involved in the architectural design phases of a project?

☐ How will you charge me for this project, what will your fee be?

☐ What might constitute a change in your fee once my project begins?

☐ It is important for me to have my choices in regard to the house design made upfront to make sure that my building budget or allowances are sufficient to purchase the items I want to include in the design of my home. Can you assist me in doing this?

☐ How will you keep track of the costs of items that I purchase when we are working together? Will I receive receipts from you?

☐ Do you have a portfolio that I can review?

☐ How do you follow-up on a project?

☐ What type of warranty or guarantee do you provide your clients for your services?

☐ Can you please provide me with three references of past clients?

Interior Designer Preliminary Review Checklist

CREDENTIALS

☐ Follow up on the designer's credentials so you can be confident of their training ability and experience to handle the project

SERVICES TO BE PROVIDED

☐ I have followed up with past clients and reviewed this designers portfolio and visited other projects that this designer has worked on and I am confident that this designer has the resources to handle my project's needs.

☐ I understand the services that this designer is going to provide me on this project.

☐ I understand how this designer is going to assist me in the initial choices that I want to make with regard to the esthetic components of my home before construction begins. These choices will enable me to confirm that my budget is adequate for the materials I want to include in my home.

☐ I am confident in this designer's abilities to be a team player when working with the architect and contractor in the initial design phase of my project.

□ I am confident that this designer can represent my desires to the architect and the contractor in the early architectural design phase as well as throughout the project's life cycle.

FEE

□ I've reviewed the costs of using this designer on this project and I'm comfortable with the way they will be compensated for their services.

BUDGET

□ This designer and I have discussed how we will break down my budget needs for the initial material choices that I have to make regarding the esthetic design elements of my home as well as the interior furnishings that this designer is going to help me with for this home.

□ I have allocated the amount of funds necessary to pay for these furnishings on the front end of my project.

□ I will be using the architectural design funds that are going to be refunded me at the end of my project from my construction loan to pay for the furnishings of my new home. (See Alan Looney's interview Chapter 6.)

SCHEDULE

□ I have confirmed that this designer's schedule is going to be compatible with my needs throughout this project.

CHANGES

□ I understand how changes to product I have ordered from this designer are going to be handled.

□ I understand how changes to the scope of the job that I ask this designer to provide would be handled.

PORTFOLIO

□ I have reviewed this designer's portfolio and I like their design approach and am confident that they will be able to help me execute my design style.

Questions to Ask Designer's References

□ Name of client.

□ Beginning and completion date of their project.

□ What type of work did the interior designer do for this client?

□ Did this interior designer help the client stay within their budget range?

□ Did this interior designer assist them in picking out their choices for their home before their project got underway?

□ Did this project come in on schedule?

□ Did this designer work well with the architect and contractor on this project?

□ Do they feel that this interior designer was able to capture their family's decor desires successfully?

□ Was the interior designer included on the architectural design process?

□ Was this interior designer a team player or did they seem to want to work independently?

□ Did this interior designer respond to the contractor's needs in a timely manner?

□ Would this client recommend this interior designer?

□ Would this client be willing to let me come and visit their home?

CHAPTER eight

YOUR PHM™ HOMEBUILDING TEAM

your specialty designer

When I refer to a *specialty designer*, I am speaking about a designer who focuses on a specific area of expertise. Whereas an interior designer can help a client with an overall esthetic look and feel with their home, a specialty designer brings more of a hands-on focus to one area of your home that will need to provide services above and beyond the norm. The kitchen tends to be one of the most common areas where homeowners will use a specialty designer.

In our home design, we had two such areas to focus on. The first was my kitchen. I am a serious cook and I was initially going to host cooking classes in my kitchen. I also like to entertain and would often cook for twenty or more people at any given time, so I needed to have a kitchen that would accommodate my lifestyle.

The second area of our home was my husband's studio office. He is a composer and needed a space he could work in that would be soundproof so he could both record music without disruption and work late into the night without bothering someone who may be asleep. We also had our home wired to take advantage of different rooms with acoustical value if he wanted to record an instrument in one of them. Whenever you are mixing the type of function needed for specific purposes beyond a normal household in a home environment, it is best to hire someone expert in combining the function along with the esthetic value that you want to keep in your living spaces.

Consider my kitchen, for example. I could make meals for 10 to 100 guests with ease. Granted, it took more prep time for the larger group of people, but the actual cooking, serving and clean up was relatively easy, thanks to Don Silvers, my marvelous kitchen designer. Making the decision to do the research necessary to identify and hire the specialty designer best suited to your needs will enhance the quality of life you experience in your home tenfold. My kitchen worked for me, not against me. It was wonderful to move from one area to another with ease. I hope that the interview I did with Don, included in this chapter, inspires you to exceed your preconceived notions when it comes to setting a standard of expectations looking for the right designer.

The following is a letter I wrote regarding Don Silvers to endorse his work and to thank him for his design services on our home. It gives excellent detail about the benefit gained from his involvement:

Our family decided to make the move from Los Angeles, California, to Nashville, Tennessee. We anticipated many changes. Topping our list was finding a place to live. We agreed on the location. Now we needed to find a house that would accommodate our lifestyle; a house with a kitchen and a floor plan that allowed us to host gatherings of all sizes.

We looked at dozens of homes ranging from 1800's historical homes to newly built custom homes, all boasting renovated or existing gourmet kitchens. We soon found this to mean beautifully appointed space equipped with the latest appliances needed to reheat already prepared foods. By prioritizing the importance of esthetics over thoughtful planning and quality products, this type of kitchen limited my options as a cook.

The decision was made that we should settle into a temporary living situation while developing plans to build our own home. I began collecting pictures and articles with ideas that we could incorporate into our house plans. In the process, I read several kitchen design books. The one that proved most helpful to me was *Kitchen Design with Cooking in Mind* by Don Silvers. The information Don laid out in his book gave me the foundation I needed to create a family cooking environment that would prove to be the heart of our home for many years to come.

I compiled my wish list. I wanted my kitchen to be:

1. User friendly.

2. To provide an intimate family atmosphere yet would accommodate parties of 8 to 80 without overload.

3. I wanted appliances that could stand the test of time while providing me with an attractive environment in which to work.

4. I wanted efficient and well-organized work and storage space, making clean-up easy for anyone using the kitchen.

5. I wanted a floor plan that tastefully united the kitchen and the adjoining rooms.

6. Finally, I wanted a cooking environment that gave guests the opportunity to help cook or simply sit nearby and visit, allowing me to enjoy their company without having to maneuver around them while preparing a meal.

Now all I needed to do was to get my extreme kitchen concept together and hand it over to Don. We planned a trip back to Los Angeles. Don's passion for educating people about fine foods, along with his gift of creating a personalized environment that enhances the abilities of a cook, quickly became evident. The concerns we had of Don being in another state during the building process were put to rest as soon as we saw Don's plans. Our architect noted the attention Don paid in providing such detailed blueprints. If a question arose on the job site, we called Don and he addressed the situation with concise clarity, getting everything back on track. With the aid of the Internet, phone, faxes and quick package delivery companies, our project with Don was free of glitches. I only wish the rest of the house came together so effortlessly.

I have numerous examples of bringing in ideas I had pulled together for my kitchen, and of Don understanding what I was trying to accomplish. He demonstrated how, in certain situations, I was actually working against myself. The best example of this was dealing with my pantry. I had designed an 8' by 9' walk-in pantry, which I was thrilled about. It would hold everything: canned goods, dog food, overnight guests — the possibilities were endless!

After reviewing my blueprints, Don suggested that I relocate my pantry to build a built-in rollout cabinet space, enclosing a hutch that I could display dishes in. This would free up the 8' by 9' space to be a baking room. I paused, caught my breath and reasoned, yes, I love to bake. In fact, I'm a serious baker. But give up my pantry? That one was hard for me. Don

assured me that I'd have more than enough storage space in his design. As a result of Don's ingenious planning, my "pantry" is the highlight of my kitchen. I'm thrilled with my baking room, and our overnight guests enjoy a spacious guest room upstairs.

We moved in over a year ago and, without hesitation, my family would say that the kitchen is the most lived-in space of our house. Whether its homework, after-school snacks, late-night talks or dinner parties, our kitchen is truly the heart of our new home.

We are grateful to Don for giving us an environment where our family and friends can gather, creating memories we will cherish throughout our lives. Don, our sincere thanks.

Dori Howard

Keep Function In Mind During Your Design

A friend of mine, who was in the process of renovating her home, was working with an architect to assure the plans were going to provide a cohesive design that matched the style of the existing house. She hired a kitchen designer to develop the kitchen plans. Once she received her kitchen plans, she asked if she could bring them over and see what I thought. When we sat down together and started going over the plans, I could see that these plans were drawn up by someone who rarely cooks. I asked Rachel," How well do you know this kitchen designer?" She said, "Pretty well, why?" I asked her if she knew whether or not this person cooks. She laughed, "Marci cook? No way. She has everything catered. Why?" I said, "Because I can tell that this layout is designed by someone who doesn't cook."

As I walked Rachel through her plans, I began asking her questions: "Give me a typical scenario of one of your dinner parties and how many guest you like to serve." Then I asked her to point out where she would prep and cook the food. Where are you going to plate the food before serving it to your guests in the dining room? Where are you going to put the dishes that you are clearing from the table between courses?" I said, "Now where are the guests

> "Cooking is like love. It should be entered into with abandon or not at all."
>
> *Harriet Van Horn*

going to be when you are in the kitchen and they want to come in and say hello?" Rachel began seeing her kitchen the way a cook would. She was able to see the bottlenecking that would happen at both entrances to her kitchen. She was also able to imagine herself wading through her guests when getting something in and out of the oven and onto the counter and over to the sink. "Oh my," she said under her breath. "I like Marci, I think she's a great lady, but this is not going to work."

I met Rachel at her house the next day and we went through the plans again. I came up with a new plan for her to incorporate some unique storage and serving cabinets in her dining area that would open up some of her kitchen space. Then I had us reenact some party scenarios in her kitchen to better understand the limitations she currently had and what needed to be done to enhance her productivity in this space. By repositioning her appliances and island we were now able to accommodate all her cooking and serving needs while opening up the entire flow of the kitchen. Guests could comfortably mingle and then intuitively knew to walk on into the dining room and family room areas without disrupting the cooking that was taking place.

Rachel loves her renovation. She hosts far more get-togethers now than she did before having the work done. I've been at a number of Rachel's gatherings and it's great to see her enjoying the new space. The reason I was able to help Rachel with her home is largely due to the learning experience I had with Don when we designed my kitchen.

I'm surprised by how often homeowners don't consider hiring a design specialist or discuss their desire to do so with their architect or contractor on the front end of their project. I've seen so many homes built or remodeled where homeowners overlook the opportunities available to them to have their needs within a space truly customized because they simply aren't

aware of their options or they don't want to take the time or they made the assumption that hiring someone like this would be too costly. On the following pages, I've included some excerpts of an interview I did with Don Silvers to give you an idea of the level of service that is available to you when you are willing to put in the time to find the right person to help customize your home.

I think that it is important for homeowners to get past the fallacy that hiring an architect, interior designer or specialty designer is going to be too costly for your project. I am speaking from experience. I admit that I go into an internal frenzy if I think I am going to get a better deal on a purchase than the rest of the public. You cannot apply that mindset to your home-building project. A pair of shoes, a piece of furniture or a vacation on St. Thomas is the place to put your need to get a deal.

The home that you and your family are going to live in for the next decade is not the place to look for good deals. The type of homebuilding professionals who offer you the deal are not the type of team members you want working on your project. Your home should outlive you and be a shelter for generations to come. Spend your money wisely. Invest in what is most important in your home, creating an environment that improves your quality of life.

Specialty Designer Preliminary Interview Information

The work you are going to have this individual do on your home will determine the type of credentials that you will want to see from them. The majority of specialty design is going to be related to the kitchen. If you are going to have work done on your home design to accommodate a health or physical need, you may want to consult with a professional in that field of expertise and have your interior designer, architect and contractor meet with them. This will help keep everyone on the same page during the pre-design/pre-conception phase of your project.

The following credentials are for kitchen and bath designers. As Don said, it is important that part of your kitchen designer's experience should be the actual cooking process.

CREDENTIALS

National Kitchen and Bath Association (NKBA) is an organization that certifies designers who have completed both experience in the field and the examination process. In order to keep this certification, the designer has to maintain a certain amount of ongoing education as well.

The designer can be certified in these different areas of expertise:

ASSOCIATE KITCHEN & BATH DESIGNER (AKBD)

To receive this certification the designer would have to prove that they have worked on kitchen and bath projects for a minimum of two years.

They would have to have thirty NKBA hours of educational training.

CERTIFIED KITCHEN DESIGNER (CKD) OR CERTIFIED BATH DESIGNER (CBD)

To receive this certification the designer would have to prove that they have worked on kitchen or bath projects for a minimum of seven years.

They would have to have sixty NKBA hours of educational training.

CERTIFIED MASTER KITCHEN & BATH DESIGNER (CMKBD)

This is a certification that a designer receives after first receiving their AKBD certification.

Add to this training an additional ten years of experience and an additional one hundred hours of NKBA education.

LICENSE (IF REQUIRED)

Some states have passed a Title Act that allows only those designers who have met the necessary educational requirements to receive their registration or licensure to be able to advertise themselves as licensed or registered interior designers. You can go on line to www.asid.org

and follow up on a candidate that you are interviewing or to find someone in your area that you might like to interview for your project.

INSURANCE INFORMATION

Ask what type of insurance this candidate carries and how it will or will not apply to your project. When you are hiring a professional who is not brought onto your project by your contractor, they may not be covered under your contractor's insurance or warranty. Go over this possibility with your attorney and get advice as to how you will need to protect your project if something were to happen as a result of this person's services. It could be a worker that they brought in or an accident with an installation, etc. You want to make sure that you have put the proper insurance and contractual modifications in place before your project begins.

AT LEAST THREE REFERRALS

You will want to see the projects that this candidate has worked on. Ask these clients if they are happy with the results from this designer. Does the space that this designer worked on provide the service that they had hoped for?

PORTFOLIO

As in working with any other professional in this industry you want to confirm that this individual has experience in the type of work that your project requires. You will want to see representation of this in their portfolio.

WHAT TO REQUEST FOR THE FIRST INTERVIEW

Credentials; License (if required); Insurance information; At least three referrals; Portfolio.

interview

Don Silvers
Author, Chef, Kitchen Designer and Cooking Instructor

"The average consumer doesn't realize the importance of the appliances they choose. They don't understand how it impacts not only the design of the kitchen but their ability to cook," Don Silvers.

The first time Don took my husband and I to an appliance store, he opened and shut oven doors with a bang! He even stood on one of the opened doors to show us how sturdy it was. Obviously the panic on my face registered with him because he assured me that the sales reps were accustomed to his thorough testing procedures and we were not going to be arrested or thrown out of the showroom. He turned a name brand convection oven around so we could see the inside components. Pointing to the convection motor, he said to my husband, "Do you see that?" To which my husband replied, "Yes, it looks a lot like something we built in Boy Scouts." Don said, "Exactly. That is the extent of the convection motor inside this range." He proceeded to show us another model with a far superior motor. Needless to say, we bought the second range for our home.

WHEN IS IT IMPORTANT FOR A HOMEOWNER TO ENLIST THE SERVICES OF A KITCHEN DESIGNER?

At the very beginning. Many times consumers wait too long and hire me towards the end and a lot of things are already framed in. The plumbing is already in. Electrical is already in. They don't need me then. They can go to a home store because all they need to do now is fill in their kitchen space.

SOME HOMEOWNERS MAY ASSUME THAT YOU HAVE TO BE A GREAT COOK TO JUSTIFY HIRING A KITCHEN DESIGNER. HOW MIGHT SOMEONE WHO MAY NOT CONSIDER THEMSELVES A GREAT COOK BENEFIT FROM YOUR SERVICES?

I've told some of my clients that one of the reasons you don't cook well is because you have always worked in an environment that manipulated you. How would you like to manipulate the environment? How would you like to be in an environment where it's a delight to cook? And not only is it a delight to cook but because it will be a delight to cook, you will begin to cook much better because you'll have the right appliances. You'll be able to move in the space with absolute ease because you won't be battling everything. You're not going to get on your hands and knees and have to dig something out of the base cabinet because you don't have roll-outs or drawers there to pull out so you can easily get to the things that are stored in back. Something as simple as that. Then, of course I go into appliances. Usually when a kitchen layout is that bad, it's done by a kitchen designer who created the design from a *kitchen triangle*.

THE KITCHEN TRIANGLE HAS LONG BEEN TOUTED AS THE BASIS FOR ANY GOOD KITCHEN DESIGN. HOW DID THIS BECOME THE FOUNDATION OF KITCHEN DESIGN AND WHAT IS YOUR OPINION OF THIS THEORY?

The beginning of the kitchen triangle design started in the early 1950s. It had to do with a house being designed and built by the University of Illinois. In designing the home, they came up with the concept of a kitchen triangle, which means that the refrigerator is at one point, the stove is at another point and the sink is another point. Well, at that time, the cabinet industry had not penetrated the kitchen industry because they couldn't figure out how to design a kitchen. When they introduced the kitchen triangle, then you could train anyone to design a kitchen. So the cabinet industry was now able to design for the kitchen industry. But at that point in time nobody asked a couple of very important questions. (Here, by the way, is the criteria for kitchen design.) They didn't ask or take into account what size the home, which was 1,000 square feet, for the returning GI. They didn't ask or take into account what size the dining room was, which was to seat four people nor did they ask or take into account the size of the kitchen, which was sixty square feet. So the triangle was most appropriate only in that space, without question. They could not project that in today's marketplace. You no longer have only a stove, a sink and a refrigerator. You have cooktops, ovens, tools, steamers, two dishwashers, microwaves and double ovens. You have lots of appliances.

They came out and said you design from locations. Nobody in our industry has ever said what you really design from, which is volume. Volume tells you the whole story. If I'm designing a condo that seats four people in the dining room, I can very well use the triangle. But if I'm designing a home that seats eight or more people, then I design by volume. Am I designing for eight, twelve, sixteen or twenty? If I'm designing for twelve, it tells me the kind of appliances I need because it has to produce X amount of volume, it tells me the kind of dry storage I need and it tells me the kind of wet storage I need (refrigeration). A kitchen needs to be designed by volume as it relates to your specific needs. So in my opinion, that's what makes the kitchen triangle a disaster.

A HOMEOWNER MAY BE MISLED BY A PROFESSIONAL WHO SAYS THAT THEY HAVE BUILT OR DESIGNED DOZENS OF GOURMET KITCHENS FOR CLIENTS. OFTENTIMES IT MEANS THAT THEY HAVE PICKED OUT OR INSTALLED NEW STAINLESS STEEL APPLIANCES AND ADDED A GRANITE COUNTERTOP. IF A HOMEOWNER IS CONSIDERING HIRING A KITCHEN DESIGNER:

1. HOW MIGHT THEY BEGIN THEIR SEARCH?

2. WHAT TYPES OF QUESTIONS WOULD THEY WANT TO ASK THE DESIGNER BEFORE HIRING THEM?

Many kitchen designers will say to you, "I've been designing kitchens for twenty years," when in reality they've been designing kitchens for one year, twenty times. So that's one of the problems we have because essentially the average kitchen designer out there is a box salesman who in turn designs kitchens in order to sell cabinetry. So the questions that I think a consumer would want to ask are:

• Do you know how to cook a meal for eight to ten people without using a microwave? Because if they understand how to cook a meal for eight to ten people, they will understand point of use, i.e., where things go for the cook to be able to use it without walking forty miles.

• Can I see some of the kitchens you've designed and how long have you been designing kitchens?

• How did you learn to design a kitchen?

• Then I would ask for four or five referrals within the last year.

When I take on a customer, the first thing I do is take them appliance shopping. I don't care where they buy the appliances. I only care that they understand what they're buying. I want them to understand all the appliances that are in the marketplace, what it will and won't do for them. I then do a layout that I call the conversation layout. And I present it to my client. The client for the most part will say, "Gee, I really like that but…" and there's always the "but," there's always the "however." And that's what I'm looking for. I'm looking for the buts and I'm looking for the howevers, because I want to fulfill their needs, not mine. And those buts and howevers are going to tell me where I missed the boat, where I can make it better, and where I can help them. Generally, I can do this within two meetings. Sometimes it takes three, and even, on occasion, four. I don't charge extra for those meetings, I charge a flat fee. And they're entitled to as many meetings as it takes to make the layout right. Then I take them countertop surface shopping, backsplash shopping, flooring and cabinet shopping. I'm after the door style and color so that we can then choose our granite, tile, laminate, butcher block or whatever material that relates well together. Now I'm able to complete a set of plans. The plans that I complete are perspectives and elevations. One elevation will show the look of the kitchen from the door point of view and how the doors line up on the cabinetry. A second set of elevations will show what's going to go inside each of the cabinets — doors, roll-outs, trash or whatever it may be — so that the cabinetmaker can see exactly what we're calling for. I do the electrical, the mechanical and the lighting. By doing all of that, I've given the client a road map that the contractor and cabinet people can use to make their bids. As long as they bid it as per the plans, then the consumer is going to get a solid bid to work with.

For local clients, once the job is finished, I will go to the client's home and let them invite eight, ten or twelve guests. Then we will cook a

Architect Nancy Hayden's attention to details and materials, makes most of limited space while saving money for clients in this custom designed kitchen. PHOTO CREDIT: RICHARD LEO JOHNSON, ARCHITECT: NANCY HAYDEN

meal together so I can teach them how to use their environment and new appliances. Having the ability to specify what goes into every cabinet and assisting the client as to where to put things is important. It's something the average kitchen designer doesn't do for their clients and I think this should be done for them.

I THINK ONE OF THE ULTIMATE COMPLIMENTS I RECEIVED ABOUT THE LAYOUT OF ONE OF MY KITCHENS WAS FROM MY DAUGHTER, WHO WAS ABOUT FOURTEEN YEARS OLD AT THE TIME. SHE WAS CLEANING UP AFTER A MEAL AND SHE SAID, "I LOVE CLEANING UP IN THIS KITCHEN BECAUSE IT'S EASY TO KNOW WHERE EVERYTHING GOES." THAT'S WHEN I THOUGHT TO MYSELF, "OH, DON SILVERS IS WORTH HIS MONEY."

Kitchens should have logic to them. One of the things that can interfere with this logic is form. And form can be difficult to deal with. With some architects, for example, the last thing they want to do is to put a prep sink on the end of the island. They want it dead center. It doesn't matter that it's only a six-foot island and that if you put it dead center, you've just ruined all your counter space.

HOW IMPORTANT IS THE EXPERIENCE THE KITCHEN DESIGNER HAS IN WORKING WITH ARCHITECTS AND CONTRACTORS TO THE SUCCESS OF THE KITCHEN DESIGN?

Very important.

EXPLAIN TO A HOMEOWNER WHY IT'S IMPORTANT THAT THE KITCHEN DESIGNER THEY HIRE ALSO COOKS.

There are two kinds of kitchens that are prevalent in today's society. One is what I call the *constipated kitchen* where everything is so jammed together that you have absolutely no room to work anywhere. And you only have one single sink. Water is the most used ingredient in the kitchen, so the first thing you need to do is to create at least two or three different water stations. When they design with the kitchen triangle, they are not going to design with two sinks.

The second kitchen, especially in a space of a couple hundred square feet or more, which is most common, is the *rollerskate kitchen,* where you need to be on rollerskates in order to get around. You have a prep sink on one side of the island and you have the refrigerator on the opposite side so you're constantly going around that island to get at something. Another big feature is when the designer builds a large pantry, and it's fifteen or twenty feet away from the kitchen. People who don't cook don't understand the concept of point of use. I need a pantry within three or four steps of where I'm cooking. When we say pantry, that doesn't mean we have to have, "a pantry". It means we have to have either wall cabinets or base cabinets that are devoted to the storage of the things you need in that area so that you can get at them within one, two or three steps.

Those are the two spaces that are the most prevalent in the marketplace. My book, *Kitchen Designed with Cooking in Mind*, helps explain this. The consumer is aware of those problems and can say, "I don't want to run around this island all the time, and I don't want to go to the pantry each and every time I need something."

YOU HAVE A COUPLE THAT YOU DESIGNED FOR ON THE BACK OF YOUR BOOK. THEY MADE THE COMMENT THAT WHEN A "REAL COOK" VISITS THEIR HOME, THEY APPRECIATE THE KITCHEN DESIGN LAYOUT. I FOUND THIS TO BE TRUE WITH MY KITCHEN AS WELL. YOU HAVE DESIGNED NUMEROUS COMMERCIAL KITCHENS ALONG WITH RESIDENTIAL. EXPLAIN WHY IT IS IMPORTANT TO HAVE AN EFFICIENT DESIGN IN THE COMMERCIAL KITCHEN AND HOW YOU INCORPORATE THIS INTO A RESIDENTIAL KITCHEN.

That's the one thing I don't understand about my industry. Why they don't look at our sister industry and say, "Oh, they design space where it has to be efficient." They don't focus solely on esthetics — they want to know — can it produce? Can it produce the volume of food in direct relationship with what's being ordered? So what I do is I design commercially at a different scale. That's essentially how I approach kitchen design. (And I design beautiful kitchens, just check out my Web site.)

In using a restaurant as an example, why in the world would you ever want the busboy crossing the cook's path. Boy, if he ever did it when I was working as a cook, I'd chop his hands off. "Get out of my space!" Yet we constantly design kitchens where people are doing that in their own homes. Not necessary at all.

I OFTEN HAVE LARGE GROUPS OF PEOPLE OVER, SO I WANTED YOU TO CREATE A SPACE THAT GAVE ME A BARRIER TO WORK WITHIN AND NOT HAVE TO MANEUVER AROUND MY GUESTS. WITHIN THIS SAME SPACE, HOWEVER, I WANTED TO GIVE MY GUESTS THE OPTION TO HELP ME COOK IF THEY SO DESIRED. THERE WAS PLENTY OF SPACE FOR THEM TO DO THAT AS WELL. AT NO POINT WAS ANYONE IN ANOTHER'S WORKSPACE, AND I LOVED THAT.

And you have a fairly large kitchen. My kitchen is 16' × 12' and has a peninsula, so it's very tight. However, when I teach cooking classes, one night out of the course I bring my class to my home and I cook a dinner for them. Generally it's between 15 to 20 students. I cook a dinner to teach them point of use. I can fit 8 to 10 people, working in my kitchen, with absolutely no problem. And it's only a 16' × 12'. That's what looking at a space from a cooking point of view allows you to do.

EXPLAIN WHAT *WORK STATIONS* ARE AND HOW THEY SHOULD FIT INTO THE DESIGN OF A KITCHEN.

There really aren't a lot of workstations. There is ample counter space so that you can do the work. The only work station I would have separate, for example, would be baking, because I don't want baking near a lot of heat. But in terms of all the rest of it, if the average home is seating 10, 12 or 14 people in the dining room, I don't need a separate garden dejour or cold station, but I do need to have plenty of counter space so that we can all be working and still have enough separation. I do need to separate the clean-up and the prep area. Clean-up for the cleaning of dishes, prepping for prepping the food. And the clean-up area becomes a secondary prep station when you're having a large party so that you can wash your bowls and so forth in both sinks and use that secondary area as a prepping station, too. But it's not like a restaurant where you have separate workstations. The National Kitchen & Bath Association (NKBA) talks about workstations. I don't agree.

HOW WOULD YOU ASSIST THE CLIENT WHO IS OUT-OF-STATE?

If it's a remodel, I have them send me pictures of the kitchen. I call them up, send them a questionnaire, they fill it out and I go over their appliances. I try to get as much information from them as possible, what their expectations are and what they're looking for. Then I go ahead and design and send them the communication plan. I get on the phone, go over it, find out if and where I've missed the boat, so to speak, so that I can redo it. Once I redo it, I get on the phone and go through the elevations: Where are we going to put this? Where are we going to put that? Then I create a set of documents to send out. Clients have told me that our documents are so good that they blow their contractor's minds.

IF A HOMEOWNER USING YOUR SERVICES TO DESIGN THEIR KITCHEN IS OUT-OF-STATE AND A QUESTION ARISES ON THEIR BUILDING SITE, HOW IS THIS HANDLED?

They call me. I'm always available to my clients. I don't believe my job is finished after the design. It really isn't. I'm available whether it's local or in New York. If it's local, I sometimes go out to the job site. If it's New York, I'm always available by phone.

I developed a business called Design Assurance for clients who know how to cook. I come in when they receive a set of kitchen plans that they know are wrong and they don't know why or what to do about it. For $690 I have them send me a set of the plans and about 70% of the time I can straighten it out for them over the phone. About 30% of the time I've got to tell them to burn it and start over.

THERE ARE SOME CONTRACTORS WHO HAVE CABINET SUPPLIERS THAT THEY CUSTOMARILY USE. WHAT DOES A HOMEOWNER NEED TO FIND OUT BEFORE SIGNING OFF ON THE COMPANY OR CABINETMAKER THAT IS GOING TO PROVIDE THEIR CABINETS?

Contractors like to use local people for a number of reasons. They will most likely get a commission on the sale, they can trust this cabinetmaker and it's done locally. If there are mistakes made, they can be fixed immediately. From that standpoint, they're trying to protect themselves and make the job easier. One of the problems I have with local-built cabinetry in kitchens — not in the rest of the house, just in kitchens — is the fact that the finishes on those may not be the best of finishes. I'm a great believer in a baked-on catalytic conversion varnish finish. Almost any major manufacturer has that kind of finish, whereas a lot of smaller factories won't. Some states allow it and some states don't. Check to see if your state does. If so, and you can get it done locally, that would be great. A cabinet with the baked-on catalytic conversion varnish will hold up over time. It will look the same in ten years as it does today.

WHAT ARE SOME OF YOUR FAVORITE FLOOR MATERIALS TO USE IN A KITCHEN DESIGN?

My favorite is vinyl.

The heart of this home is an all-inclusive kitchen that was designed and built for a homeowner who loves to cook and entertain. Subway brick tile raps around the ventilation system for easy maintenance. PHOTO CREDIT: REED BROWN, CONTRACTOR: CASTLE CONTRACTORS

WHY?

Vinyl isn't to be confused with linoleum. You have to understand my concept with flooring. I don't want to see it. I don't want to know about it. And the reason for that is that I don't want anybody to walk into one of my kitchens and say, "What a beautiful floor you have." I want them to walk in and say, "What a beautiful kitchen you have." You will want to have a darker floor than the cabinet color. The purpose behind that is to float the kitchen. I like vinyl because it's easy on the knees and feet. I could duplicate your wood floor in vinyl and you'd never know that it was vinyl — in any color you want. That's how good they are, and, they will last twenty years, so it's a great value. That's my first choice. Second choice is a wood floor, even though there is maintenance with it, as long as you run three coats of polyurethane on it, you could live with it. Third choice is stone, which I hate in any kitchen.

HOW IMPORTANT IS LIGHTING IN A KITCHEN DESIGN AND WHY?

It's extremely important. If you don't have good lighting, it doesn't reflect what you've put in the kitchen and it doesn't allow you to see worth a darn. Lighting is functional. As you well know, there isn't a spot in your kitchen that is not well-lit, and that's because it was balanced out properly. When you're working with machines, knives, opening up cans, you'd better be able to see what you're doing. I have fluorescent lights underneath wall cabinets, spots over counters and smaller spots on each side of the sinks.

to do list

Whatever area of expertise that this specialty designer works on, you will need to confirm that they actually have experience in this area. So as Don pointed out, if you are hiring a kitchen designer, you want to know that they actually cook as opposed to creating just an esthetically pleasing space.

Specialty Designer Interview

☐ How long have you been designing in this area of expertise?

☐ What makes you a specialist in this area of design?

☐ What type of training have you received?

☐ If designing a kitchen, do you cook? Tell me about your cooking experience.

☐ Have you worked on other projects similar to mine?

☐ Are you confident that you have the resources to provide me with all that I will need for this project? Please elaborate.

☐ Do you carry insurance?

☐ Do you see any specific challenges to my project?

☐ How is a change in the product that we ordered handled?

☐ Give me an example as to when a change can be made and when a change cannot be made.

☐ Have you worked with an architect and/or a contractor on a project before?

☐ Give me an idea as to how that process would go?

☐ Have you been involved in the architectural design phases of a project?

☐ How will you charge me for this project, what will your fee be?

☐ What might constitute a change in your fee once my project begins?

☐ It is important for me to have my choices in regard to the house design made upfront to make sure that my building budget or allowances are sufficient to purchase the items I want to include in the design of my home. Can you assist me in doing this?

☐ Do you have a portfolio that I can review?

☐ How do you follow up on a project?

☐ What type of warranty or guarantee do you provide for the services you provide?

☐ Can you please provide me with three references of past clients?

Specialty Designer Preliminary Review Checklist

CREDENTIALS

☐ I have followed up on my specialty designer's credentials and am confident of their training ability and experience to handle my project.

SERVICES TO BE PROVIDED

☐ I have followed up with past clients and reviewed this specialty designer's portfolio and visited other projects that this specialty designer has worked on and I am confident that this designer has the resources to handle my project's needs.

☐ I understand the services that this specialty designer is going to provide me on this project.

☐ I understand how this specialty designer is going to assist me in the initial choices that I want to make with regard to the schematic design of my home before construction begins. These choices will enable me to confirm that my budget is adequate for the materials I want to include in this area of my home.

☐ I am confident in this specialty designer's abilities to be a team player.

☐ I am confident that this specialty designer can represent my desires to the architect and the contractor in the early design phases as well as throughout the project's life cycle.

FEE

☐ I have gone over the costs of using this specialty designer's services on this project and I am comfortable with the way they will be compensated for their services.

BUDGET

☐ This specialty designer and I have discussed how we will break down my budget needs for the material and/or product choices that I have to make regarding the design needs of my home to help me establish a realistic

"Stonybrook" walls and "Cappuccino Muffin" ceiling add to calming master bedroom, French doors open to covered porch and outdoor entertaining area. PHOTO CREDIT: REED BROWN GENERAL CONTRACTOR: CASTLE CONTRACTORS, ARCHITECT: KEVIN COFFEE

budget for these design needs before my project begins.

SCHEDULE

☐ I have confirmed that this specialty designer's schedule is going to be compatible with mine for this project.

CHANGES

☐ I understand how changes to product I have ordered from this specialty designer are going to be handled.

☐ I understand how changes to the scope of the job that I ask this specialty designer to provide will be handled.

PORTFOLIO

☐ I have reviewed this specialty designer's portfolio and I am confident that they will be able to help me execute my design needs.

Questions to Ask References for Specialty Designers

☐ Name of client.

☐ Beginning and completion date of their project.

☐ What type of work did the specialty designer do for this client?

☐ Did this specialty designer help the client stay within their budget range?

☐ Did this specialty designer assist them in picking out their choices for their home before their project got underway?

☐ Did this project come in on schedule?

☐ Did this designer work well with the architect and contractor on this project?

☐ Do they feel that this specialty designer was able to capture their family's decor desires successfully?

☐ Was the specialty designer included on the schematic design process?

☐ Was this specialty designer a team player or did they seem to want to work independently?

☐ Did this specialty designer respond to the contractor's needs in a timely manner?

☐ Would this client recommend this specialty designer?

☐ Would this client be willing to let me come and visit their home?

CHAPTER nine

YOUR PHM™ HOMEBUILDING TEAM

your landscape architect

As Evy, the interior designer, pointed out in her interview, the last person considered for funds on a project is most often the landscape architect or the landscaper. If the homeowner has to start cutting back on their budget during the project, the landscape architect is the first one to take the hit. On the majority of projects, the architect or contractor will have someone they work with and will allocate funds accordingly. It is my experience that this number is usually too low. For me, putting in all the time and expense to build or remodel your home and not finishing off with adequate landscaping is comparable to planning an amazing night out on the town and wearing Birkenstocks with your evening gown.

A great landscaping plan can make a huge difference on the exterior of your home. If done correctly, it pulls everything together, blending your new construction into the land it inhabits. When you think of landscaping, think long-term. It's very much a part of your investment that will only add value to your home with each passing year.

When you are interviewing your architect and contractor, ask them, "Who is going to be responsible for your landscaping needs?" Meet with this person. Ask for some references of other clients who they have done work for. Go and visit these homes. Get one or two references from clients of a couple of years ago. This way, you can see how the assortment of plants that were chosen and installed have filled in over this time. Is it attractive? Are the plants spaced properly or are they crowded? Is there an irrigation system installed? If so, does the lawn look like it is growing evenly? Walk the property. If you are with the landscape architect while visiting this client, ask them to show you some of the features that they are most proud of. Once you are home again, you can follow up with this customer one-on-one and ask more user-friendly questions, like, how is the overall maintenance of the property? Did this landscape architect show the homeowner how to use their irrigation system properly? Have any plants died, and if so, how was that handled?

Were there any specific challenges to this project that this landscape architect had to deal with, i.e., soil and drainage conditions?

Determine how important the outdoors are to you. Do you like to take walks, garden, set out bird feeders, swim, etc.? Parks, library gardens, resorts and neighborhood walking paths didn't just happen — they were intentionally designed by someone for our enjoyment. Landscape architects are responsible for creating the outdoor spaces that we often take for granted. Being able to incorporate the existing landscape with this huge intrusive building structure we call home and make it feel like it belongs is a true talent.

One of my favorite memories from my childhood is when it started to rain. I would haul out a sleeping bag and set myself up with a coloring book and crayons in the back of my family's station wagon. The rhythm of the raindrops hitting the roof relaxed me.

Other days, I would pack a lunch and hike over to a neighboring field. I'd carefully scope out just the right spot to settle into. Standing on my tiptoes, I'd hold the edge of my blanket, shake it out into the air and let it drift down atop the tall grass. I'd then toss my lunch in the center of the blanket and watch it plummet to the ground. I jumped into the hole and proceeded to stomp. Working my way from the inside out, round and round until my blanket lay flat on the ground. The golden wall around me rustled in the breeze while I lay basking in the warmth of the sun, hidden from the busy life of everyone around me. I would eat my lunch, listen to the birds and dream the day away.

It's obvious that the outdoors mean a lot to me. As an adult, would I like to have fields of land to wander my days away? Yes, if someone sprayed for wood ticks and cut paths into the tall grass, and, if I wander too far, come and get me in a golf cart. What would be more realistic is for me to bring this story to my landscape architect and ask how can they create this emotional comfort zone for me outside my back door. And let them do their magic.

Even if your budget is tight, consulting with a landscape architect will provide you with the opportunity to make the most out of a small amount of space and add on as you're able to. I talked with this young couple that just got married. The house they bought was a very sweet beginning home. The yard, however, was in dire need of help. Their parents went together on a house-warming gift, and purchased a five-year landscape plan. How cool is that? This couple can now look forward to each Spring in anticipation of adding new landscaping! On an emotional note, this is a wonderful way for the parents to embrace this new life that their kids have begun together. Each section of plantings will come with its own set of stories and memories that will be shared for years to come. On the more practical side, this gift will enhance the value of this couple's investment.

Include the Landscape Architect From the Start

Just as with any other team member, it is best to include your landscape architect on the front-end of your project, for a number of reasons. This professional will be able to assess your building site and help you determine how to best marry your plans to the land you build on. If your city, state or federal government regulates how, what and where you build due to the protection of wetlands, historic sites or communal property that you need to know about, your landscape architect can work alongside your architect to ensure that your plans meet these laws. And in the process, make the most of your property usage.

Early on, you can include them in on how you might plant trees to cut back on your need for air-conditioning in the summer. Live privacy barriers can be more attractive than fences. The ability to create an outdoor space for socializing or just reading and bird watching is certainly a therapeutic aspect to my lifestyle.

If you are hiring this landscape architect independent of your architect or contractor, you will want to confirm during your interview that they are experienced in working with both an architect and a contractor and that they can help you determine your budget on the front-end of your project. Also, determine with this professional what constitutes a change order, and how far into the design you can still make changes. And, how will it be handled if you don't like a plant that is brought onto your property or planted during construction? What types of resources do they have? Can they handle all your project's needs? Are they skilled in using CAD to help you envision your design?

You need to determine what your needs and desires are for the outside of your newly built project. Depending on your needs, you may want to hire someone with a degree. Visit the American Society of Landscape Architects, ASLA at asla.org.

If there are trees and plants that are indigenous to your state, you will want to know that this person is knowledgeable as to what they are and the types of soil, sun, shade and water needs they have. Are they compatible with the other plants that you may want to use? The more experience the landscape architect has, the more creatively they are going to be able to work within your budget. When it comes to landscape architecture, the rule applies — a builder builds, an architect designs homes, a landscape architect designs the outside space. You don't want your contractor deciding on what types of plants would look best around your house. As the homebuilding climate is changing and more and more people want to incorporate the natural environment with their everyday living spaces, the importance of hiring a professional with the proper training is essential to you project.

It is important that you interview a number of landscape architects for your project. When we were interviewing for our home, the irrigation prices alone varied by thousands of dollars. We threw out the high and low and chose between the two in the middle. As with any professional you are going to hire, do not let money be the only deciding factor. You need to Proactively follow up with past clients and actually see the work that was done before making your final decision.

to do list

Interviewing a Landscape Architect

☐ What level of experience do you bring to my project?

☐ Do you have a portfolio to show me?

☐ Can you provide me with a number of references of past projects that you have worked on and please include one or two clients that have at least three years of growth to their plans?

☐ Do you see any challenges to my project?

☐ Do you guarantee your work?

☐ If you hire this professional independent of your contractor, you will want to know what type of insurance they carry. Talk with your provider to see if you need to gather any information from this professional.

☐ How do you charge for your services?

☐ Can you give me an estimate as to how much you think it will cost me to landscape my project?

☐ Would you be willing to design a progressive plan for me, one that I would add to over the next year or two?

☐ Tell me about the irrigation system that you are considering for this project.

☐ Have you worked with sustainable design? (Ask this question if this is important to you. For example, do you want to save on energy, do you have historic property that you need to take into consideration before you begin building or do you have an irrigation system that needs to be set up for recycling water?)

☐ How knowledgeable are you about this state or this region's indigenous plant species?

☐ Discuss any specific needs or desires that you want to have incorporated into this design to determine that this individual is able to implement the concept that you are looking for

☐ If you are having a pool, pond or fountain installed, ask this person to tell you about how they would incorporate this element along with the rest of your property.

☐ If you have any privacy issues how does this person suggest you handle them?

☐ What is this landscape architect going to use to help you better visualize their design concepts? Are they experienced in using CAD?

☐ What type of time commitment will this professional need from you for this design?

☐ Have you worked with an architect and/or a contractor on a project before?

☐ Do they consider themselves to be a team player?

☐ How long will this landscape architect take to finish the installation of your landscape design?

When you are interviewing both your architect and your contractor, ask about landscaping and how they see this aspect of your project being played out. If the landscape architect is going to be brought in by your architect, it is likely that they will be included in the early phases of design. However, in not wanting to assume this as fact, ask the architects that you interview how this will be handled. If this landscape architect is going to be brought in by your contractor, ask your contractor to show you some other projects that this person has worked on. Meet with them and ask them what they have in mind for your project. If you feel that you may want to hire someone else for your project, this needs to be communicated with your contractor before your contract is signed. You also want to keep in mind how important it will be for the landscape architect to be a team player. They will be working within your contractor's schedule so that will have to be agreed upon up front by both parties.

Landscape Architect Preliminary Review Checklist

CREDENTIALS

☐ I have followed up on my landscape architect's credentials and am confident of their training, ability and experience to handle my project.

SERVICES TO BE PROVIDED

☐ I have followed up with past clients and reviewed this landscape architect's portfolio and visited other projects that this landscape architect has worked on and I am confident that this professional has the resources and connections needed to handle my project's needs.

☐ I understand the services that this landscape architect is going to provide me on this project.

☐ I understand how this landscape architect is going to assist me in the initial choices that I want to make with regard to the landscaping of my home before construction begins. These choices will enable me to confirm that my budget is adequate for the plan.

☐ I am confident in this landscape architect's abilities to be a team player in the initial design element of my project.

☐ I am confident that this landscape architect can represent my desires to the architect and the contractor in the early architectural design phase as well as throughout the project's life cycle.

FEE

☐ I have gone over the costs of using this landscape architect's services on this project and I am comfortable with their fees.

BUDGET

☐ This landscape architect and I have discussed and agreed upon the sum of money it will take to implement my landscape design needs.

SCHEDULE

☐ I have confirmed that this landscape architect's schedule is going to be compatible with my needs throughout this project or is going to be compatible with my contractor's needs throughout this project.

CHANGES

☐ I understand how changes to product I have ordered from this landscape architect are going to be handled.

☐ I understand how changes to the scope of the job that I ask this landscape architect to provide would be handled.

PORTFOLIO

☐ I have reviewed this landscape architect's portfolio and/or visited client's homes that they have worked on and I like their design approach and am confident that they will be able to help me create and execute my design style.

INSURANCE

☐ I have followed up on this landscape architect's insurance with my insurance provider and am confident that my project is adequately covered if an accident were to occur. (This would be necessary only if this landscape architect is subcontracted by me and not by my architect or contractor.)

Questions to Ask References for Landscape Architects

☐ What type of work did this landscape architect do on your project?

☐ Were you happy with the results?

☐ How has the design held up?

☐ Did you have an irrigation system installed?

☐ Do you know how to control the system?

☐ How was the follow up on the work that this landscape architect did for you?

☐ Did this landscape architect stay within the budget that was originally allocated for your project?

☐ Would you recommend them?

building green and sustainable housing

Going Green

Building green is an intentional implementation of specific materials and applications to achieve an anticipated outcome. It is essential that you consider green building at the front-end of the design process. This will ensure maximum function and make the most of natural resources. For example, you can opt to use engineered wood products. These products use 50% more of the log for constructional lumber, thereby cutting down on the waste that is created in using lumber product for conventional homebuilding. It is much harder to incorporate green elements into a home plan once the design is completed. If the green element is included in the front-end of the building process the architect and contractor can plan for heating and air efficiency by how the house is initially prepared — how it is insulated from the outside in. As Nancy Haden, AIA architect says in her interview, everything affects everything. How you begin determines how things are going to play out.

Adhering to the PHM™ in your desire to build green will prove to be very beneficial not only to the decisions you make on the front-end of your project but with regard to your upkeep and maintenance of your newly built home as well. If you Proactively commit to caring for your newly built green home, you will assure yourself of the long-lasting benefits that incorporating green building will have in your sustainable design. When I talk about care, I mean simple things like changing your air filters every month and using light bulbs that conserve energy. These are not major inconveniences. On the contrary, the sustainable lifestyle is meant to decrease the amount of upkeep and energy that you expend in your everyday life within your new home. Simplify and conserve.

If you do not follow through with the care and maintenance procedures necessary to keep your green design working at its optimal level, you can cancel out the benefits you spent your time and money on.

You can go online and research some of the green building options you have before you begin your interview process. Be prepared to get green information overload once you go online! Take notes, and if a product looks interesting to you, jot it down. Keep track of the sites you are most interested in. Visit my site to help you get focused. This information can be valuable when you begin your interview process and once you have hired the people who are going to design and build your home.

Some basics to get you started:

• Green building focuses on the products that you incorporate into your home's design, beginning with the site planning, onto the construction and finally with the upkeep of both the inside and outside environments of the house once it is built.

Sustainable Design

Sustainable design is the implementation of the Green products in the design of your home to create an overall better living environment for both the family that resides in the house and the ouside world around them.

Leadership in Energy and Environmental Design (LEED)

LEED is a nationally accepted green building rating system that was developed in 2000 by the U.S. Green Building Council (USGBC), which was established to move the construction market towards sustainable building. Currently, twenty-two states across the country are encouraging LEED standards as the basis of their commercial construction projects. However, the residential market is gaining strength and complying with LEED standards as more and more people are becoming educated to the positive effects of building green.

The LEED measure of green building has set credits or points that a builder can receive, depending on how many steps are taken to include green building throughout the overall design of the home. The construction industry uses LEED as the standard of measurement for the way a green building is designed and constructed and the way it functions with regard to sustainable building principles. There are five key areas that LEED focuses on:

1. Sustainable site development
2. Water conservation
3. Energy conservation
4. Materials used
5. Environmental quality level of your indoor living environment

Sustainable site development focuses on adapting your building envelope to maintain and incorporate as much of the natural resources on your property as possible.

Water conservation can be achieved both inside and outside the home. Inside, you can conserve on your water usage by installing products designed to use less water consumption throughout your everyday lifestyle. Outside, this is achieved by incorporating a landscape design that will include drought-tolerant plants that naturally grow in your climate zone and by creating a natural drainage/filtering system that will allow you to reuse household water and rainwater for irrigation purposes.

Energy Conservation is very important in sustainable design and can be implemented with an energy-efficient HVAC system put in place for your heating and air unit. Also, you will determine how you place the building envelope on your building site to obtain more shade in the summer and more sun in the winter. You will also focus on how your house is insulated from the outside of your structure before the exterior is applied to the inside, i.e., the design of your HVAC system.

Materials used refers to what types of materials are going to be used on your home. These materials are eco-friendly in their manufacturing aspects, their ability to enhance sustainability and the overall living environment in your home and are designed to be more eco-conscience when being disposed of. Use wood from sustainable forests. The forests are meant to replace the wood that is used for buildings as opposed to the continuous depletion of one of our world's natural resources. Use engineered wood products that use 50% more of the log for construction lumber.

Environmental quality level of your indoor living environment is focused on improving your indoor living environment by increasing energy efficiency, quality of air and the alleviation of pollutants found in typical materials such as paints and stains currently used in the building of homes. This is good, given the current rise of allergy and respiratory conditions.

LEED Certified Point system
26 – 32 Points ....Certified
33 – 38 Points ....Silver
39 – 51 Points ....Gold
52 – 69 Points ....Platinum

Along with the point system, go over the cost of implementing this credit and determine whether or not its impact and cost to your design is a viable option for you. In a recent conversation I had with Sarah Nettleton, AIA architect in Minneapolis, and author of *The Simple Home; The Luxury of Enough*, I asked Sarah, who specializes in sustainable design, "How do you begin the process with a client who is interested in green building, but new to the process?" Sarah said that she begins by asking the client if they are able to spend an additional 1% of their overall building budget or 5%, 10% or 25%? This helps define the realities of what the homeowner can incorporate into their design. She tells her clients not to feel guilty if they cannot afford to do all that they would like to do in incorporating a sustainable design.

I think that this is an important point. It's going to be easy to get caught up in the green frenzy and feel like you are building less of a house if you are not able to obtain all that you think you should. Focus on the improvements that this project will have over the home you are currently living in. Building a home should be a joyful experience that a lot of homeowners never get to have.

You can incorporate many responsible lifestyle choices into the way your family lives that won't cost you a cent. Go online and type in "green living" or "green lifestyle" and see for yourself. Also ask your interior designer to help you come up with ways to incorporate a green lifestyle inside your living spaces.

Diano Realle marble tops, cherry furniture-style cabinets, heated tile floors, Kohler Sok tub with overflowing bath and directional Kohler Water Tiles in the shower create an ideal place for relaxing and rejuvenating. PHOTO CREDIT: REED BROWN, GENERAL CONTRACTOR: CASTLE CONTRACTORS, ARCHITECT: KEVIN COFFEE

Some critics challenge the LEED certification standards and say that they fall short on the amount of energy that can be saved on any given project. The 2030 Architecture Initiative adopts a plan that doubles the amount of energy saved in building design. The NHBA, National Home Building Association, has also come up with it's own standard of measure for green building practice. The NHBA established this standard of measure to fill a need of contractors across the country who are building homes for clients who cannot afford high-end construction costs and still want to benefit from green building standards. This standard of measure or point system is similar to the LEED standards, with added considerations such as providing for building in different regions and climate zones.

If you are not able to afford all that you would like to include in this phase of your building project, ask your architect and contractor to help you plan ahead. How might you design your home to continue adding green elements in the future? There may be ways that you can prepare your design now to receive these options when you are able to afford them. An experienced and knowledgeable professional can also council you as to how to best spend the money that you do have to realize the most beneficial outcome of a sustainable design concept for your project.

I met an architect who expressed his frustration with the inability to receive LEED certification on his projects because his clients build very large-sized homes. He was saying how he incorporates green building into his designs and expends a lot of energy educating his clients to the advantages of the sustainable design. As a result of his insight most of his clients have cut their building size in half, going from 20,000 square feet to 10,000 square feet. While some of us may think that 10,000 square feet is huge, it's relative to your lifestyle and cutting your original plan in half does deserve credit.

Even though you may not receive LEED certification, you can still have a positive impact on the environment by implementing Green building elements to your home.

If not being certified is of concern to you, keep track of all the green building elements that your architect included in the building of your home. This can be helpful if you decide to sell.

Remodel Green

Those of you who are going to remodel your home can make green building choices too. Just because you are building onto an existing structure doesn't mean you can't incorporate green elements into this addition. You may be able to add something to the remodel plans that will benefit the rest of your house as well. Ask your architect and contractor when you do your initial walkthrough to offer their ideas, suggestions and what potential challenges exist.

There are going to be more and more opportunists taking advantage of this green building wave and you want to be able to keep your head above water. I was talking with an industry professional the other day and he told me that he could purchase a LEED certificate for $100 if he wanted to. His point was that homeowners need to be careful as to who they do business with.

It's important that you hire the right professionals who are knowledgeable and experienced in Green home building and sustainable design and have your financial investment and your family's home as their priorities.

to do list

Green/Sustainable Design Questions for an Architect, Contractor or Interior Designer

☐ What type of experience do you have with green building and sustainable design?

☐ Can you give me some names of other clients that you have done work for that includes this type of design?

☐ Do you have a portfolio that I can review?

☐ Do you see any specific challenges with my project?

☐ How much will using the green building elements in my design increase the cost of my project?

☐ How will you help me learn about these green building elements?

☐ Do you consider yourself to be a team player? How will you enlist the services of the other team members to enhance the overall design and building of my home?

☐ Tell me about the products that you suggest I consider using on my project.

☐ What type of research have you done with regard to these products?

☐ Why did you choose these products over others?

☐ Is your staff experienced in working with green building product?

☐ How is using these products going to increase my overall quality of living?

☐ What are the long-term benefits going to be from building with these green products?

☐ Will I have to adjust my family's lifestyle to use these products?

☐ What kind of upkeep am I looking at once my project is completed?

☐ What will you provide me with at the end of my project that will help me learn how to maintain my new green-built home?

☐ Do you guarantee your work?

☐ What types of follow-up should I expect from you with regard to these green building products?

Questions To Ask Client References

☐ Did you feel that this professional was knowledgeable in the application of green building and sustainable design?

☐ Did you stay within the budget that was originally provided for you?

☐ Has your family's quality of life been enhanced as a result of building green?

☐ Is there anything that you would do differently if given the opportunity to do it again?

☐ Have you maintained your home's green elements over the time you have lived in it?

☐ Were there any challenges that occurred on your project as a result of choosing this professional or from implementing green product into your design?

☐ What do you like the most about your new home?

☐ How did the architect or contractor carry out the whole green building concept on your project, i.e., site preparation, landscaping, design and construction?

☐ Are you LEED certified? What is your level of certification?

☐ Also consider asking your mortgage lender about special incentive packages for homeowners who are incorporating green building into their home design.

Visit my Web site to check out how my Proactive Homebuilding Method product line is contributing to the Forest Stewardship Council, www.FSC.org.

Woodmeister Master Builder's close attention to detail brought this contemporary unit in Back Bay Boston back to it's traditional roots of a Boston home. PHOTO CREDIT: ALEX BEATTY, ARCHITECTURAL MILLWORK: WOODMEISTER MASTER BUILDERS, INTERIOR DESIGNER: SELDOM SCENE INTERIORS, INTERIOR DECORATOR: SANDRA OSTER

CHAPTER eleven

hidden costs of pre-designed plans

When I make reference to pre-designed plans, I am not speaking about stock plans that you receive from a builder or developer offering you a limited amount of choices that fit within a set price for that home. The pre-designed plans that I am talking about here are the types of plans that you can order online, from a design book or that a contractor has provided for you. These plans don't come with predetermined choices. Two different homeowners could purchase the same set of pre-designed plans and one could finish out their home for $70,000 and the other for $1,200,000. It all depends on the choices you make.

These are plans that you decide on or purchase because you like the general layout, square footage and exterior. It's the main skeletal structure of a house and you are going to customize the inside and possibly exterior surface to suit your style and taste. You may move some rooms around or place your garage on the opposite side of the house, but for the most part, you are happy with this layout. And, by using this set of plans you assume that you are going to save the time and money that you would have to pay an architect to draw them from scratch.

You may be building in a development that has specific requirements such as the size of home you build and the style of architecture you choose. Most likely your plan is going to have to go through an approval process by a designated board representing the interests of the development you're building in. Whether your budget is $300,000 or $3,000,000, the majority of homes that are being built today are being built from pre-designed plans. Either the homeowner has found a plan or their contractor has provided them with one.

Oftentimes the homeowner either assumes or they are told that by building their home from a pre-designed set of plans they are going to save the time and money it would take to have an architect custom-design a home for them. What a homeowner does not know and oftentimes is not informed of, is that unlike the set of plans that you can get from an architect,

these plans don't come with a detailed set of specifications. Specifications are all the details that are going to go into the house as it's being built. This would include everything from the type of air conditioning unit to a Kohler faucet that is going to be installed in your home. These would be defined in the construction document that your architect provides to you.

Specifications Needed to Confirm Cost

Generally, a contractor is able to determine, given the amount of square footage that is in your plans, along with the types of materials you say you want to have included in your home, what the overall cost will be to build this house for you. They can tell you that your home is going to run you $200 or $300 a square foot. You calculate that price per foot and assume that you are in agreement as to what this house will cost to build. If you have not detailed or spec'd this out to confirm this price, how will you know what your allowances will pay for? You may purchase materials for one room that costs $200 a square foot and another room that costs $400 per square foot. Then, when you get into the process and discover that your allowances don't provide you with the amounts you need, you receive change orders for upgrades.

Remember, a contractor entering into a cost-plus agreement with their client to build this house is not taking the risk. They are going to get paid their fee regardless of the choices you make. It's you who is put at risk if you don't have your decisions made and your specifications spelled out at the front of your project.

Many builders will offer these types of plans to homeowners because the builder has already built from this plan or others similar to it. This makes the builder's job much easier. They know the product that they will order ahead of time. They have agreements with vendors that provide the materials that are used in building from these plans. A lot of builders will receive discounts from these vendors if they keep coming back to them for materials. The discount the contractor receives from this agreement is rarely passed on to the homeowner. By offering the client these plans, the contractor can also build more homes in less amount of time. The subs are well-versed in the applications called for in these plans and are able to move along quickly once construction begins.

Consider All Price Factors

Some pre-designed plans come with the cost to build included. What you don't know is what part of the country that these costs are based upon. Your state's building cost could be much higher. Also, you need to consider whether or not this plan was designed to be built on a site like yours. Perhaps you have a steep slope on one side of your property that is going to require a very expensive retaining wall. If your lot has a stone slab or colluvial soil to deal with, your excavation and footing costs could put you way over budget before you begin building. You may even have to add a basement instead of the crawlspace that your plan calls for. This type of information has to be worked out by someone at some point in your project's process. Without these details upfront you are susceptible to walking into a quagmire of home-building mishaps and expenses.

Before you decide to build a home from a pre-designed set of plans, I want you to consider this. To be successful and to build this home within your budget restrictions you are going to have to follow my PHM™ and make use of the tools I offer. You do not have the benefit of working with a proactive design team that has integrated both your specifications and budget restrictions throughout the development of these plans. And you didn't have their expertise to guide you in making your decisions on the front-end of your project. An equally serious limitation in building from this pre-designed set of plans is that you don't have the opportunity to fine-tune the design and customize it to your and your family's needs. In a design process with an architect or home designer you have the ability to develop and define the spaces, if need be, meaning, you can adjust the space in the developing floor plan. When working with

an already existing set of plans you are more at the mercy of working within its parameters or limitations.

If you are serious about setting a budget on the front-end of this project, you will have to spend the time it takes to define your specifications just as you would with an architect. You and whoever makes up your homebuilding team are going to have to flesh out these details. You want to make sure that you have hired an experienced proactive thinking contractor that is willing to be up-front with you and take the necessary time to educate you as to the information that is not included in the plans that will affect your costs. Then, you want to know how they are going to help you fill in the blanks, defining the specifications and providing adequate allowances or educating you about your limitations before construction begins. Make sure this contractor understands that you plan on taking the extra time upfront to make all the choices that you are responsible for before you begin building.

You also want to make sure that this contractor can handle any changes that you might want to make to this set of plans. Walk through this information during the interview process. Ask for references of other clients for whom they have done similar work. Visit those homes. Confirm that these changes are on the same scale as those you want to make.

If you are building in a development and you are limited as to whom you can hire to build your home, interview a number of your choices. Use the interview process just as you would if you were able to choose builders outside the development. Don't assume that because you are moving into a development, even if it's high-end homes, that you are going to have a great experience because this builder is considered a master builder by the development's standards. Neither should you assume that the owners of the development are going to take responsibility for your project, should something go wrong.

Visit homes in your neighborhood that each builder has built. When you receive references from these builders, ask if they can provide

Walnut cabinets aged using a multi-step glazing technique, ceiling is hand-painted fabric, and raised panels in the home office are just some of the exquisite details that Woodmeister brought to this contemporary high-rise unit located in the heart of Boston. PHOTO CREDIT: ANDREA BRIZZI, INTERIOR DESIGNER: RICHARD FITZGERALD & MICHAEL LEE OF RICHARD FITZGERALD INC., GENERAL CONTRACTOR: WOODMEISTER MASTER BUILDERS.

you with a couple of extra references outside of this development. That way, you will be talking with people other than potential neighbors who are likely to say everything is wonderful (or they wouldn't still be living there.) Ask these references if you can visit their homes as well. I strongly urge you to hire an experienced interior designer for this project, too. When you are interviewing both the builder and the designer, determine if they are team players and would welcome each other's insight in getting your plans spec'd out so you can establish a realistic budget before construction begins.

Don't expect a builder to put in hours of their time and not be compensated for this consultation process. Tell each builder in the interview that you know their time is valuable and you plan to compensate them for their consultation. Some may offer to include this cost as part of their building fee if you hire them.

If a builder tells you flat out that they don't have the time it would take to help you with this phase, move on. There could be a number of reasons why they don't want their clients to have this information — none that you want to stick around for. If you are in a position to have to work with this builder, and, after meeting

them, you still want to live in this development, I would set up a meeting with the board of directors. Explain your process and have them help you come up with a solution. Being proactive in this situation may take some effort, but it will be vital in limiting the costly surprises that are likely to occur during construction.

Some contractors that I have interviewed have no problem working with pre-designed plans. Their opinion is that these plans have been thoroughly developed and have been built so many times that the kinks are ironed out — the building process goes smoothly. I have also talked with contractors who will not work from a pre-designed set of plans because of the lack of information provided. I had one contractor tell me straight-out that anyone who would consider building from a set of pre-designed plans is crazy.

The attorney that you have hired based on the information in this book should also be of help to you. Have them review any legal documents that you receive from your contractor and the developers. Get a clear understanding of what you will and what you will not be getting from both parties as to the protection of your homebuilding assets.

interview

Richard Dykman
Architect/Contractor
Executive Vice President, Boran Craig Barber Engel Construction Co., Inc.

Richard is a 35-year veteran of the construction industry. He was an architect for the first fifteen years of his career and has been a contractor who uses his architectural background for the last twenty. I visited some of Richard's condos when I was in Sarasota, Florida. The first thing that I noticed about his company's work was the quality with which his condos were built. They weren't just esthetically attractive; there was cohesiveness between the quality, craftsmanship and esthetics that I appreciated. The units under construction were clean and orderly. It was obvious the attention to detail was important to his company and the developers he works for. Richard's construction firm builds both high-end high-rise condominiums and high-end homes. He attributes his business's success to his and his staff's proactive mindsets when it comes to working with their clients; both the end user (the buyer client) and the developer.

WHAT TYPE OF RELATIONSHIP DO YOU HAVE WITH THE CLIENTS YOU BUILD RESIDENCES FOR?
In my end of the business, most of our clients are high-end developers who build high-rise condominiums for buyers, but we do interface with each buyer. We have a field person at the level of what types of changes we make and we have a staff person on site to work with the end user on changes.

IS THAT FIELD PERSON LIKE A PROJECT MANAGER?
Yes, we call them a buyer-change coordinator. They get involved with each unit owner for changes that they may want to make in their unit. We also have a person that remains in the job six to twelve months after the project is completed and they interface with all the owners. They would be the post-construction coordinator, helping with those little things that don't quite work right during that period.

IN YOUR OPINION, WHAT ARE SOME OF THE MOST COMMON MISTAKES WOMEN MAKE WHEN DEALING WITH THE CONSTRUCTION ENVIRONMENT?
Not understanding the process and how important their role is going to be in it. Men are the same way. They don't understand our business, how it works and what they're going to get. It all comes down to the need for good communication between the builder and the client. Many times the client thinks they're going to get something that they may not get because of the limited depth of communication between them and the contractor or them and the architect. Then the problem becomes, what you thought you said, or, I heard that differently.

AND WHAT DO YOU SUGGEST BE DONE TO IMPROVE ON THAT?
There has to be better education of the end user. In my business this would be the client. There's got to be better education from the contractor side, and even from the architect's side, if they're involved on a single-family house.

WHAT TYPE OF INFORMATION DO YOU THINK WOULD BENEFIT THE HOMEOWNER AND HELP THEM UNDERSTAND BETTER?
A lot of times a homeowner will go to an architect and say, "This is what I want, give me this," but they don't follow through with that information to make sure that what they wanted actually got placed into the design. They assume that by simply tossing that information out to the architect that that's what they're going to get. They can't assume, they have to follow through. I know the guys in our single family home division spend a lot of time, after the drawings are done, sitting down with the owners and going through each room again — each facet of their home — and getting the homeowner to sign off on it.

What we have found is that during this review process, they'll make a comment to us or to an architect, and generally speaking, what they had in their mind can be different from what we have in our mind. For instance, someone will say, "You know, here's a bar area but you don't have a sink," and the owner will say, "What do you mean I don't have a sink? I told the architect to add it in." But no one followed through. Follow-up is very important to make sure everyone is on the same page. We are pro-active with the end user to make sure that they are getting what they want. I think that that's how you have to be — totally proactive.

Also, it's important for the homeowner to educate themselves about the products they want in their home so they're not surprised by something they did or didn't get. For example, I've chosen my master bath countertop from a small sample of marble. Once it's installed I didn't realize it would have so many veins running through it because I didn't take the time to see a full slab before I said OK.

That happens all the time. We have 12" by 12" marble samples that we show to an owner. When they see the 8'-long by 2'-wide bathroom top, they say, "This isn't what I picked out." Marble is a natural product and has a lot of variations. We try to get five pieces of that marble to show them the variations, otherwise, they'll ask us to rip things out of a building even though stones are natural and will vary — it's just a lack of communication. The customer will like this color, but this is not Corian, it's stone, so it's not going to look the same. The customer needs to understand what they are getting.

IN YOUR YEARS OF EXPERIENCE AS AN ARCHITECT INVOLVED IN THE DESIGN PROCESS OF A RESIDENCE AS WELL AS BEING A CONTRACTOR THAT OVERSEES THE CONSTRUCTION OF THE RESIDENCE, WHAT ARE SOME OF THE PITFALLS YOU SEE PEOPLE FALLING INTO THAT MIGHT MAKE THE BUILDING PROCESS OF THEIR HOME MORE COMPLICATED THAN IT HAS TO BE?

One of the things that happens quite frequently with homes is that people make a lot of changes during construction. There's nothing worse for a builder then to have the momentum of a project disrupted to where it throws the schedule off. The project is sailing along, being built off the set of plans that everybody has agreed to and all of a sudden, whoops, we're going to spend $100,000 because we don't like the way the kitchen is and we're going to move all kinds of stuff around. That's just detrimental to the whole process.

GIVE ME A BIG PICTURE AS TO WHY.

For example, the homeowner is limited in understanding why that would be such a big deal. They don't understand the process.

EXACTLY, SO EXPLAIN IT SO THE HOMEOWNER CAN UNDERSTAND. WHEN A HOMEOWNER MAKES A DECISION TO CHANGE SOMETHING LIKE THAT, HOW DOES THAT AFFECT THE BIG PICTURE OF THEIR OVERALL PROJECT?

The process of construction is like getting a big ship out of port. You have all these materials arriving on site. You also have all these people that are working together to make this project come together. There are schedules to be met and all of the subcontractors have set up their schedules in anticipation of this project. They estimate, "I'm going to have to give this job four days and then my business plan is that I move on to my next project to hang the drywall, then I've got the next project to go to and then I've got the next project." They have their schedules arranged to do these things in an expeditious way that keeps things moving.

Think about it. A drywall guy is on this project and he hangs all the drywall. Then the cabinet guy comes in and starts hanging the cabinets. Different subcontractors have to poke holes in the drywall to add electrical outlets and wire. Same thing with the plumbing and everything else needed to bring life to the house.

Then the homeowner comes in and says, "Oh, wait a minute. I don't like this. We've got to change it, how much is it going to cost me to rip this kitchen out, I want to move the sink over here and I want to do this and that." Guess what? Now you've got to go back and pull the subcontractor that is four jobs down the road and has started the framing and the sheetrock on another project. He's got to leave that project and come back. The cabinets need to be taken out because the electrical and plumbing holes are in the wrong place for this new change. He's got to patch and refinish the drywall. The plumber's got to come back in, the electrician's got to come back in to run new wires, etc. Now everybody is in a backwards slide. There are a lot of people involved in building a home, and they have business plans for numerous projects so that they can run their business in a certain time frame.

Schedule, schedule, schedule — that's the most important thing to a builder, the most important thing. If you keep your jobs on schedule, you'll be a successful builder. If you don't keep your jobs on schedule, you're in trouble all the way down the line. So changes disrupt schedules. Disruption of schedule is detrimental to the process. It not only costs money, but it causes chaos.

IT'S IMPORTANT FOR A HOMEOWNER TO UNDERSTAND THEIR RESPONSIBILITIES. EITHER THEY GO ON THEIR OWN OR WITH THEIR DESIGNER OR ARCHITECT OR CONTRACTOR TO A SHOWROOM, OR TO ANOTHER HOME OR RESIDENCE, WHERE THEY SEE PRODUCTS INSTALLED. IT'S GOING TO MAKE A DIFFERENCE AS TO WHETHER OR NOT THEY'RE GOING TO LIKE IT VERSUS ASSUMING THIS IS WHAT I WANT, HAVING IT PUT IN, IT'LL BE FINE AND THEN HAVING TO MAKE A CHANGE.

That's right. The more homeowners can go and see a finished product of a builder or an architect, the better off they're going to be. They need to spend the time doing it.

WHEN A HOMEOWNER LOOKS AT A SET OF PLANS AND THEY FEEL LIKE A DEER IN HEADLIGHTS AND THEY GO, "OKAY, I CAN'T VISUALIZE WHAT THIS IS GOING TO LOOK LIKE," WHAT DO YOU SUGGEST THE NEXT STEP BE FOR THEM TO GAIN CLARITY?

I think they need to spend more time with it. If they don't understand, they should never say, "Okay." They should say, "I don't understand. Show me what I'm getting. Make me a three-dimensional drawing, use the CAD or take me someplace and show me what it will look like." The homeowner should not let the building process start until they fully understand what they're getting.

IN THE HIGH-END CONSTRUCTION INDUSTRY, IT IS COMMON FOR A HOMEOWNER TO HAVE BUILT OR RENOVATED NUMEROUS HOMES. WHAT DO YOU THINK THAT HOMEOWNER LEARNS ALONG THE WAY REGARDING THE HOMEBUILDING PROCESS THAT COULD BENEFIT A HOMEOWNER THAT WILL MOST LIKELY BUILD ONE HOME IN THEIR LIFETIME?

Experience. I was talking to our home guy the other day about a current project for a high-end client. It's about an $8,000,000 house for this client who was the CEO of a major corporation in the United States. This client told our guys, "I've built seventeen homes in the last twenty to thirty years." Then he said, "Working with you guys has been the best experience I've ever had. My wife and I have learned lots of lessons, but I've never seen someone as proactive as your company in terms of telling me what I'm going to get and explaining each and every component of my house before I started construction."

That is so important for any contractor and architect, as a team, to explain to an owner what's on those two-dimensional drawings that's now going to be converted to a three-dimensional space. An owner has to have that desire to want to understand and push to get it, because all contractors and architects aren't that proactive.

THE PEOPLE THAT HAVE BUILT NUMEROUS TIMES UNDERSTAND THE IMPORTANCE OF WORKING AS A TEAM. WHEREAS, SOMEONE GOING IN FOR THE FIRST TIME DOESN'T. UNFORTUNATELY FOR MOST HOMEOWNERS, THEY HAVE BUILT THEIR ONE AND ONLY HOME AND NOT HAD THE BENEFIT OF ALLOWING THE EXPERTISE OF AN ARCHITECT TO IMPROVE THEIR OVERALL EXPERIENCE.

That's why it's so important not to jump into this process. Don't get so focused on the price of something right out of the gate — don't look for the cheapest deal. Bottom line: You get what you pay for, and things won't work successfully one-hundred percent of the time. But, if you put that aside and focus on hiring good people that have great track records and may charge a little more and work on having good communication, you're going to be better off in the long run. The builder and architect — they're working for you. You're paying them. You need to hold them accountable to explain things to you if you don't understand what it is they're giving you based on what you want. It's important that you realize you're the boss on this project. Don't let the architect and the builder run over you. You need to listen to them, but you're the person that makes the decisions, and that's what you have to understand. There's no stupid question. If somebody's telling you something you have no concept of, you need to say, "Wait a minute, time out. I don't understand this. We're not going any further until I do, so you guys start explaining it to me."

WHEN A HOMEOWNER EITHER PURCHASES OR IS GIVEN A SET OF PRE-DESIGNED PLANS FROM THEIR BUILDER, THOSE PLANS ARE VAGUE AS FAR AS SPECIFICATIONS AND OTHER INFORMATION

THAT IS IMPORTANT TO THE HOMEOWNER. HOW WOULD THEIR BUILDER SET REALISTIC ALLOWANCES FOR THEM?

You would be much better off not having any allowances. Get everything defined and get a final price for what you want. Never start a project with anything that's vague in terms of specifications, money or anything else. I know building a house is an emotional issue but you've got to put that aside. It's a business, it needs to be treated like a business. I don't want any allowances. I want to know what my specs are, I want to know what I'm getting and I want to know what I'm spending. I want to understand it and then we'll go forward. That's what has to happen. You've got to put the emotion aside and become a businessperson.

WHEN YOU ARE BUILDING A RESIDENCE FOR A CLIENT, WHAT TYPES OF INFORMATION DOES THAT CLIENT OR SOMEONE REPRESENTING THE CLIENT USUALLY REQUEST TO SEE FROM YOU OR YOUR COMPANY?

- When you're hiring a contractor, a builder and an architect, it's important to research their history.
- Talk to three or four individuals about the builder and/or architect they've hired. You shouldn't say, "Oh, well, they gave these names to me and I know they're going to give me good references so I don't have to call and talk with these people.
- Ask the builder about their financial strength, who their banker is and follow up with that banker.
- Confirm that the builder has the size and the financial strength to build your project.
- Ask what subcontractors they do business with in the community.
- You want to make sure that your contractor has the knowledge of the product type, what your home's requirements are and that they can meet those requirements.
- You need to find someone who has a personality that can work with the team. It's very important to have a personality fit between the client, the architect, and the builder. That just makes the whole process go so much better.

WHAT QUESTIONS WOULD YOU SUGGEST A HOMEOWNER ASK WHEN FOLLOWING UP WITH A REFERENCE PERSON?

- I would start by saying, "I got your name from so-and-so builder or so-and-so architect. They said that they had worked with you. I'm thinking about hiring them and I'd like to know your opinion of how the process went."
- What were their strengths, what were their weaknesses?
- Did they get the project done on time?
- Were the change orders excessive?
- Did they treat you professionally?
- Did they follow up afterwards?
- Were they proactive in the design phase, the building phase and the financial part?
- Have them give you a complete run-down. Spend time with them. Ask them these questions and you may find they'll start off by saying, "They really did a great job," and then further into the conversation you'll find out that "while they did a great job, they were two months late and the project cost twenty-five percent more than the original bid. I didn't make too many changes and I'm ticked about it." Maybe there's a trend there.

WHAT MIGHT BE SOME WARNING SIGNS FOR THE HOMEOWNER, SIGNALING THAT THIS MAY NOT BE SOMEONE THEY ARE GOING TO WORK WITH?

- Of course, there's the gut feeling that you get when you talk to anybody about doing business.
- There's no free ride. I think that people tend to think that contractors are like automobile manufacturers, that all cars run. The Mercedes looks better than the Chevy, but they all run. Unfortunately, in the construction industry we're not selling cars. You've got people out there building a car for you, so to speak. They're building a building for you. Don't expect it to be too cheap — never go with the cheapest guy.
- I'd be leery of contractors that ask for a bunch of money upfront before they do anything on your project.
- You need to find out what their workload is.
- If they're not going to give you any references, not going to tell you about themselves, not open, honest and upfront, you stay away from those kinds of people.

YOU HAVE TAKEN GREAT CARE IN COMPILING A HOMEOWNER'S MANUAL ON BEHALF OF YOUR CLIENTS. TELL ME WHAT THIS MANUAL CONSISTS OF AND HOW AND WHY YOU CAME TO DEVELOP IT.

We developed a homeowner's manual because we felt that we needed something to give our developer's clients. When the job is over, we tell them what they have in their unit, who the subcontractors were, what they need to do if they have a problem, what they need to do for maintenance — of all these issues. I hate to go back to the car thing, but when you buy a car you get a DVD or a book that tells you all of these things. We feel that the new owner of a condominium — many who come out of single family homes — have no idea of what to do, because condominiums are different than homes. The manual works for homes too, but you have to be able to graphically and verbally portray how you take care of the railing on your porch, who to call if you've got a problem, what's going to happen long-term and how to maintain it.

I NOTICED IN YOUR MANUAL THAT YOU REFERENCE ALL OF THE SUBCONTRACTORS THAT DO THE WORK, WHETHER IT'S THE ELECTRICIAN OR THE PLUMBER AND THEY PUT THEIR WARRANTY INFORMATION IN THERE. SHOULD A HOMEOWNER WHO IS BUILDING A RESIDENCE HAVE ONE OF THESE MANUALS?

Absolutely. That would be great for anybody. I don't know how many homebuilders give those books out. Perhaps the small guys don't, but the homeowner should know who the subcontractors are. Obviously, in a warranty or a problem situation, they'll call their contractor. But if the contractor is out of business or has moved, it's nice to know who the subcontractor was, because sometimes the subcontractors will honor warranties.

IT WOULD BE THE INFORMATION REGARDING THE SUBCONTRACTOR'S, THEIR COMPANY'S NAME AND WHAT THEY DID.

Yes, you just say electrical so-and-so subcontractor, list their phone number and the contact person. Think about it this way — in the future, an owner may want to add three lights, move two switches and add an electrical outlet. Instead of getting someone that doesn't know the project, you've got someone that has already worked on it. If there's a problem with the original subcontractor, you might want to make a change. In the condominium business, that's very important, because in Florida we have some very stringent warranty requirements by statute. We like the same subcontractors to be involved in any changes.

HOW CAN THE ROLE THE HOMEOWNER TAKES ON HELP AND/OR HINDER THE PROGRESS OF THE CONSTRUCTION PROJECT?

A Proactive homeowner who's involved in the process of design and construction can help immensely by knowing what they want, making decisions early and making sure they are getting everything they want in the plans. I think that they need to spend enough time in the selection process to get the right people — people who have a track record of doing the kind of product that this homeowner likes, that have great reputations and have good financial backing. If you get the right architect, the right contractor and the right owner, the three of them can work together to develop a product. If they're communicating well, they're asking questions and it's all an open book, they're going to come out of the gate with 90% of it behind them.

REGARDING INSURANCE COVERAGE OF THE BUILDER WHEN HE'S BUILDING IN A DEVELOPMENT, THE HOMEOWNER MAY ASSUME THAT THE DEVELOPMENT TAKES CARE OF INSURING THE BUILDER. IS THAT THE CASE?

No, there are several kinds of insurance that the builder needs to have. First, any home needs a builder's risk policy, which the owner needs to make sure the builder provides. The builder's risk policy is an insurance policy that protects against fire, damage and things like that during construction. The builder has to have a GL (general liability) policy, workers comp, automobile, etc. When you ask your builder for a certificate of insurance, you'll get his GL. Each state has statutory limits for what builders need to have.

WHAT IS FLORIDA'S STATUTE LIMIT?

It's two million dollars on liability — a company like ours has a lot more because there's a lot more expense. It's important to talk to the builder and their insurance provider about their policy. Find out what your state requires builders carry for general liability insurance.

A Woodmeister designed kitchen incorporates both a clean–up area for storage and prep area for that is conveniently located by the pantry, fridge and sink. PHOTO CREDIT: GARY SLOAN, ARCHITECTURAL MILLWORK: WOODMEISTER MASTER BUILDERS, GENERAL CONTRACTOR: KISTLER & KNAPP

And then, of course, after the house is completed and you get the certificate of occupancy, the homeowner has to make sure that they have homeowner's insurance in place to cover fire and all those kinds of things.

IT'S COMMON FOR A BUILDER TO WARRANTY THEIR WORK FOR A YEAR. THERE IS A STATUTE WITHIN EACH STATE AS TO HOW LONG THE BUILDER IS ACTUALLY RESPONSIBLE FOR THAT WORK.
That's true. I know in condominium work, again, because that's what I'm most familiar with, it's one year on the unit and three years on the common element, and it can be a lot more depending on if there's some late defects. It could be up to fifteen years. That's the Florida statute. In the single-family arena I'm not sure.

IS THERE ANYTHING ELSE THAT A HOMEOWNER MIGHT ASSUME THE SUBDIVISION IS TAKING CARE OF AND IN FACT THEY LEAVE THE RESPONSIBILITY UP TO THE HOMEOWNER?
You need to make sure that you've got sewer, water and road access. Most developments provide sewer, water, road access and you pay to hook up to their system. Homeowners need to verify certain impact fees that municipalities charge to hook up at permitting time. In Florida, a building permit will cost a certain amount — say you build a house and a building permit might cost $8,000. There are also $25,000 of impact fees. You need to be clear with your builder about who pays the impact fees and what they are. The impact fees can be for schools, fire, water, sewer, regional parks, libraries, etc.

Development is paying for development. Road impact fees are excessively high. So make sure that you understand, as a homeowner, what you can afford to pay. When you're building a two or three million dollar house, you're not worried about twenty-five, thirty or forty thousand dollars, but if you're building a $500,000 or $600,000 house, that's a lot of money. When you get a price from your builder, make sure that he outlines all these fees. A lot of builders might leave that out and later on say, oh, that's something you pay for.

The same thing can happen with soil. Most of the time, when you buy in a community that already has lots and builders, soil borings or any kind of exploratory work are probably ironed out. But, that's another thing to ask the builder, the architect or the development community when you go in and buy the land.

remodeling
your home

When it comes to taking on a remodeling project, adopting a PHM™ mindset is one of the most important homebuilding essentials that I can pass on to you. I received an email from Tammy Swenson, a Public Relations representative in Minneapolis. At the time, Tammy was working with one of her clients in New York. This particular morning she happened upon the Today Show while in her hotel room. The featured topic was titled, "How to not get ripped off by your contractor." When I followed up on the story, the homeowners being interviewed were mostly people involved in remodeling projects. These homeowners had made the unfortunate mistakes I address and help you to avoid in this book. They went into their projects ill-prepared and unknowledgeable as to how to identify, follow up on and hire the right professional to help them protect their home remodeling investment.

First Considerations

Professionals admit that renovating a home is different than building a new home. Whether renovating your existing home or renovating a house that you are going to purchase, your project will come with a special set of circumstances that you need to consider before the process begins.

Characteristically, homeowners new to the remodeling process tend to be even more lax in identifying with the seriousness of viewing their remodeling project as a financial venture than homeowners who are building new construction. They tend to let their guard down when it comes to preparing and following up on the professionals they are going to hire. They make the assumption that because they are working on a smaller area of their home it will need a lesser degree of their attention. This is evidenced by who they hire, how they manage their remodeling budget, not getting proper design elements in place before they begin their project and rushing the process to accommodate misguided priorities — such as making the decision in June to get the kitchen and dining room done before the family comes out for Thanksgiving. When a homeowner takes on the challenge

to remodel, it's just as emotionally charged as building new, if not more so. You have been living in this space for years, dreaming about how great it would be to make a change. Then, once the potential for making this change becomes a reality, the excitement kicks in, followed by the impatience to get it done. Now!

You do not want to be making decisions from this highly emotionally charged mindset. Think long term, the bigger picture. This remodel, if done poorly, now affects your entire home value, not just the space that was worked on.

If you log onto the National Association of the Remodeling Industry's web site, www.nari.org, and review what the professionals say about the types of questions homeowners are asking them during an interview, it sheds some light on how and why millions of dollars are lost annually by homeowners entering into their remodeling projects ill-prepared and short-sighted. A PHM™ homeowner will enter into their remodeling project with the understanding that they need to be thorough in following up on the information from every potential team member before making the decision to hire them to work on their home.

Regardless of the size of your budget or if your project requires one contractor or a builder and their crew, you've most likely settled on this amount because it is what you can afford or it's what your home can sustain at this time. It's all relative; it's still a costly investment. And if not managed correctly by you from the very beginning, starting with who you hire, a relatively low budget remodel can become a very expensive heartache. You are responsible for making these important decisions and, as I pointed out earlier in the book, if something goes wrong on your project, it is ultimately you that will be held financially responsible to a lender and you who will suffer the consequences.

In a renovation, you want to hire a professional who is experienced in the type of work that your project is going to require. You do not want to hire a contractor who has not done renovation projects. An architect or contractor who has only worked on new construction is not going to have the experience to anticipate and deal with the hidden surprises that are inevitable in a renovation, especially if your home is older and requires someone who is knowledgeable with integrating different materials. You will want someone who you can depend on to give you an accurate estimate of costs. You do not want to be halfway through your project and out of money because the estimate you received upfront was not adequate for the work you needed done.

An architect can help you draw up plans and coordinate spaces so they flow seamlessly from the existing part of the home onto the addition. If you are renovating a historical home, an architect and interior designer who is experienced in the style appointment of that era will be invaluable in keeping true to your home's details that are so important in a historical renovation.

The first person you want on your team is your loan officer. Once you have determined who that is, walk through your intentions with this person, and get pre-qualified for your loan. This is going to help you enter into your project with a realistic budget in mind.

Start Out in the Know — Get Prequalified

• Talk with a realtor who is familiar with the neighborhood in which you will be doing the work. Confirm that this neighborhood will support the cost of this renovation. Ask to see specs from other homes in the area that are currently the same size and quality that yours will be once your remodel is completed.

• Depending on the scale of your renovation, ask an architect or contractor to walk through the property to provide you with an expert opinion and reality check as to how much this renovation is going to cost you. This professional can tell you, given the age and condition of the house, if you can expect additional costs, i.e., asbestos removal or extra foundation support, etc. You don't want to purchase a home assuming that you can afford both the house and the renovation only to find that the hidden costs of the renovation are so extensive that you can't afford to do the work.

• Also check with the city or county codes department to confirm that the work you want to do is within the parameters of what is being accepted. Some areas are reestablishing their building requirements, changing their codes and restricting what homeowners can and cannot do. You may live next to a neighborhood where homeowners are permitted to build a certain size house. However, in your neighborhood you may be limited as to the amount of square feet you can build. Your neighbor may not want you to build a second story onto your home because it obstructs their view. If the architect or contractor that you are consulting with has recently done work on a house close by, they will be able to provide you with this information as well.

• If purchasing a home with plans to renovate, combine the cost of this house along with the cost of your remodel. If the total amount is within keeping of the homes around you, you can be confident that this is going to be a good investment for you.

• Bring the above information, along with your financial records, to your loan officer and have them pre-qualify you for your loan.

If you are planning on buying an already existing house and remodeling it before you move in, do so only after you have walked through your intentions with an architect and contractor. When you look at an already existing structure, you are able to pick out the flaws and obvious problems that are easily distinguishable. However, it takes a trained eye to also include the surprise scenarios that are hidden behind the walls. Before you begin spending too much time and energy contemplating what could be, you need to enlist the services of a professional or two to help you assess the reality. Enlisting the counsel of a professional early on can also provide you with creative alternatives that you would not have considered.

FINDING YOUR BUILDING TEAM

There are numerous ways to find a potential home designer, architect or contractor — first being word of mouth. If you have a friend, neighbor or work associate who has recently gone through this process and they are pleased with the outcome, get their referral information. Drive around the neighborhood that you want to remodel in and see what type of work is being done. If you find a project that interests you, ask the homeowners about the contractor they are using to do the work. Another great resource is an architect, realtor or an interior designer that you may have a relationship with. All are used to using contractors for their work. If you are new to an area or don't have any personal contacts to confer with, check out these web sites: NARI (National Association of The Remodeling Industry) www.nari.org, AIA (American Institute of Architects) for information about architects, AIA.org, NHBA (National Home Builders Association) NHBA.org. These sites will guide you to professionals in your area who will be knowledgeable in remodeling. Always follow up on these professionals by using the PHM™ interview and review process.

Your goal is to get professional advice before making a purchase that may limit your possibilities or cost much more than you anticipated when renovating. If you are remodeling your existing home, you will need the insight of a professional as well. At this point of the process the professional is hired as a consultant. How they handle this initial meeting may help you determine whether or not you want to hire them to actually do the work on the project. Meet with a number of individuals to get their opinions and perspectives on your project.

Once you have found the professionals that you want to come look at your project, ask them if there is going to be a fee involved to have them assess your situation. Some contractors and architects may want to be compensated for their time. Others will consider this to be an opportunity to get to know you and your project, just as you want to get to know them. Either way, consider paid and gratis professionals as possibilities. If the fact that one of the contractors or architects charges you for their time is a bit off-putting to you, bear in mind that if this person were to meet and advise every person who called them up, and they didn't get compensated for that time, they would not be able to sustain their business.

Most contractors and architects who charge you for this time will throw that fee into their total budget mix if you hire them to do the work. Make the initial phone call, describe briefly what your plans are and ask if they are interested and what their current timeframe is. Ask how they handle consultant fees. If you are talking with a contractor, ask how he likes working with architects or home designers. When talking with an architect or home designer ask how they like working with contractors. Let them know that it is your intention to have a collaborative team of professionals working on this project.

From this initial visit you will get a feel for whom you want to set up formal interviews with. Reschedule an interview time to meet and discuss your project in more detail. At this time you will use the information from my preview, interview and review section of this book. While you are scheduling your interview dates, set aside time to meet up with an attorney as well.

Your Attorney

You will want to have your attorney in place before you sign any agreements with someone you hire. The PHM™ homeowner would not hire anyone without having a signed contract that has first been reviewed by their attorney who is specialized in construction law. The attorney will help you review any contracts that have been provided by your architect or contractor. If, during your interview with a homebuilding professional, it is determined that they do not have a contract that they typically use, this can be a red flag. You can check out examples of contracts by going to Web sites such as www.uslegalforms.com, American Institute of Architects, www.AIA.org (they provide a great owner/contractor agreement), National Association of Remodeling Industry, www.nari.org and National Association of Home Builders, www.nahb.org. Use the information from these and other resources to learn about the points that you will want to see in the contracts that are presented to you. If you purchase a contract from one of these sites, you still need to have your attorney review this contract and confirm that you understand everything that it is or is not providing for you. It is not a Proactive move on your part to pay hundreds of thousands of dollars for a remodel and not take the additional time needed to protect that money. It's better to pay a few hundred dollars upfront on legal fees than to lose your remodeling investment.

The amount of work you are going to have done will determine the details you need to include in your contract. If it's a small project you can simply include the project specifications, cost and schedule of time it will take to complete, along with the contractor's personal information such as name, phone number, fax, license number and their insurance certificate. For a larger, more complicated project, you will want to include all of the above along with more specific detailing that pertains to your project. Things to consider are:

- Name and all contact information of contractor.
- License number of contractor.
- Contractor's warranty agreement listing the warranty information along with a list of all manufacturers and subcontractors who are warranting their work and products.
- Insurance certificates with current information and your name on them as additional *name insured*. Include a clause that says the contractor will only hire insured workers to work on your project.
- Certificate copy of a bond ,if you are requesting one, can be important for remodels.
- Blueprints, drawings and other visual representation that will be used in clarifying the work that is to be done on your project.
- The builder obtains permits for work to be done; a description of the project, specifications detailing all materials to be used, i.e., product brand name, model, size, color, etc. Include all warranty information on products to be used, where it was purchased or who supplied it.

(Architect's construction documents will have this information on them.)

- Phases of project and what work is to be done with each phase.
- Overall cost of your project with detailed line items including allowances.
- Sequence of payments to be paid out during the project — after review and acceptance of work by homeowner. Ask for phases to be broken down for you by the contractor with the percentage of work to be done at each draw request.
- Upon draw request, receipts need to be provided for project costs to date.
- A penalty clause to protect you the homeowner. Talk to your architect and contractor about this clause when doing a remodel. Given the extent, "hidden work" needs to be considered. Then talk with your attorney.
- Lien releases to stipulate that your contractor is responsible for any liens filed against you and your project for non-payment to their workers or to their suppliers during and after work is completed on the project.
- No work is to be done until a change order is issued. Detailed information about the change is laid out, the scope of the work to be done and the homeowner and contractor have signed off on the change at the cost agreed upon by the homeowner.
- Project schedule should include beginning date, completion date and dates for progress and financial report meetings.
- You have the right to fire the contractor if they or their subcontractors are doing work that is defective, incompetent or detrimental to your home and your project.
- Resolution-of-conflict information (Read the section in chapter one about arbitration versus mediation.)
- You have a right to cancel your contract within three days if it was signed someplace other than the business place of your remodeling contractor (Federal Trade and Commissions, FTC cooling-off rule).
- Add any other details that may relate to your property or your home while work is progressing. For example, where to and where not

to park cars, off-limit areas of the house and the hours the workers are going to be working.

• If you are renovating a historical home you will want to specify how things like asbestos testing, lead paint testing and removal of these materials are going to be handled. (A contractor would most likely handle the hiring and coordination of a sub for this, or you will have to hire a specialist. Find out during your interviewing process.)

• If you're having work done on a damaged home, ask your attorney how to best provide any additional information resulting from this damage, in your contract. For example, mold removal, smoke and fire related damage, water damage.

• If you are having any work done that will require a specialist, such as a sound studio, computer wiring for a home office or installation of special equipment, provide this information in your contract. You will want to know who is going to do the work required and get any necessary warranty, insurance and contact information.

When using the services of an architect on your project, they can also help you navigate through the contractual process. After getting a contract completed with your architect, run it by your attorney before signing it.

PHM™ Remodeling Interview

The PHM™ interview process can be one of the most enjoyable stages of your building project. This will be the beginning of your hypothetical newly-built house coming to life. It's exciting, and it will be your first opportunity to exercise your role as CEO (Chief Executive Officer) of your homebuilding venture. Emotionally charged, and new to the homebuilding experience, homeowners can be vulnerable to hiring someone prematurely out of the desire to start right away and under the assumption that all architects know how to design homes and all builders know how to build them. Remember the homebuilding mantra — *don't assume, confirm*. You are going to be using this mantra throughout your entire project.

In the interview process, don't assume that because one person had a good experience with someone that you automatically will. Don't assume that because someone goes to your church, coaches your kid's softball team, is a neighbor of yours or is related to you or your friend who recommended them, that that guarantees you a good homebuilding experience. Don't assume that someone is going to be loyal to you because they have a great personality.

Like attracts like. If you start out with someone who isn't qualified, experienced, reliable, trustworthy and truly desiring to work on your project, rest assured that the people that work for them will be like-minded as well.

Communication will be the key element to the success of your homebuilding experience. You need to establish a PHM™ communicative environment from the beginning so everyone you involve yourself with understands that this will be the basis for how your project will run. This means that on your end, you will be forthcoming with any and all questions or concerns you may have about entering into the design and building process of your project, as well as answering questions posed to you from the professional you are interviewing as honestly as you can. You cannot hold back or skip over something you are not clear on. The professionals you are going to be working with don't expect you to know how the homebuilding profession works. (And you'll be surprised at how quickly you'll catch on.) What you will be looking for on the other end is that the professional you are interviewing is more than willing to explain their process to you in a manner you easily comprehend. Even if it means going over something more than one, two or three times — you need to know that when a question arises, you are going to be working with someone who welcomes the opportunity to include you, rather than make you feel inferior, or, a nuisance who is disrupting the flow. (At the point of hiring someone, this is the type of information you will be seeking from referrals who have worked with this professional.) Any successful professional who is experienced in design, development and homebuilding will welcome a homeowner who takes the initiative to stay in the know and stay on top of their responsibilities because this will make the entire job run smoother for everyone involved.

Defining New Boundaries

In talking with both homeowners and homebuilding professionals about the adjustments that have to be made when a family opts to stay in the home during construction, there was one element of the process that came up most frequently — setting appropriate boundaries. An experienced contractor who specializes in remodeling has most likely gone over this with their workers. These subcontractors come to your project with an understanding of how they should respect your living space. Still, it is your responsibility as CEO of this remodeling venture to clearly delineate boundaries with your contractor before work begins. If you do not want subcontractors using your refrigerator, microwave or bathroom, this is the time to bring that up. If there is a specific place for them to park their vehicles during the workday, let the contractor know that as well. Or, if you have prescheduled dates or events coming up when you cannot have workers present at your house, discuss it on the front-end. Contractors are used to accommodating homeowners who are living in their homes while work is being done. They understand that even though your property is their place of work, it is still your home and you and your family will need to function in it as such.

The concept of the need to set boundaries is more difficult to grasp for the homeowner who is new to the remodeling process. The natural response you have to all who enter your home is to be hospitable and welcoming. When you are host to a remodeling crew, the manner in which you express your hospitality and welcoming nature needs to take on a different persona. This is important, because your home and the purpose that the areas being remodeled once served are now going to change. The area that is getting remodeled is no longer your living space as you once knew it to be, it is now going to become another person's workplace. Though temporary, it is your responsibility to make this transition on the worker's behalf. When in doubt, a good reference point would be to consider any manner of conduct from you and your family members (kids) that would be out of place in an office setting where people are working. This conduct will now become out of place in this new construction space where the subcontractors are working.

If you have young children, begin to help them prepare for this remodel by talking about what is going to be happening. If they are emotionally connected to the area that is getting remodeled, a week or two before the work begins, have family times in this area. Picnic on the floor, have a camp-out and talk about the things you all did in this space. Address the fact that while this space is changing, new space is going to be created to allow for more opportunities. Let the kids draw pictures on walls that are going to come down. Put a time capsule together and plan on putting it inside a wall or floorboard. Some kids may enjoy having the opportunity to hit the wall with a hammer. If it is your child's room that is getting worked on, encourage them to draw pictures to show the architect and contractor. You never know what creativity can surface if given the opportunity. One of your family members may come up with a great concept you can integrate into your new design. These are the types of things you'll want to include in your family's home-building legacy. Visit my Web site for additional ideas in documenting your family's homebuilding experience.

Kids need to understand that this new space is no longer a place where they can run freely and bring friends or toys into. If workers leave tools on the site, they are not to be touched. Some phases of the project can be hazardous and the last thing the workers or the contractor want to be concerned about is where your kids are while work is going on.

We were having a renovation done on our home in Los Angeles. The workers had left for the day and I was making dinner when it occurred to me that the house was a bit too quiet. I went to check on our son, who at the time was just over two years old. I opened the door to our master bedroom that had just been painted, wood floors still drying and found him exuberantly flinging a paintbrush that had been soaking in a paint can, up and down. He was covered from head to toe, thoroughly enjoying one of those tactile cause-and-effect learning moments. Pale pink paint from our daughter's room was being strewn all up and down our newly painted walls and finished floors. Timing my tackle on a down swing, I was able to get the brush out of his hand before he made it to the closet doors.

Setting up a physical boundary for kids is helpful. You can use some hazard tape, or other material to signal off-limits. Obviously, in some situations, the project may make interaction between the homeowner and the workers inevitable to some degree. You will need to find a constructive balance.

Another aspect of boundary setting is avoiding the inclination for chitchat. Contrary to the regular guests that visit your home, these workers are okay with you not chatting with them while they are working. Not chatting with them does not translate into being rude. You can be very cordial with them by greeting them when you see them and commend them on the work they are doing. Just be mindful that lost time equates to lost dollars for your contractor. The more time you take up with the subcontractor chatting, the less work they're going to get done for their boss. You talking with the subcontractors puts them in the uncomfortable position of having to choose between being polite to you or getting their work done. Also, you could inadvertently cause confusion between workers if you were to ask one of them their opinion about something or to make a change in the way they are doing a task that they were assigned to do — no matter how miniscule that change may seem to you. Instructing your contractor's subcontractors in any way, shape or form is off-limits. If you have a concern or a change to make, always talk to your contractor or the project manager and let them convey the information to the workers.

Think of it this way, you've left your three kids at home with specific instructions as to what they need to do in order for your family to be ready by 5:00 tonight to leave for your family's trip. One child is in charge of gathering and sorting the dirty clothes to be washed, one is in charge of washing and drying them and one is in charge of folding them and putting them in the suitcases. You leave to do last-minute errands, confident that with everyone's help, you can actually make this happen. Those of you who are parent's of kids and find yourself chuckling at this thought — bear with me. Your spouse comes home early and asks the child who's waiting for the next batch of clothes to finish drying, to come and help clean out the car. It's 4:30 and you return home to find laundry piled up in the laundry room and only one of the three suitcases you laid out has clothes in it. You talk to the child who was in charge of washing and drying the clothes and they tell you that they were asked to do something else so they didn't get your work done. Your husband comes in from the garage and says that the car is clean and he's ready to go!

Blurring The Lines Between Work and Friendship

This story is one of my favorites in this book. It illustrates the importance of setting clear boundaries between you and the people you hire to work on your remodel:

I knew a woman — I will call her Julie Anderson — who hired a man, Sam, to do restoration work on her house. Because this was a historical house, the work being done was much more labor intensive than a newer house remodel would have been. Julie and her husband, Jack, knew heading into the project that time and money could only be determined by the information gathered from carefully lifting layer upon layer of paint to get down to the original colors used in the early 1800s.

Julie and Jack were excited to see history literally unveiled before their eyes. They welcomed Sam into their home as if he were part of the family. Sam showed up for his first day of work. Julie greeted him and asked if there was anything he needed from her to get his work started. He said, "No, I think I've got everything I need, thank you." He began setting up the area he was going to work in. As the day progressed, Julie started making her lunch and asked Sam if he had brought a lunch for himself. He said, "No ma'am, I was planning on going out and picking up something in the next thirty minutes or so."

Julie decided, since she was already preparing her own lunch, that she would go ahead and make Sam lunch, too. When she informed Sam that she would be making him lunch, Sam said, "Really Mrs. Anderson, I'm fine. I'll just go over to McDonald's and get a burger." Julie insisted. She took pride in her spirit of hospitality. Sam sat down to a plate of salad, fresh fruit and a sandwich. They talked about the progress of the work he was doing. Julie was beside herself with anticipation as she cleared the lunch dishes from the table. Before she knew it, it was time to pick the kids up from school. Heading out the door she yelled to Sam, "There's iced tea in the fridge. Help yourself if you get thirsty."

As the days turned into weeks and weeks into months Julie had established a routine for Sam's lunch hour. Julie started planning out the lunches earlier so she could accomplish her normal day's activities and still have everything for lunch prepared on time.

One Sunday afternoon Julie, Jack and the kids were relaxing. The house was quiet, the football game was on and Julie had started putting together a large tray of food, buffet style, for her family to eat from at their convenience. There was a knock at the door. Jack got up and opened the door to find Sam, his wife and their son smiling back at him. Jack welcomed them in and called Julie to greet the visiting family. Sam proceeded to tell Jack and Julie how much he appreciated working in their home and wanted to know if he could show his family the house and the restoration work he'd been working on. Sam's wife oohed and aahed over the Anderson's home as Julie explained the his-

(continued on page 153)

interview

Salem Forsythe
Remodeling Contractor

I met Salem while he was working on a renovation for a friend of mine. She couldn't say enough good things about him so I thought he would be a good contractor to meet, I was right. If you are considering remodeling your home, Salem represents the type of contractor you need to look for.

HOW DOES A CONTRACTOR DETERMINE WHAT HIS OR HER FEE WILL BE TO OVERSEE A PARTICULAR RENOVATION PROJECT?

I like to meet with the clients, understand what the project is and then give them a budget for the way I would do the project. First, I determine the project's cost.

If it costs $200,000, I'm going to say, "For a project of this size, I can perform the work for 20%, or $40,000, which I would propose as a fixed fee. If, when we get finished, you've changed your bathtub to a more expensive one, and we spend over $200,000 in costs, my fee does not increase. What this does is give the client and the builder a relationship where there is no incentive for the contractor to increase their costs. The American Institute of Architects has several sample contracts. I generally propose, for this type of project, that their contract stipulate, *projects of limited scope, where the basis of payment is cost plus a fixed fee.*

On a small job, a client might say, "Hey, come on in and let's get it done. I'm ready. You've worked for me before." I just say, "Well, cost plus 20 okay?" They'll say, "Yeah, cost plus 20 is okay." If not, as always, everything is negotiable. And it never hurts to ask.

WHEN A HOMEOWNER IS CONSIDERING RENOVATING THEIR HOME, HOW IMPORTANT IS THE EXPERIENCE OF THE CONTRACTOR THEY ARE CONSIDERING HIRING TO DO THE WORK TO THE SUCCESS OF THEIR PROJECT?

I think it's important. There are a lot of fine young men who are going to work hard and try to get the job done, and, perhaps, for half the fee. There may be additional costs incurred.

HOW?

Because the guy might order the stuff wrong, it might take longer to do it, he might not know which subcontractors to use because he has not had the time to build those relationships yet. He wasn't experienced enough to know if he needed to provide the homeowners with a realistic bid, etc. A standard comment that I make to a new client is, "I know you're going to be looking at some other builders. That's a great thing to do. Keep in mind that through the experiences that I've had over the years, while money is an important factor in who you choose, your feelings for the contractor and the way your personalities work together is just as important. Do you feel like you want to trust this person with this amount of money and that you can tell them something and they're going to listen to you?" Within the interview process, I am attempting to get a feel for how well this client and I will work together.

HOW MIGHT A HOMEOWNER DETERMINE WHETHER OR NOT THE REMODEL THEY ARE CONSIDERING IS GOING TO BE VALUED AT THE AMOUNT OF MONEY THEY ARE SPENDING ON IT?

If these people are getting a construction loan, they're going to have an appraisal of the property in its current shape and what it's going to look like after it's completed. They can make a judgment on what they've got in it, what they plan on putting into it and whether it's worth it to them or not. Sometimes people will spend more to get what they want. It's their choice. It's their house.

HOW IMPORTANT IS IT FOR THE HOMEOWNER TO HAVE THE POTENTIAL CANDIDATES DO A WALK THROUGH OF THE EXISTING HOUSE, TO GO OVER WHAT THE HOMEOWNER WANTS TO DO?

Imperative.

WHAT TYPES OF QUESTIONS SHOULD THE HOMEOWNER BE PREPARED TO ASK THE CONTRACTOR ON THIS WALK THROUGH?

Do you see any problems with my design? Is this a project that you're interested in? Does this excite you? See if you can get any level of excitement. For me, if I get excited or I don't, you'll notice it.

WHAT TYPES OF QUESTIONS SHOULD THE HOMEOWNER BE PREPARED TO ANSWER FROM THE CONTRACTOR ON ONE OF THESE WALK-THROUGHS?

I generally won't ask many questions during the intial walk-through. I'll wait until we do an actual interview. Then I would ask:

- What are we going to do with all your things?
- What have you got in mind for storage?
- What areas do you not want us going into?
- What times are you going to be out of the house on vacation?
- Do you have any parties that we are heading towards for a particular termination date?
- Any problems with where we're going to park?
- Where do we put the port-o-let?
- The list can go on and on.

DOES BUDGETING FOR A RENOVATION DIFFER FROM BUDGETING FOR A NEW HOME CONSTRUCTION?

Yes, I'd say there's more chance of a change in the budget for a renovation project than in a new construction project. On new construction, you can better predict your costs, because you have a set of blueprints without existing construction in the way.

HOW WOULD A HOMEOWNER COME UP WITH A REALISTIC BUDGET FOR THE RENOVATION OF THEIR HOME?

- Hire a competent contractor.
- Use an architect to assist in the planning process.
- Interview several contractors. Each proposal from a contractor should have a schedule of values, and that schedule of values will be broken up into a series of divisions that are called out by the architect in his specifications. It's generally framing, interior sheeting, exterior millwork, windows, etc. Analyzing proposals from different contractors is key to helping you get a realistic budget.

HOW MIGHT A HOMEOWNER INCLUDE THEIR CONTRACTOR'S EXPERTISE WHEN IT COMES TO ARRIVING AT A REALISTIC BUDGET FOR THE WORK THEY WANT DONE?

It would be nice if a homeowner would give a contractor a broad concept of what his or her budget is early on, because it can save the contractor a lot of work. For example, if a homeowner tells me, I want to have all this work

English Country design built by Castle Contractors features a natural limestone surround on fireplace, vaulted ceilings with distressed wood beams and custom full-length windows. PHOTO CREDIT: REED BROWN, GENERAL CONTRACTOR: CASTLE CONTRACTORS, ARCHITECT: KEVIN COFFEE

done but I can only spend $100,000, I can look at the amount of work and tell them that this is going to cost $200,000. So what are we going to do? Do you want me to price it at $200,000 or are there areas we can reduce the scope of work by using less expensive finishes? Give me some good information on the front end so this process doesn't go on and on.

IN YOUR EXPERIENCE, HOW OFTEN DOES THE REMODEL OR RENOVATION PROJECT GO OVER THE ORIGINAL BUDGET AMOUNT?

Most of the time. There are many variables to consider. Usually a client will ask for more work to done than was originally scheduled.

WHAT, IN YOUR OPINION ,CAUSES MOST OF THE BUDGET INCREASES IN A RENOVATION PROJECT?

Unanticipated framing, demolition costs, change in scope of work, specifications and the ever-present unexpected!

WOULD YOU SUGGEST A HOMEOWNER PAD THEIR BUDGET FOR THE UNEXPECTED BEFORE THEY BEGIN THEIR RENOVATION?

Yes. Generally, a 10% contingency is sufficient.

WHEN SOMETHING UNEXPECTED COMES UP DURING THE RENOVATION THAT CAUSES THE COST OF CONSTRUCTION TO GO UP, HOW DOES THE CONTRACTOR HANDLE THIS NEW INFORMATION AS IT PERTAINS TO THE HOMEOWNER?

I inform the homeowner as soon as possible. In fact, the AIA document mentions the critical path. That's how much you're spending on these budgets and that while it is cost plus a fee. It's the responsibility of the contractor to, *in a timely fashion* (the way it's worded), alert the homeowners of additional costs. Sometimes

things happen so fast in a renovation that it's already done, but it's the contractor's responsibility to stay on top of it and know when it's going over and let the homeowner know right away. When possible, tell the homeowner before it's happened so they can make a decision with regard to the change.

HOW DID YOU ARRIVE AT THE METHOD YOU USE FOR THE ACCOUNTING FOR YOUR BUILDING PROJECTS?

I base it off the guidelines of the divisions that are standard within the architectural industry. My particular budgets follow a chronological aspect to the construction of the home. For example, foundations are listed before framing. Roofing after framing. Then you can put the windows and exterior millwork after that. As a layman looks at it, they see it in sections that are distinct parts of the work. It follows down the spreadsheet as the project is being built.

SO IT'S ORGANIZED THROUGH THE PROGRESS OF THE PROJECT, WHICH IS EASY FOR THE HOMEOWNER TO UNDERSTAND.

Yes.

HOW DO YOU ASSIST THE HOMEOWNER IN KEEPING ON TOP OF THE FINANCES OF THEIR CONSTRUCTION PROJECT?

Many of them say, "Oh, gosh, this is too much paperwork. How much do I write the check for?" They write the check and they write the check, etc. I say, "Things are going over." They get to the end and say, "I didn't know it was going to be over this much! What is going on?" I say, "I tried to explain it to you but you never had the time to really go over it." So, homeowners need to take the time to review each progress billing and compare it to the schedule of values in the initial budget.

Authors note: The tact being taken by the above-mentioned homeowner is not a Proactive perspective when it comes to managing a building budget. Please note my comments with Kimberley Collins-Ripmaster with regard to financing your project and managing your homebuilding budget.

HOW OFTEN DO YOU GO OVER THE FINANCES OF THE PROJECT WITH THE HOMEOWNER?

There's a thorough going over the budget every month. We bill monthly. But if a particular aspect of the work is going to change in scope from my budget, there could be daily meetings, weekly meetings or hourly meetings. It's as needed, but definitely monthly. When I give them the bill, they see the continuation sheet, which shows how the schedule of values is accumulating and how the receipts, the labor and materials and subcontractors' draws have been applied to the various schedules.

A HOMEOWNER MAY ASSUME THAT SINCE THE CONTRACTOR IS TAKING CARE OF THE BUDGET, HE OR SHE DOESN'T HAVE TO WORRY ABOUT IT. HOW IMPORTANT IS IT FOR THE HOMEOWNER TO UNDERSTAND THE SIGNIFICANCE OF THEIR RESPONSIBILITY WHEN IT COMES TO KEEPING TRACK OF THEIR REMODELING FINANCES?

It's imperative.

WHAT SUGGESTIONS DO YOU HAVE FOR THE HOMEOWNER TO HELP THEM DETERMINE WHETHER THE CONTRACTOR THEY ARE CONSIDERING TO HIRE IS COMPETENT IN KEEPING UP WITH A BUILDING BUDGET?

Ask to see an example of a budget from a different project and how it went. It's easy for a contractor to white out the address and the personal information. For example, here's a $300,000 project and it ended up costing $400,000. You say, "Why did this go over?" As I said earlier, ask a lot of questions and you start to get a feel for how this person operates.

IF A HOMEOWNER, GOING INTO A BUILDING PROJECT, KNOWS THAT THEY ARE NOT GOOD AT KEEPING UP WITH PROLIFIC PAPERWORK AND ACCOUNTING PROCEDURES, DO YOU THINK IT IS IMPORTANT FOR THEM TO HIRE AN OUTSIDE BUSINESS SOURCE, I.E., ACCOUNTANT OR ATTORNEY TO WATCH OVER THE BUILDING BUDGET ON THEIR BEHALF?

Absolutely. In fact, I recommend it to any client.

WHAT SORT OF THINGS DOES THE HOMEOWNER NEED TO CONSIDER WHEN MAKING THE DECISION AS TO WHETHER THEY SHOULD LIVE IN THE HOME DURING THE RENOVATION OR NOT?

They need to examine their degree of ease, from a stress standpoint, about people being in their house and do they get upset about dust. If they're A-type personalities, I think they'd be better off renting and having peace of mind. If they're laid-back, funky folks and they don't mind insulation in their oatmeal, it can be a fun thing for them.

TELL ME ABOUT SOME OF THE CREATIVE WAYS YOUR CLIENTS HAVE COPED WITH LIVING IN THEIR HOUSE WHILE UNDER RENOVATION.

On my last project, we initially fixed up the basement a little bit. It was called Le Cave, and it provided the owners with a nice little nest. They knew that not much work would be going on down there until we got everything done up top. Then we'd come and spiff up that space. This gives them an area that they know is still theirs. A lot of times that can be achieved, but I've seen people washing dishes in their bathtub, as well. I think trying to create a nest-like environment, a sanctuary and private place, is great if you can achieve it. I've also had people live in a secondary building on their property or move to a nearby apartment.

I RECENTLY TALKED WITH A FRIEND OF MINE. HER NEIGHBOR HAS DONE RENOVATION. THEY JUST BOUGHT THIS HOUSE, AND THEY WANTED TO RENOVATE BEFORE THEY ACTUALLY MOVED IN. THEY RENTED A TOUR BUS AND PUT IT IN THE DRIVEWAY. THEY LIVED IN THE TOUR BUS AND WERE ABLE TO BE CLOSE TO THE SITE., BUT, THEY HAD THEIR OWN SPACE. SO INSTEAD OF LE CAVE, IT WAS LE BUS.

That's an excellent idea.

AS FAR AS SETTING BOUNDARIES, IF A HOMEOWNER FINDS THEMSELVES LIVING IN THE HOME WHILE THE WORK IS BEING DONE, HOW WOULD THEY BEST SET BOUNDARIES AS TO WHAT IS AVAILABLE TO THE WORKERS AND WHAT IS NOT? FOR EXAMPLE, USING THE BATHROOMS, PHONES, MICROWAVES, ETC.

First of all, I don't like to do any jobs without a port-o-let on site. I think this is an important little thing. A CFO might look at that expense and say, "That's 75 bucks a month on a 6-month project — $300. Wow, I could have bought my vanity fixtures with that." Don't try it, because, ultimately, it's going to become a problem. The contractor and his crew must respect the homeowner and their private things.

IF A HOMEOWNER DECIDES TO LIVE IN THEIR HOME DURING THE RENOVATION, HOW WOULD THEY SET CLEAR BOUNDARIES OF THEIR LIVING SPACE WITH THE CONSTRUCTION CREW?

It's best to communicate with the contractor, who would then communicate to his employees, so the appropriate chain of command is established. Sometimes a client speaks to the workers, but I've seen more problems with that than not. The worker wants to please, but doesn't understand, and now I am out of the loop. That may not appear crucial to the client. However, the worker doesn't understand and it causes a problem.

Let's say, hypothetical, that the homeowner knows that I've set a port-o-let and I've told everybody not to use the homeowner's facilities. All of a sudden she hears the toilet flush in the house and somebody's coming out. I recommend her calling me and I would take care of it. That's my job, as opposed to the homeowner talking with the sub directly. I feel strongly about that.

IS THERE ANYTHING IN THE HOME THAT MIGHT BE AN EXCEPTION AS TO WHAT THE SUBS MIGHT NEED TO USE?

This is a training process of your employees and subcontractors, and it has always caused me grief when these rules are transgressed. A guy doesn't have his hammer, so what does he do? He goes into the basement, finds a hammer and at the end of the day the homeowner calls me and says, "My grandfather's hammer is laying on my workbench and it's broken in half."

We are there to respect your place and do the work, but we've got to establish and adhere to those boundaries. My subs don't borrow tools and don't use the homeowner's refrigerator. If they need some water, fine, but they don't go into the refrigerator. There are exceptions. A lot of my clients that I've been working with for twenty years are coming back and wanting more renovation work done. Yesterday I sent a carpenter over to a house we'd done a few years ago. I'm sure that the homeowner fixed him a cup of coffee, then they sat down and caught up for ten minutes and she knew she was paying for it. Once a situation of trust and a relationship has developed, these rules do bend a little bit.

DO YOU HAVE A PROBLEM WITH HOMEOWNERS GOING TO THE SUBS DIRECTLY AND SAYING, "AS LONG AS YOU'RE IN HERE…"

Absolutely. I do not want them doing that.

EXPLAIN WHY A HOMEOWNER SHOULD NOT DO THAT.

Then I'm not able to be in control of the situation — I'm not in the loop. For example, I might have a recommendation about doing something that you didn't' know about. I have already anticipated what's going to happen when this work commences. The subcontractor won't have any idea as to what might happen. It can cause a multitude of problems.

THERE'S A BIG DIFFERENCE WHEN YOU'RE ACTUALLY WORKING IN THE ENVIRONMENT AND THE COUPLE IS DEALING WITH SOMETHING IN YOUR MIDST, SO TO SPEAK, VERSUS IF THEY GO UP ON THE SITE ON A WEEKEND AND THE CREW'S GONE. THEY CAN GO OVER WHATEVER THEY NEED TO HASH OUT THERE IN THE HOUSE. WHEN YOU'RE WORKING THERE AND SOMETHING COMES UP, YOU AND THE HOMEOWNERS ARE IN EACH OTHER'S FACE. EXPLAIN THE IMPORTANCE OF THE HUSBAND AND WIFE COMMUNICATING TO EACH OTHER.

Oh, I think that definitely needs to be entered into your book. The husband and wife, it's like raising kids. It's us against them, meaning the homeowners and myself. The mother and father must be united so that the children don't divide them. The husband and the wife, the CEO's, try not to let the workers see that there's turmoil going on. The workers don't know if their contractor's going to get kicked off the job. It stops productivity because they're asking, "Did you hear what they said?" The workers watch ten minutes and that's a percentage of your work efficiency. A good builder is never going to divide his clients because that will backfire on them.

I'm doing a project right now and I love these people. I've been working with them forever, but they can get together and get a plan going. Then I say, "Okay, no changes. Everything's fine." As soon as I'm gone, the husband goes out and changes things around. Now they want to have some work changed because it's not what the wife wanted, but it's what the husband told the carpenter to do.

AND HOW DOES THAT AFFECT THE JOB?

It's raises the cost of the job and slows it down.

IS THE INSURANCE THAT A CONTRACTOR CARRIES FOR A REMODELING PROJECT DIFFERENT THAT WHAT THEY WOULD CARRY FOR A NEW-HOME CONSTRUCTION?

No, it's the same, with one caveat. Homeowners should purchase their own builder's risk insurance. The builder's risk is insuring the value of the goods as they are put into the house. The general liability insurance the contractor has may not cover them. If I burn your house down that I'm renovating and I'm found to be at fault, my policy will replace everything and put everything back. In a new construction project, if the appliances get delivered and they haven't been installed and get stolen, my general liability policy won't cover that. The builder's risk policy has to capture it. I think this is one of the crucial areas where homeowners get confused, so they need an insurance agent who understands what their needs are going to be, will stay on top of the project for them and increase their limits as the project increases in value. The agent can look at a builder's insurance certificate and say, "Yeah, this is a good one," or "No, this doesn't work."

THE HOMEOWNER SHOULD TAKE RESPONSIBILITY FOR THIS BECAUSE THE REMODELING CONTRACTOR WILL NOT CARRY A RISK POLICY THAT COVERS THE EXTRA AREAS THAT NEED TO BE INSURED?

That is correct. A homeowner can assign a builder to get the risk policy and ask to be put on the policy. I always have my homeowners purchase their own, so they are responsible to pay the premiums and are always aware of their coverage.

HOW MANY HOMEOWNERS HAVE ASKED YOU ABOUT YOUR INSURANCE COVERAGE OR IF THEY COULD SEE YOUR INSURANCE CERTIFICATE?

You know what, a lot of them forget and a lot of them don't know to ask. I make sure that every client gets an insurance certificate with their name on it the day I start work.

WOULD YOU RECOMMEND A HOMEOWNER DO THIS WITH THE CONTRACTOR THEY ARE CONSIDERING HIRING, ASKING FOR THE CERTIFICATE?

Absolutely. In fact, it would be smart to do it prior to choosing the final contractor. It's easy for a builder to do it. They call their carrier and have them print it up.

HOW WOULD YOU SUGGEST A HOMEOWNER, WHO IS REMODELING THEIR HOME, PROTECT THE VALUABLE ITEMS THAT ARE IN THEIR HOME WHILE THE WORK IS BEING DONE?

- Make sure that all the necessary insurance is in place.
- Remove all valuables such as pictures, mirrors or other items hanging on the walls.
- Clear all built-in cabinets of contents. In the kitchen, remove all the dishes, glasses, etc.
- Ask the contractor what needs to be removed.
- Ask the contractor, "What do I need to move out?" This makes him liable, in a sense, because if damage occurs, it is now clearly the contractor's responsibility to have protected it.

AT WHAT POINT DOES A HOMEOWNER NEED TO HIRE A CONTRACTOR VS A HANDY MAN?

Always. I will do an entire project for $500. I'll do it for a couple of reasons. One, because I'm here to provide a service, and two, if I do a $500 job now, later on, when that homeowner has a $50,000 job, I've laid the groundwork. A typical markup on a handyman's work is about 50% over actual costs. When I do a small job, I increase my fee, but only to cost plus 25%. The homeowner is not really saving any money if they go with a handyman. Sometimes these guys are handymen because, for some reason, they don't fit the mold for standard construction.

WHEN A HOMEOWNER ASSUMES, WELL, ALL I'M DOING IS ADDING ON A COUPLE OF ROOMS, IT REALLY DOESN'T TAKE A LOT FOR SOMEONE TO DO THAT. WHY IS THAT A MISCONCEPTION?

When adding on a couple of rooms you've got foundations, framing, electrical, roofing and you're tying to an existing structure. You've got a microcosm of an entire house structure. The handyman might not have the proper license and he might be trying to do all the work himself. The project might take longer.

HOW MIGHT A HOMEOWNER DETERMINE WHAT CONTRACTOR WOULD BE BEST SUITED TO WORK ON THEIR REMODEL/RENOVATION PROJECT? WHAT ARE SOME OF THE IMPORTANT QUESTIONS A HOMEOWNER SHOULD CONSIDER ASKING WHEN INTERVIEWING A POTENTIAL CANDIDATE TO DO THEIR RENOVATION?

- What's your insurance status?
- What's your license status?
- Can you give me a half a dozen projects that are similar to this with the names of the

people that I can call and talk to them about? What's your time schedule right now?

- How many projects are you working on?
- Can you do this?
- How long is this project going to take?
- What hours will the men be working?

Ask everything.

Find a number of contractors to interview and ask:

- What is their comfort level with these contractors?
- Go look at some of their jobs.
- I would be honest with your contractors at the front end and say, "Hey, I'm having three people look at it and here are their names." Many times they're hesitant to tell the builder who the other builders are. Could that be because they think we're going to get together and rig up a price? I've never even heard of that in twenty-five years and it's not going to happen. By letting each contractor know who they're bidding against lets the builder know who his competition is. I will tell you right then and there, because I know most of these builders, "Oh, that's a good guy that I'd be glad to bid against and give you a price compared to him." Or, "I don't know that fellow but I'll be glad to give you a bid." Or, "If this is the kind of person that you're interested in using, I can tell you right now I'm going to do a different job than they're going to do." I don't say a better job, but I say, "I'm going to go at it differently. My attention to detail is such that my cost is going to be higher. If your budget is being driven by the fact that you want to have that level of work, that's fine and I'm cool with it, but I want to let you know right now I cannot compete with this guy's price."

WHAT TYPE OF DESIGN INFORMATION SHOULD A HOMEOWNER HAVE WHEN THEY FIRST MEET WITH A POTENTIAL CANDIDATE THEY ARE CONSIDERING HIRING?

As much as possible.

DO YOU THINK THE AVERAGE HOMEOWNER UNDERSTANDS THE IMPORTANCE OF HAVING A WELL-EXECUTED AND DETAILED PLAN OF THE RENOVATION OF THEIR HOME TO PROVIDE THE CONTRACTOR?

No, I don't think most do. Some homeowners think they can jot an image on a napkin.

HOW WOULD THIS BENEFIT THE HOMEOWNER?

I think the money is well spent. Without a set of documents or specifications, a homeowner cannot hold the contractor's feet to the fire. It's additional money up front, but the homeowner is going to have a level of comfort knowing that they are going to get what they see in the set of plans. If it's on a napkin and the builder builds it one way and the homeowner says, "That's not what I wanted," then the builder says, "Well, I did the best I could to interpret what you wanted."

HOW WOULD HAVING A SET OF PLANS DRAWN UP BY AN ARCHITECT BENEFIT THE CONTRACTOR?

I can give you a more realistic budget. I'll have clear documentation to pass on to my workers to help get the job done.

AT WHAT STAGE OF THE DESIGN PROCESS WOULD YOU SUGGEST A HOMEOWNER CONSULT WITH THE CONTRACTOR THEY ARE CONSIDERING HIRING TO DO THE WORK ON THEIR HOUSE?

In the preliminary stage, to help them get some ideas of their total budget. You could spend $10,000 with an architect designing something you can't afford. Then you've got to spend $5,000 more to cut it out. Everybody's unhappy. Many times, when it works well, is when the client first makes contact with his architect or her architect, they should give clear information to the architect of what their budget is so the architect can begin to design that project around that budget. And, before line drawings are drawn, while it's still in the conception process, it's okay to ask the architect if they have one builder they trust to give them some preliminary ideas. This is something that the builder is not going to spend more than an hour on. They will just work some square-foot numbers and give an idea of the costs.

HOW OFTEN ARE YOU BROUGHT IN ON THE BEGINNING OF THE DESIGN PROCESS AS A CONSULTANT FOR A RENOVATION PROJECT YOU ARE WORKING ON?

Not often enough.

HOW LONG WOULD YOU SUGGEST A HOMEOWNER LIVE WITH THE DESIGN OF THEIR NEW HOME BEFORE CONSTRUCTION BEGINS?

A month. Don't get in a hurry. For some people it's going to take more time than others. They need to feel knowledgeable and comfortable with the new changes.

AND WHY IS IT IMPORTANT WHEN YOU SAID DON'T GET IN A HURRY? WHAT HAPPENS IF THE HOMEOWNER HURRIES THAT PROCESS, HURRIES THE TIME THAT THEY WOULD TAKE TO UNDERSTAND THE PLAN?

They'll end up in the framing process and say, "Oh, I don't want that."

WHAT TYPE OF FOLLOW-UP DO YOU OFFER YOUR CLIENTS ONCE THE PROJECT HAS BEEN COMPLETED?

I tell them that, over the next year, I can guarantee them that there are going to be some cracks in interior millwork, nail pops in the sheetrock and other minor adjustments when things are settling. Within a year's time I will come back. If we finish a project in the fall, I say let it go through the winter process because it's going to contract to a large extent. We'll let it go through whatever seasoning it's going to do through the winter period and we'll come catch it in the early spring for you.

BONUS INFORMATION:

I have done projects in this town for twenty-five years and I've had three bad ones — all for high maintenance and wealthy people. I didn't see it coming. I never sued, but those three people have never hurt me a bit because they're nuts and people know they're nuts. But, if there's a bad recommendation or something went wrong, you need to get a second opinion about who that person was that gave the bad opinion and check into it. A bad recommendation may not be the end of the thing, but it's certainly something to raise your eyebrows and to talk to the contractor about. Say, "Hey, I talked to these folks and they said that you didn't satisfy them. What happened?" It will be interesting to hear the two stories. At that point you're going to get a good feeling as to whether that contractor is backpedaling and who's right. Not only are you the CEO but you're the judge.

(continued from page 146)

torical significance of each room. After the tour, Julie thought it only fitting that she invite her guests to serve themselves from the buffet tray.

Sam's work on the house ended up taking far longer than the Anderson's could have imagined. Before Sam's job was completed, Jack and Julie had employed numerous relatives of Sam's who, according to Sam, were also experts in the art of restoration work. Sam's family started attending traditional celebrations, along with longtime friends of the Anderson family. By this point, Julie had worked her employee meal plan into a normal day's activity. Sam had become more relaxed with his work schedule, so Julie gave him their security code so he could let himself in if no one was there when he arrived. Sam also felt more comfortable making personal decisions as to how the Anderson's should esthetically improve on their original concepts of restoring their home.

As the months grew into years and thousands of dollars into tens of thousands of dollars, the Anderson's realized they had to make a decision. Either they include an addition on their home to accommodate Sam and his family, or they set a date of completion for Sam to get him out of their house. The latter took precedent, as they were quickly running out of money. Breaking the news to Sam was what they anguished over. Julie and Jack had so blurred the line of employer and employee in their relationship with Sam that the decision to bring his daily routine to an end felt more like terminating a relationship with a family member than closing out an account with an employee.

Believe it or not, the end of this story wasn't when Jack handed Sam his last paycheck. The Anderson's had recommended Sam to friends of theirs. Sam was to start work the day after he left the Anderson's house. While Julie was sitting in her kitchen enjoying the long overdue solitude of her now empty home, the doorbell rang. Julie walked to the door and opened it. There stood Sam. Julie, somewhat confused, invited him in and asked, "Did you forget something?' To which Sam replied, "No, it's lunchtime isn't it?"

I've come to enjoy the reaction that I get from people reading this story. More times than not I will have a homeowner gasp and say, "I would do that!" or "I've done that!"

When I first relayed this story to my editor, he informed me that when he would work on construction sites, he would purposely schedule his lunch hour early to avoid this very situation. He said that even if the kids were home and they all ate together, it was uncomfortable for him.

Setting A Bad Precedent

When women homeowners don't set proper boundaries with their workers it continues to keep the stereotypical gender bias alive in this male-dominated work environment. I've included this next story that happened to a friend of mine to demonstrate how the consequences of one woman's mishandling on her project come back around to affect another woman's project.

I received a call from a friend of mine who was familiar with Julie and Jack's story. Rita and Carl recently purchased a home that was on a large wooded lot. The homes in their neighborhood were not yet connected to city water so everyone had their own septic system. A year after they moved into their home a developer bought land adjacent to their property. This developer was connecting the new homes he was building to the city waterline. Our friends inquired as to the possibility of having their home connected as well. The developer gave them a reasonable price and agreed to do the work to change them over to city water.

Rita and Carl have two children and both parents work. Rita's job and the type of work she does can be emotionally draining. One day, a client of hers canceled, freeing up a few hours of her afternoon. Rita went home in anticipation of using this much-needed time to get caught up on some things around the house.

While working in her backyard, one of the workers installing the waterline yelled over to Rita, "We'd like to have some pizza for lunch." Rita was dumbfounded. She began questioning her responsibility to these men and wondered, am I supposed to get them their lunch?

Am I responsible for that? I don't want to be rude and they are working on my property. Remembering the story of Julie and Jack, Rita called me. "Your book says I'm not responsible to feed the subcontractors that are working on my house, right?"

Upon hearing her quandary, punctuated with, "I have to go back to work and then pick up my kids from school. I don't have time to get them lunch!" I suggested to Rita that maybe this worker was joking with her. Rita said it didn't seem like he was joking. I told her to go outside and finish up her work. If the worker brings it up again, she should laugh and say, "Right, and would you like a six-pack with that as well?" This would give them both a chance to acknowledge each other and get past this awkward exchange.

Two minutes later I received a second call from an exasperated Rita. "He brought it up again and I said what you told me to say." "So, what did he say back?" I asked. "He said, we're not thirsty, we're just hungry." Then I told her she was being tested — so to speak. It was obvious that these workers had had some success in getting their lunch from homeowners before, most likely in the development behind Rita's house. And most likely it was the women of those houses that acquiesced. Now they were hoping Rita would do the same. Think about it, wouldn't it be great to have someone treat you to lunch and a refreshing drink in the middle of your workday? Then ask yourself, how many times is that luxury afforded you? How often does someone bring lunch to you or your husband while at your workplace, whether that's an office or your home? On a more personal note, how often do you bring lunch to your husband when he's at work? If you wouldn't do it in an office, don't do it on this job site either.

I came up with a new strategy. Rita went back outside and when the worker approached her again, she politely but firmly said, "I'm busy working — do you need to borrow a phone book for the number of a restaurant in the area?" The worker got the message and he and his buddies

(continued on page 156)

interview

Sharon Lester
Retired Contractor

Sharon is a 30-year veteran of the construction industry who established herself as a successful contractor who approached her projects with a no-nonsense attitude.

"One of the most important elements in a homeowner's relationship with their contractor is trust. It's the contractor's responsibility to really listen to the homeowner and maintain that trust throughout the construction process."

WHAT IS ONE OF THE MOST COMMON MISCONCEPTIONS THAT A HOMEOWNER NEW TO THE PROCESS OF HOMEBUILDING MAKES?
That a contractor knows how to build homes. Contractors should know how to do the things they are asking their subcontractors to do. That's why I've built two homes for myself. As a woman, I knew that I had to literally be able to show a subcontractor what I needed done. Then I could say to them, "I don't want you to do it like that, here, let me show you how I want it done." That would get their attention quicker than anything I could say.

AS A WOMAN CONTRACTOR, HOW DO YOU STAY IN CONTROL OF THE BUILDING PROJECT WHEN THE MAJORITY OF YOUR SUBCONTRACTORS ARE MEN?
My role with my subcontractors is different than any man's role with them because my relationship with them as a woman is different, and I've had to be very careful of that from the beginning. When we first meet, I try to be genderless. They know I'm in charge. It's dirty work — and I'll do whatever it takes to get the job done, and they know this. As long as they're doing what we have agreed to do, I will support them to the death.

The same with my customers. I've got to help them understand from the beginning that they're not hiring me to be their friend. I work very hard to set boundaries between the homeowner's I work with and me. I am there conducting business. I focus on building the home. My goal is to build them the very best house that can be built.

HOW SHOULD A HOMEOWNER HANDLE DISCUSSING THEIR PROJECT WITH THE SUBCONTRACTORS THAT ARE DOING THE WORK?
One of the things I try to make clear to my customers from the outset is that I don't want them to talk to my subcontractors — period. I don't even want them asking their opinions about something on the job. Hello is about it.

Not that we don't all get together if it's necessary to discuss something, because there's a huge, collaborative, warm, friendly atmosphere on my jobs. There's respect. I know what's going on with any sub at any time. If the homeowner has a question regarding anything on their project or with a sub of mine, I need to be the one made aware of it first. Then we all can get together and talk about it. The sub appreciates knowing that his direction is always going to come through a specific channel — me. Confusion makes for disharmony and ambivalence on a job.

WHAT IS THE ROLE OF THE HOMEOWNER AS IT PERTAINS TO BUILDING THEIR HOME?
To understand as best they can what they want. To sit down and to create specifications, what these specifications mean and how they relate to the house. If they do, they'll have a better understanding of what's going into their house. I always like to know what they think they're going to get for their money.

BEING A WOMAN YOURSELF, WHAT ADVICE WOULD YOU OFFER THE WOMAN HOMEOWNER WHO FINDS HERSELF HAVING TO MAKE DECISIONS AND ANSWER QUESTIONS IN AN ENVIRONMENT THAT IS FOREIGN AND MAYBE INTIMIDATING TO HER?
Admitting vulnerability, and owning it, and to not be afraid to ask their contractor questions about something she doesn't know about. And not to act like she is not important or she knows the answers when she doesn't. I've had many women tell me how discomfited they were by their contractor and the workers on their project. They were made to feel like they were incapable of making the right decisions for their project. The contractor must provide an environment of appreciation and respect. And the woman in this case must learn to set proper boundaries and assume that respect.

(continued from page 154)

got their own lunch. The waterline was installed and Rita learned a valuable lesson with regard to the role she plays when hiring someone to do work on her house.

This is a good example of how one homeowner's behavior can affect the way another homeowner is treated on their project. It's obvious that these workers had gotten away with this behavior enough times to feel confident in approaching my friend the way they did. Using a common workplace as an example, can you imagine any situation where an employee would get away with this entitlement type of attitude with the person they are working for? By you assuming a PHM™ mindset and establishing clear professional boundaries between you and the people that you hire to do the work on your home, you will create an environment of mutual respect between you and your home-building employees. You will be communicating that while these subcontractors are on your project you expect them to treat you and your home with a professional attitude. If, after your work is completed, you would like to have a thank you builder's brunch to show your appreciation, that would be most appropriate.

Your Home's Personal Insurance Policy

If you are remodeling a home that you are living in, you will want to make sure that you obtain the proper insurance coverage for all your property. This would include everything inside the house as well as outside the house and around your property. Meet with your insurance provider and let them know what your plans are. Show them a copy of your contractor's insurance policy to determine what types of coverage you need to take out to compensate for what your contractor's insurance does not cover. Get copies of everything and keep them together.

Determine what type of insurance coverage you need to add to your home while the work is being done and the value of your property is being increased. Builder's risk is the most

important. You might need to get more homeowner's insurance.

Preparing the Space for Your Remodel

Once you have hired your contractor, do a walk-through to determine how you need to prepare the area or areas where you are going to have the work done. Make a list as you go along. Ask what you need to do or need to have done to prepare the areas that are going to be worked on before the work commences. Ask what the contractor and his workers will do for you to prepare these areas. The contractor will have a way of handling some things that can minimize the preparation work you need to do.

Take into consideration that the subcontractors may have experience in moving furniture — however — that is not their expertise. Don't put them in the position of having to deal with your great-grandmother's hutch. Valuable items need to be taken care of professionally. Call a local moving company to either move the items into a room of the house that is not going to be bothered or rent a temporary space and have your valuables moved there.

The more you can do to create a low stress productive work environment versus an obstacle course for the workers, the better for everyone involved. Ask if there are adjoining areas as well that need to be cleared out.

Don't wait until the last minute to start cleaning out areas to be worked on. You may assume that you have days to clean your kitchen out if the workers start on another area of the house first — but you won't. Take the time needed before the workers come in to prepare the areas properly in an organized manner so you are in control of where everything ends up. Once two or more subcontractors get working on demolition or prepping a room, the work moves along quickly.

They will be ready to move into your kitchen space before you know it. You don't want to be running ahead of them rushing to get things out of their way.

If you are planning on running the project

Some homeowners consider themselves able to run a remodel versus a new construction because "it's just a remodel." Assess your project's needs wisely. If it is a project that is not going to involve structural changes or other modifications that you would not be knowledgeable about, and if you have the time to devote to the needs of you project, you may be able to manage it. You will essentially become the general contractor and most likely the project manager.

These are things that you need to go over with an attorney before you hire anyone for your project. This meeting will assist you in writing up a project description and the responsibilities of the people you hire for your job.

Estimate
☐ Once you get bids from the subcontractors that you are going to hire you can compile an estimate of what this project is going to cost.

Hire Subcontractors
☐ You are going to be responsible for hiring the subcontractors that will be doing the work on your project. This means that you need to follow up with each subcontractor as you would a contractor (See Chapter 5). For example, are they licensed (if it applies)? Check to confirm that they are listed in a local phone book.

Contracts
☐ Don't hire anyone or begin work without a written contract that clearly specifies what is expected from both you and the subcontractor.

Insurance
☐ If the subcontractors are working for you, you may need to purchase worker's compensation insurance. Call your local NAHB, National Association of Home Builders, and ask about it. Follow up with your insurance agent and your attorney. Understand what types of insurance you need for coverage on all that you are doing before you begin your project.

☐ Confirm that every subcontractor you hire is properly insured. Follow up on their certificates. Follow up on their monthly premium payments as well.

Designate Work Areas and the Work in Those Areas That is to be Done
☐ You need to have a clear understanding of your project. What work you want done, what work you don't want done. You can instruct your workers as to what they need to do.

Pull Permits
☐ You need to determine if you will be responsible for pulling the proper permits for your project.

Know Code Requirements
☐ You are responsible to make sure that you are following the code requirements in your city or county before you begin work on your project. Ask if and at what point you may need your project to be inspected and approved before moving on to the next phase.

Bond
☐ Are you requiring a bond from those you hire on your project?

Lien Releases
☐ Are the subcontractors going to purchase product and materials for your project?

☐ Are they responsible for paying helpers? If so, ask your attorney about aquiring lien releases.

Site Preparation
☐ You will have to make sure that the area to be worked on is ready to receive the workers when they get to your home. The amount of prep work you will have to do is dependent

on the work you are having done. Be clear as to what that is before you schedule your workers to arrive on your site.

Work Schedule (Sequence of Work to be Done)

☐ You will be determining your work schedule. Once you know the amount of work that is needed and you have hired the subcontractors to do the work, you can take the information they have provided you and whatever other research you can do to determine a time frame for your project. You will also have to properly schedule your subcontractors if you have numerous workers who are responsible for different tasks. For example, electrical and plumbing have to be scheduled before the drywall installers.

Budget Management

☐ You will be responsible for managing your finances of this project. You will not be getting an itemized draw sheet from a contractor. You are going to have to produce that yourself. Your subcontractors will present you with their bills. You will need to combine these along with the project receipts that you have accrued from material purchases. This will become the financial record of your project that you oversee.

Provide Materials for Subcontractors

☐ You will be responsible for making sure that the materials for the project are available when needed.

☐ Disposal of waste and debris from project. Your subcontractors can clean up after themselves, meaning what they have brought to the site; their tools, etc. The debris or accumulated waste may be something that you are responsible for at the end of the day.

MAKE SURE YOU CAN HANDLE THE PROJECT

☐ Do you have the time to spend from start to finish of this project? (Allow a month or two extra just to be safe)

☐ Is the money you save worth the amount of time and effort you are going to have to take to make this happen?

☐ What if you get started and you find out that there are more extensive aspects to the project than you had anticipated?

☐ What if you have a subcontractor or two who starts to tell you that things need to be done that you had not anticipated? Are you in a position to make the call as to whether or not that work needs to be done?

☐ If a subcontractor comes to you and says you will save a lot of money if you do not do something that you had planned on doing — it may be the case or maybe that subcontractor either does not know how to do it himself or he doesn't want to do it. Will you be in a position to make that call?

☐ Are you able to check the work to determine if the work is being done correctly?

☐ Are you confident in your ability to manage a work schedule that keeps the project moving in a timely fashion?

☐ Will you be able to follow up on the insurance coverage that you and your subcontractors will have to carry?

☐ Are you willing to pull all the necessary permits needed to execute the work to be done on your project?

☐ Are you confident in your ability to find competent subcontractors to work on your project?

☐ Can you take on this full-time job along with managing your family's priorities?

If your project is esthetic in nature and does not require any structural modification, your research is going to be less involved. If you are going to be tearing down walls and adding new space, it is in your best interest to enlist the services of an architect and a contractor to help you evaluate your project's needs.

I recommend that you hire a remodeling professional who has a good reputation and can provide you with trustworthy subcontractors to do your job. It may cost a bit more, but the benefits of having someone else oversee the work being done, thereby freeing you up to continue with your everyday life, will prove to be worth the upcharge.

in closing

If you have the opportunity to build or remodel your home and gift your family with a better quality of life, consider yourself blessed. Take this commitment seriously and prepare wisely. The fruit of your labor will be greatly rewarded. Your new home will be the source of many memories shared by the people who mean the most to you. The walls will wrap around to embrace the most intimate moments of your family's life together. I wish you a wonderful homebuilding experience.

Please share your experiences with me. I'd love to see pictures and hear your stories. Log on to my Web site, Proactivehomebuildingmethod.com, click on BUILDING COMMUNITY and begin to build new relationships with other homeowners across the country who are going through the same process. Encourage one another. Offer tips. Strengthen the homeowner-to-homeowner homebuilding experience. Pass on knowledge that will enhance someone else's process.

Log on to watch my interviews with industry professionals. Ask questions and get answers in a manner that will benefit other homeowners as well. If you want to brag on your architect, contractor, designer, landscape architect or one of your subs, go for it! We will be featuring professionals from across the country regularly on our Web site — people who work hard to provide their clients with a great homebuilding experience. Contribute your builder's brunch recipes and ideas to our BUILDERS BRUNCH section of the site for other homeowner's to review.

When you're done with the building-phase of your project, move onto the other areas of the Web site to see what may be of interest in maintaining your home, landscape, future additions and surprise homebuilding events that will change the life of a homeowner forever. For those of you who have purchased my book, I am offering an interactive CD that will allow you to begin using the PHM™ tools right away. Log onto www.proactivehomebuilding.com. It's never too early to begin your homebuilding process. There will always be something happening at Dori Howard's Homebuilding Essentials, the door's open, come on in.

Sincerely,

Dori

index